CW00833539

NARRATOLOGY AN

Narratology and Classics

A Practical Guide

IRENE J. F. DE JONG

Great Clarendon Street, Oxford, OX2 6DP,
United Kingdom

Oxford University Press is a department of the University of Oxford.
It furthers the University's objective of excellence in research, scholarship,
and education by publishing worldwide. Oxford is a registered trade mark of
Oxford University Press in the UK and in certain other countries

© Irene J. F. de Jong 2014

The moral rights of the author have been asserted

First Edition published in 2014

All rights reserved. No part of this publication may be reproduced, stored in
a retrieval system, or transmitted, in any form or by any means, without the
prior permission in writing of Oxford University Press, or as expressly permitted
by law, by licence or under terms agreed with the appropriate reprographics
rights organization. Enquiries concerning reproduction outside the scope of the
above should be sent to the Rights Department, Oxford University Press, at the
address above

You must not circulate this work in any other form
and you must impose this same condition on any acquirer

Published in the United States of America by Oxford University Press
198 Madison Avenue, New York, NY 10016, United States of America

British Library Cataloguing in Publication Data
Data available

ISBN 978-0-19-968870-8

Links to third party websites are provided by Oxford in good faith and
for information only. Oxford disclaims any responsibility for the materials
contained in any third party website referenced in this work.

Preface

The idea of writing this practical guide occurred to me when I heard from different sources that colleagues were using the glossary of my *Narratological Commentary on the Odyssey* (2001) in their teaching as a kind of 'crash' introduction to narratology. This made me realize that, while there is no shortage of general introductions to narratology, there might be a need for a book that is geared specifically to classical students and that offers a practical introduction. The current volume is 'practical' in several senses. First, it presents a selection of concepts that I have come to rely on for the analysis of classical texts over the past twenty-five years. Second, it explains those concepts on the basis of examples from actual texts, both ancient and modern. This juxtaposition of ancient and modern examples is both pedagogical, the modern ones being easier to process, and ideological, the ancient ones showing the roots of our modern European literature. Third, apart from a brief historical introduction that sketches the emergence of narratology and its introduction into classics, I refrain from giving a full, diachronic overview of how terms and concepts have been modified over time. Rather, I present a systematic and clear set of terms and definitions, which, so to speak, are ready for use.

For this is what theoretical concepts are for: not to be introduced for their own sake or to be nit-picked endlessly, but to be applied to texts. They should sharpen and enrich our interpretation of texts. At the same time, theory should never become a straightjacket. Inevitably, as in grammar, there will be passages that are difficult to label as device A or B or perhaps as both. In such cases the function of theory is to highlight textual complexity, not to straighten it out. Used with 'sprezzatura' narratology can be a powerful instrument, one among many developed in and after antiquity to increase our understanding and appreciation of what classical literature has to offer us.

In order to show the interpretative benefits to be reaped from putting on a pair of narratological glasses, the second part of the book contains a series of close readings of texts. Here the concepts introduced systematically in the first part are shown at work *in situ*. Such literary close readings are my personal favourite of the many applications for narratology. Others will use it for different purposes, for example to uncover ideologies or relate formal devices to historical contexts.

In writing this book I have made use of much earlier work, in particular the Introductions that I wrote for the edited volumes in the series Studies in Ancient Greek Narrative: *Narrators, Narratees, and Narratives in Ancient Greek Literature*; *Time in Ancient Greek Literature*; and *Space in Ancient Greek Literature*. They have been expanded and revised considerably, however, and I have added a chapter on focalization, a subject not (yet) covered in the series. These three volumes also provided me with a treasure trove of passages from which I have thankfully culled many of my examples. I have added examples from Latin literature, which meant a pleasant return to texts I had hardly read since my student days. The three close readings in the second part are also reworkings of earlier studies, but they have been revised, expanded, and updated almost beyond recognition. I quote ancient texts mainly from Oxford Classical Texts or Teubner editions. Translations are my own adaptations from existent ones.

Although written primarily for an audience familiar with classical literature, this book may also be of interest to narratologists in other fields. The days of Erich Auerbach or Ernst Robert Curtius, when scholars would as a matter of course be steeped in classical as well as modern literature and thus aware of the long pedigree of novelistic devices, are long past. The following pages offer non-classicist readers a quick introduction to early manifestations of the narrative phenomena they are investigating in their own texts.

I would like to thank a number of my Amsterdam colleagues and graduate students who read (parts of) the penultimate version of this book and provided valuable comments: Aniek van den Eersten, Jo Heirman, Niels Koopman, and Marietje van Erp Taalman Kip. I would also like to acknowledge my great pleasure and gratitude for the generous suggestions I received in a masterclass at Corpus Christi College, Oxford, 1 March 2013, from a group of extremely talented PhD students: Sophie Bocksberger, Chrysanthos Chrysanthou, Camille Geisz, Dan Jolowicz, Tom Mackenzie, Iarla Manny, Enrico Prodi, Athena Siapera, Helen Todd, and Lucy VanEssen-Fishman. Finally, I would like to thank the two anonymous readers of OUP for valuable suggestions and corrections, and Elizabeth Upper for polishing my English.

This book is dedicated to a person who does not 'give a hoot' about narratology but who is a patient narratee of my endless narratives of academic daily life, Tjang Chang.

Contents

Contents

Part I

A Narratological Primer

1

Introduction

1.1. A BIRD'S-EYE VIEW OF THE HISTORY OF NARRATOLOGY

The term 'narratology' was coined in 1969 by Tzvetan Todorov in his *Grammaire du Decameron*, but the interest in the theory of narrative is, of course, much older. In fact, narratology can be said to have started in antiquity, when a number of central concepts were developed. One example is the crucial distinction between narrator-text and character-text or speech, as made by Plato in his *Republic* III.392–3:

> [Socrates:] 'Is not everything that is said by mythologists or poets a narration (διήγησις) of past, present, or future things?' [Adeimantus:] 'What else could it be?', he said. [Socrates:] 'Do they not proceed either by one-layered narration (ἁπλῇ διηγήσει) or through representation (διὰ μιμήσεως) or both?' [...] 'Do you know the first lines of the *Iliad* in which the poet says that Chryses implored Agamemnon to release his daughter, and that the king was angry and that Chryses, failing of his request, cursed the Achaeans?' [Adeimantus:] 'I do.' [Socrates:] 'You know then that up until these verses "Chryses had come to the ships of the Achaeans to gain release for his daughter [...] He began to entreat the whole body of the Achaeans, but especially the two sons of Atreus" the poet himself is the speaker and does not even attempt to suggest to us that anyone but himself is speaking. But he delivers what follows as if he himself were Chryses and tries as much as possible to make us feel that not Homer is the speaker, but the priest, an old man: "Sons of Atreus, and you other well-greaved Achaeans [...] release my dear child to me".'

Plato distinguishes between the poet speaking as himself and speaking as if he were one of the characters, that is, impersonating one of the characters. In other words, he recognizes the difference between *dihēgēsis* and *mimēsis*, or between narrator-text and character-text.

Another example of ancient 'proto-narratology' is the notion of plot, as developed by Aristotle in *Poetics* 7:

> We have already laid down that tragedy is a representation of an action which is complete, whole and of a certain magnitude [...] By 'whole' I mean possessing a beginning, middle, and end. By 'beginning' I mean that which does not have a necessary connection with a preceding event, but which itself can give rise naturally to some further fact or occurrence. An 'end', by contrast, is something which naturally occurs after a preceding event, whether by necessity or as a general rule, but need not be followed by anything else. The 'middle' involves causal connections with both what precedes and what ensues. Consequently, well-designed plot structures ought not to begin or finish at arbitrary points, but follow the principles indicated.

And even the modern distinction between 'telling', a style of narration whereby a narrator continuously refers to himself and expresses his opinions, and 'showing', when events seem to tell themselves, has ancient roots, as witness Aristotle *Poetics* 24:

> Homer is to be praised for many other things but especially because he alone of all (epic) poets knows very well what he should do himself. For a poet should speak as little as possible himself (i.e. in person). For when he does so he is not engaging in *mimesis*. Other epic poets are commenting on their story all the time and engage in *mimesis* only rarely and briefly. But Homer after a brief proem immediately introduces a man or a woman or another character, all of them fully characterized.

Aristotle here distinguishes between narrators who constantly discuss the accounts they are presenting (telling) and Homer, who hardly refers to himself but leaves the stage to his characters (showing).

The ancient scholia (comments that are usually extracted from preexisting monographs or commentaries and that are written in the margins of ancient manuscripts) in particular are rife with 'narratological' concepts, some even anticipating modern terminology such as prolepsis or flash-forward. Thus in a comment on *Iliad* 15.610–14, when the Homeric narrator announces that Hector's death is imminent, they write, "And prolepsis ($\pi\rho\delta\lambda\eta\psi\iota\varsigma$) is a poetic device. It renders the reader attentive and emotionally more engaged."[1] In modern times it was novelists who, reflecting on aspects of their art, further developed the theory of narrative. Thus Henry James, himself

---

[1] Nünlist 2009: 37.

a master of the device of perspective, wrote about it in one of his prefaces (collected in *The Art of the Novel*):

> The house of fiction has in short not one window, but a million [...]
> every one of which has been pierced, or is still pierceable, in its vast
> front, by the need of the individual vision and by the pressure of the
> individual will. [...] at each of them stands a figure with a pair of eyes,
> or at least with a field-glass which forms, again and again, for observa-
> tion, a unique instrument [...] He and his neighbours are watching the
> same show, but one seeing more where the other sees less, one seeing
> black where the other sees white, one seeing big where the other sees
> small, one seeing coarse where the other sees fine.[2]

Another novelist, E.M. Forster, published a series of lectures on *Aspects of the Novel*, in which he discussed amongst other things the central importance of 'time' in narrative:

> in the novel, the allegiance to time is imperative: no novel could be
> written without it. Whereas in daily life the allegiance may not be
> necessary: we do not know, and the experience of certain mystics
> suggests, indeed, that it is not necessary, and that we are quite mistaken
> in supposing that Monday is followed by Tuesday, or death by decay. It
> is always possible for you or me in daily life to deny that time exists and
> act accordingly even if we become unintelligible and are sent by our
> fellow citizens to what they choose to call a lunatic-asylum. But it is
> never possible for a novelist to deny time inside the fabric of his novel:
> he must cling, however, lightly, to the thread of his story, he must touch
> the interminable tapeworm, otherwise he becomes unintelligible, which,
> in his case, is a blunder.[3]

Around the same time, the beginning of the twentieth century, another number of central concepts were contributed by the Russian formalists, who wanted to define the 'literary' essence of literary texts. An example is the well-known opposition between *fabula/fable* and *sujet*:

> Fable refers to the total number of interlinked events that are reported
> in a work ... Contrasting with the fable is the sujet: the same events, but
> in their representation, in the order they are communicated in the work,
> and in that combination in which the information on it is conveyed in
> the work.[4]

[2] James [1934] 1953: 46.   [3] Forster [1927] 1979: 43.
[4] Lemon and Reis 1965: 137.

But the real heyday of narratology was the 1960s and 1970s, when the classical models of Bal, Booth, Genette, and Stanzel were developed. Two of these, Bal and Genette, form the basis of the present book and will be introduced in detail in Chapters 2–5.

Since the 1990s narratology has both become postclassical (Alber and Fludernik, Herman and Vervaeck) and branched out to include as subjects of its research film (Branigan, Chatman), historiography (Cohn), drama (Jahn), and lyric (Hühn and Kiefer).

Another recent trend is to introduce a historical dimension to narratology and to look at the development of narrative techniques over time. Monika Fludernik, who advocates such a 'diachronization of narratology', suggests possible programmes:

> The historical approach to narrative can take a number of forms. For instance, one can look at narrative genres in each historical period and discuss how they develop over time. Or one can find out when certain techniques or constellations were first used, or when they became current and, even later, predominant, but also it will be exciting to take up the question of refunctionalisation. Do certain features and techniques acquire a different function at crucial points of the restructuring process of the narrative paradigm?[5]

Such diachronical narratology offers many possibilities to the study of the history of classical literature, as will be set out in the next section.

At present there are many general introductions to narratology (e.g. Bal, Bonheim, Fludernik, Herman, Martínez and Scheffel, Molino and Lafhail-Molino, Porter Abott, Prince, Rimmon-Kenan, Schmid), two companions to narratology (Herman, Phelan and Rabinowitz), an encyclopedia of narratology (Herman, Jahn, and Ryan), a dictionary of narratology (Prince), an electronic handbook of narratology (<http://hup.sub.uni-hamburg.de/lhn>), and a history of narratology (Martin).

1.2. THE INTRODUCTION OF NARRATOLOGY INTO CLASSICS

For a long time, classics, as the oldest philology, which was moreover armed from antiquity with an impressive arsenal of terms and concepts with which to analyse and interpret texts, was the leader in the

---

[5] Fludernik 2003: 332–4.

field of literary interpretation. When from the beginning of the twentieth century the modern philologies were born and started to develop their own models, classics suffered under the dialectics of progress: it did not feel the need to catch up with those developments of modern literary theory and became somewhat isolated and withdrawn within the confines of its own discipline. This situation was diagnosed in the 1960s, and gradually papers and volumes started to appear which especially addressed the issue and offered samples of the application of modern literary theories (Segal, Rubino, de Jong and Sullivan, Hexter and Selden, Harrison), with telling titles such as 'Ancient Texts and Modern Literary Criticism', 'Innovations of Antiquity', or 'Modern Critical Theory and Classical Literature'. The introductions of these studies mark the gradual process of the integration of modern theory. Thus, the early ones ask why classics was slow in adopting modern theory. Segal comes up with the following analysis:

> When we come to consider specific methods of criticism, it is clear that classical critics have not of late been pioneers or innovators of new approaches, as they were in the early part of the century. No new critical theories have arisen from classical studies *per se*. We cannot today claim a Nietzsche, a Frazer, a Cornford, or even a Gilbert Murray, nor do we have a critic of the theoretical scope or synthetic imagination of a Northrop Frye. The reason for this is perhaps that classical studies have grown more cautious about generalisation. Critics prefer to work in the securer, more manageable areas of a single author or work.[6]

In other words, the tradition of close reading prevented classical scholars from coming up with large, sweeping literary theories. Rubino brings up another relevant point: the structuralist theories of the 1960s, which were mainly developed by French thinkers, were simply very hard reading.

When modern theory became increasingly embraced by classical scholars, the volumes' introductions likewise became more confident, for example that of Sullivan and de Jong:

> In recent decades the study and teaching of literature in Europe and the Americas have been radically influenced by modern critical theory in its various forms. Although the influence and the leading exponents of these various theories and approaches have been most noticeable in the

---

[6] Segal 1968: 10.

study of modern literatures and culture, there has also been a perceptible impact of these theories in the study of Greco-Latin literature [...][7]

Hexter and Selden's introduction, written at about the same time, is more open about the tensions that the introduction of modern theory created within classics:

> to judge from recent conferences, convention sessions, courses, books, and journals, critical appreciation of Greco-Roman literature is itself in a state of significant transition. Partly under the influence of intellectual energy drawn from neighbouring fields [...] the received forms of linguistic and historical positivism are undergoing transformation. For some the critical right has condemned this development as a degeneration of science [...] into speculation, while the critical left has hailed the trend as the belated displacement of a moribund philology by an ethically more conscientious hermeneutics.[8]

To appease such tensions the introduction of Harrison in 2001 has the conciliatory title 'Working Together'. The volume sets out 'to promote a simple idea: that, in the contemporary context of the study and interpretation of classical literature at universities, conventional classical scholarship and modern theoretical ideas need to work with each other in the common task of the interpretation of texts'. In particular, the editor hopes 'that this volume will encourage sceptically inclined literary classics to believe that the application of literary (and other) theory can provide new and enriching resources for their traditional scholarship, and remind the more theoretically inclined that they need and rely on traditional scholarship'.[9]

Along with these studies, which discussed whether modern theory could be applied to classical texts and merely offered samples, monographs that simply used such modern theories have appeared since the 1970s. It is not possible to list all of those here, but one may fruitfully consult the overview by Thomas Schmitz in *Modern Literary Theory and Ancient Texts*. In twelve chapters, he first introduces a branch of modern literary theory both historically and systematically, ranging from formalism, structuralism, via narratology and intertextuality, to deconstruction, psychoanalytic and feminist theory, and then gives an overview of applications of this branch to classical texts.

---

[7] De Jong and Sullivan 1993: 1. [8] Hexter and Selden 1992: xii.
[9] Harrison 2001: 1, 17.

In his introduction Schmitz gives a clear and helpful discussion of
all the old classical prejudices against modern theory and ends with a
passionate plea for the intelligent, creative, and eclectic use of the
many good things modern theory has to offer the classical scholar. He
rightly observes that the slowness of classics in adopting modern
theory can also be seen as an advantage in retrospect:

> Classics as a field has been rather slow to come to grips with modern
> literary theory [...] It could be argued that this belatedness is an
> advantage rather than a drawback: while the turmoil of the last
> century has subsided and given way to a more dispassionate view,
> the fundamental questions that literary theory has raised remain with
> us. [...] this situation should be considered an opportunity to take a
> calmer look at all these questions and problems, at a safe distance from
> the sound and the fury of earlier times [...] we can now examine the
> contributions of the theoretical positions and the individual theorists
> with a less polemical eye—you no longer have to surf the latest
> theoretical wave to be considered hip.[10]

One of the most successful and fruitful modern theories absorbed by
classical scholarship is narratology. In the mid-1980s, pioneers like
John Winkler (Apuleius), Massimo Fusillo (Apollonius of Rhodes),
and Irene de Jong (Homer) published the first book-length narratological studies. Since then narratological studies on virtually all Greek
and Roman narrative genres have appeared. This is not the place to
provide a full overview, but between them the chapter on narratology
in Schmitz's *Modern Literary Theory and Ancient Texts*; the introduction of Grethlein and Rengakos's *Narratology and Interpretation*;
the electronic bibliography 'Narratology and the Classics' compiled
by Antonios Rengakos and Chrysanthe Tsitsiou-Chelidoni;[11] and the
bibliographies at the end of this and the other four introductory
chapters give a good impression of the work that has been done.
Actually, the number of narratologically based studies is at present
growing so rapidly that it is no longer possible to give a complete
picture, just as it is no longer possible to summarize all intertextual
studies within classics.

A possible explanation for the success of narratology within the
field of classics is that its terms resemble those of rhetoric, which has
been of old the framework within which ancient literary texts are

analysed. The French narratologist Genette in particular introduced numerous neologisms, such as analepsis, prolepsis, paralepsis, paralipsis, and metalepsis, that mirror or build on ancient rhetorical terms. They will be explained in chapters to come.

What has narratology brought classics? Some broad lines may be sketched. First, the notion of a narrator as distinct from the historical author has been a welcome correction of the trend towards an all-too-biographical reading of ancient texts (e.g. in connection with Hesiod or Ovid). Second, the crucial narratological distinction between narrator-text and character-text has spawned important stylistic research into the vocabularies of narrators versus that of characters (e.g. in Homer or Apollonius of Rhodes). Third, the notion of focalization or point of view has proven helpful in laying bare the ideologies of texts (e.g. in Virgil and Propertius). Fourth, the category of time has turned out to be a useful instrument to pinpoint generic characteristics (e.g. in archaic Greek choral lyric or in Latin elegy). Fifth, narratology has generally enriched the toolkit for the close reading of texts. Classical texts have been read and interpreted for centuries, and every new set of scholarly 'spectacles' that opens our eyes to new facets is welcome.

Narratology has also been instrumental in renewing age-old instruments of classics. One example is the commentary. Classical commentaries traditionally summarize scholarship on all aspects of a text in the form of line-by-line lemmata and are aimed primarily at explaining difficulties: they elucidate problematic grammatical constructions or obscure words, provide the historical or archaeological background needed to understand what is said, and summarize interpretations of puzzling passages. Narratological commentaries, such as now exist for Homer's *Odyssey* and Ovid's *Metamorphoses*,[12] are not comprehensive but concentrate on one aspect of the text: its narrative art. They discuss the role of the narrator and narratees, the methods of characterization, the handling of time, matters of focalization or point of view, and the role of space for the whole of the text, not only those words or passages that in the past have been deemed problematic. They also proceed by larger lemmata than the traditional line-by-line format.

Another instrument of classical scholarship that has received a new impetus from narratology is literary history. While traditional literary

---

[12] De Jong 2001; Tsitsiou-Chelidoni 2003.

histories concern the author and his works and readers, the multi-volume narratological history of ancient Greek narrative, Studies in Ancient Greek Narrative,[13] focuses on the narrative techniques in those works. It combines the synchronic and the diachronic, offering not only analyses of the handling of a specific narrative device by individual authors but also a larger historical perspective on the manner in which techniques change over time. It explores how they are put to different uses and achieve different effects in the hands of different authors, who are writing in different genres about different material. The series thus is the first large-scale example of the diachronization of narratology advocated by Fludernik (see §1.1), and it covers some twelve centuries of literature.

If classics has benefited greatly from the introduction of narratology, the time has come to give something back. About fifty years ago, two literary scholars, Robert Scholes and Robert Kellogg, wrote in *The Nature of Narrative*:

> To understand the present we must possess the past. The literature of Greece and Rome is still of interest to us in the twentieth century because of its intrinsic merit, but for our special purposes in this investigation it has an even greater interest. The classical literature provides us with prototypes of virtually all later narrative forms and with paradigms of the processes which govern their interaction and evolution.[14]

Classical scholars can now lay bare the literary DNA of the most popular literary form of our times, the novel, in ancient narrative texts. This book aims at providing new generations of students with a practical guide for doing so.

FURTHER READING

Classics and literary theory

Harrison, S.J. (ed.), *Texts, Ideas, and the Classics: Scholarship, Theory, and Classical Literature* (Oxford 2001).
Hexter, R., and D.L. Selden (eds), *Innovations of Antiquity* (New York 1992).

---

[13] De Jong, Nünlist, and Bowie 2004; de Jong and Nünlist 2007; de Jong 2012.
[14] Scholes and Kellogg 1966: 57.

Jong, I.J.F. de, and J.P. Sullivan (eds), *Modern Critical Theory and Classical Literature* (Leiden 1993).

Rubino, C.A. '"Lectio difficilior praeferenda est": Some Remarks on Contemporary French Thought and the Study of Classical Literature', *Arethusa* 10, 1977, 63–83.

Schmitz, T.A., *Modern Literary Theory and Ancient Texts: An Introduction* (Malden 2007; first published in German 2002).

Segal, C.P., 'Ancient Texts and Modern Literary Criticism', *Arethusa* 1, 1968, 1–25.

Narratology

Alber, J., and M. Fludernik (eds), *Postclassical Narratology: Approaches and Analyses* (Columbus 2010).

Altman, R., *A Theory of Narrative* (New York and Chicester 2008).

Bal, M., *Narratology: Introduction to the Theory of Narrative* (Toronto 1997; first published 1985).

Bonheim, H., *The Narrative Modes: Techniques of the Short Story* (Woodbridge, Suffolk and Rochester, NY 1982).

Booth, W.C., *The Rhetoric of Fiction* (Chicago 1983; first published 1961).

Branigan, E., *Narrative Comprehension and Film* (London and New York 1992).

Chatman, S., *Story and Discourse: Narrative Structure in Fiction and Film* (Ithaca, NY 1978).

Chatman, S., *Coming to Terms: The Rhetoric of Narrative in Fiction and Film* (Ithaca, NY 1990).

Cohn, D., *Transparent Minds: Narrative Modes for Presenting Consciousness in Fiction* (Princeton 1978).

Cohn, D., *The Distinction of Fiction* (Baltimore 1999).

Fludernik, M., *Towards a 'Natural' Narratology* (London and New York 1996).

Fludernik, M., 'The Diachronization of Narratology', *Narrative* 11, 2003, 331–48.

Fludernik, M., *An Introduction to Narratology* (London and New York 2009; first published in German 2006).

Forster, E.M., *Aspects of the Novel* (Harmondsworth 1979; first published 1927).

Genette, G., *Narrative Discourse: An Essay in Method* (Ithaca, NY 1980; first published in French 1972).

Genette, G., *Narrative Discourse Revisited* (Ithaca, NY 1988; first published in French 1983).

Herman, D. (ed.), *Cambridge Companion to Narrative* (Cambridge 2007).

Herman, D. *Basic Elements of Narrative* (Malden, Oxford, and Chichester 2009).

Herman, D., M. Jahn, and M.L. Ryan (eds), *The Routledge Encyclopedia of Narrative Theory* (London and New York 2005).

Herman, L., and B. Vervaeck, *Handbook of Narrative Analysis* (Lincoln, NE 2005).

Hühn, P., and J. Kiefer, *Narratologia: The Narratological Analysis of Lyric Poetry: Studies in English Poetry from the 16th to the 20th Century* (Berlin 2005).

Jahn, M., 'Narrative Voice and Agency in Drama: Aspects of a Narratology of Drama', *New Literary History* 32, 2001, 659–79.

James, H., *The Art of the Novel: Critical Prefaces* (New York 1953; first published 1934).

Lemon, L.T., and M.J. Reis, *Russian Formalist Criticism: Four Essays* (Lincoln, NE 1965).

Martin, W., *Recent Theories of Narrative* (Ithaca, NY 1986).

Martínez, M., and M. Scheffel, *Einführung in die Erzähltheorie* (Munich 1999).

Molino, J., and R. Lafhail-Molino, *Homo fabulator: théorie et analyse du récit* (Montreal 2003).

Phelan, J., and P.J. Rabinowitz, *A Companion to Narrative Theory* (Malden, Oxford, and Carlton 2005).

Porter Abbott, H., *The Cambridge Introduction to Narrative* (Cambridge 2002).

Prince, G., *Narratology: The Form and Functioning of Narrative* (Berlin 1982).

Prince, G., *A Dictionary of Narratology* (Lincoln, NE and London 2003; first published 1987).

Rimmon-Kenan, S., *Narrative Fiction: Contemporary Poetics* (London 1983).

Schmid, W., *Elemente der Narratologie* (Berlin 2008; first published 2005).

Scholes, R., and R. Kellogg, *The Nature of Narrative* (London 1966; a revised and expanded version, co-authored with J. Phelan, appeared in 2006).

Stanzel, F., *A Theory of Narrative* (Cambridge and New York 1984; first published in German 1979).

Narratology and classics
See also the bibliographies at the end of later chapters.

Barchiesi, A., 'Narrative Technique and Narratology in the *Metamorphoses*', in P. Hardie (ed.), *The Cambridge Companion to Ovid* (Cambridge 2002), 180–99.

Fowler, D.P., 'Deviant Focalisation in Virgil's *Aeneid*', *Proceedings of the Cambridge Philological Society* 36, 1990, 42–63 (reprinted in *Roman Constructions: Readings in Postmodern Latin* (Oxford 2000), 40–63).

Fusillo, M., *Il tempo delle Argonautiche: un analisi del racconto in Apollonio Rodio* (Rome 1985).

Fusillo, M., *Naissance du roman* (Paris 1991; first published in Italian 1989).

Fusillo, M., 'Apollonius Rhodius as "Inventor" of the Interior Monologue', in T.D. Papanghelis and A. Rengakos (eds), *Brill's Companion to Apollonius Rhodius* (Leiden 2008), 147–66.

Gale, M., 'The Story of Us: A Narratological Analysis of Lucretius' *De Rerum Natura*', in M. Gale (ed.), *Latin Epic and Didactic Poetry: Genre, Tradition, and Individuality* (Swansea 2004), 49–72.

Grethlein, J., *Das Geschichtsbild der Ilias: Eine Untersuchung aus phänomenologischer und narratologischer Perspektive* (Göttingen 2006).

Grethlein, J., and A. Rengakos (eds), *Narratology and Interpretation: The Content of Narrative Form in Ancient Literature* (Berlin 2009).

Hägg, T., *Narrative Technique in Ancient Greek Romances: Studies of Chariton, Xenophon Ephesius, and Achilles Tatius* (Stockholm 1971).

Hornblower, S., 'Narratology and Narrative Technique in Thucydides', in S. Hornblower (ed.), *Greek Historiography* (Oxford 1996), 131–66.

Jong, I.J.F. de, *Narrative in Drama: The Art of the Euripidean Messenger-Speech* (Leiden 1991).

Jong, I.J.F. de, 'Narratology and Oral Poetry: The Case of Homer', *Poetics Today* 12, 1991, 405–23.

Jong, I.J.F. de, *A Narratological Commentary on the Odyssey* (Cambridge 2001).

Jong, I.J.F. de, 'A Narratological Commentary on the Odyssey: Principles and Problems', in R.K. Gibson and C.S. Kraus (eds), *The Classical Commentary: Histories, Practices, Theory* (Leiden 2002), 49–66.

Jong, I.J.F. de, *Narrators and Focalizers: The Presentation of the Story in the Iliad* (London 2004; first published 1987).

Jong, I.J.F. de, 'Aristotle on the Homeric Narrator', *Classical Quaterly* 55, 2005, 616–21.

Jong, I.J.F. de, 'Where Narratology Meets Stylistics: The Seven Versions of Ajax' Madness', in I.J.F. de Jong and A. Rijksbaron (eds), *Sophocles and the Greek Language: Aspects of Diction, Syntax, and Pragmatics* (Leiden 2006), 73–94.

Jong, I.J.F. de, R. Nünlist, and A. Bowie (eds), *Narrators, Narratees, and Narratives in Ancient Greek Literature*, Studies in Ancient Greek Narrative 1 (Leiden 2004).

Jong, I.J.F. de, and R. Nünlist (eds), *Time in Ancient Greek Literature*, Studies in Ancient Greek Narrative 2 (Leiden 2007).

Jong, I.J.F. de, (ed.), *Space in Ancient Greek Literature*, Studies in Ancient Greek Narrative 3 (Leiden 2012).

Lively, G., and P.B. Salzman-Mitchell (eds), *Latin Elegy and Narratology: Fragments of Story* (Columbus 2008).

Lowe, N.J., *The Classical Plot and the Invention of Western Narrative* (Cambridge 2000).

Lowrie, M., *Horace's Narrative Odes* (Oxford 1997).

Markantonatos, A., *Tragic Narrative: A Narratological Study of Sophocles' Oedipus at Colonus* (Berlin 2002).

Munson, R.V., *Telling Wonders: Ethnographic and Political Discourse in the Work of Herodotus* (Ann Arbor 2001).

Nikolopoulos, A.D., *Ovidius Polytropos: Metanarrative in Ovid's Metamorphoses* (Zurich 2004).

Nünlist, R., *The Ancient Critic at Work: Terms and Concepts of Literary Criticism in Greek Scholia* (Cambridge 2009).

Paardt, R.T. van der, 'Various Aspects of Narrative Technique in Apuleius' "Metamorphoses"', in B.L. Hijmans and R.T. van der Paardt (eds), *Aspects of Apuleius' Golden Ass* (Groningen 1978), 75–94.

Pausch, D., *Livius und der Leser: Narrative Strukturen in ab urbe condita* (Munich 2011).

Richardson, S., *The Homeric Narrator* (Nashville 1990).

Rood, T., *Thucydides: Narrative and Explanation* (Oxford 1998).

Rosati, G., 'Narrative Techniques and Narrative Structures in the Metamorphoses', in B.W. Boyd (ed.), *Brill's Companion to Ovid* (Leiden 2002), 271–304.

Stoddard, K., *The Narrative Voice in the Theogony of Hesiod* (Leiden 2004).

Tsitsiou-Chelidoni, C., *Ovid, Metamorphosen Buch VIII: Narrative Technik und literarischer Kontext* (Frankfurt 2003).

Wheeler, S.M., *A Discourse of Wonders: Audiences and Performances in Ovid's Metamorphoses* (Philadelphia 1999).

Wheeler, S.M., *Narrative Dynamics in Ovid's Metamorphoses* (Tübingen 2000).

Winkler, J.J., *Auctor and Actor: A Narratological Reading of Apuleius' The Golden Ass* (Berkeley, Los Angeles, and Oxford 1985).

2

Narrators and Narratees

Perhaps the most central concept in narratology is that of the narrator. For most narratologists, his presence is the necessary condition for a text to be deemed a narrative: a narrative text is a text in which a narrator recounts a series of events. Adopting this criterion, this book discusses the following types of narrative texts in Greek and Latin literature: *purely narrative texts* (epic, novel, narrative types of lyric such as the dithyramb), what could be called *applied narrative texts* (historiography, biography), *narratives that are incorporated in non-narrative genres* (such as the myths or historical narratives of lyric, the messenger-speeches of drama, and the *narrationes* of oratory), and what Gérard Genette called *pseudo-diegetic texts*, that is, texts with a suppressed narrator. He used this term in explicit reference to Plato's philosophical dialogue *Theaetetus* 143 c, where the narrator says that he avoids the tag 'and he said'. Here, it is also applied to the so-called mimetic *Idyls* of Theocritus and *Eclogues* of Virgil, poems that purely consist of dialogue but that belong to genres that also have instances *with* a narrative frame and a narrator. For historiography and drama, see also Chapters 7 and 8.

2.1. AUTHOR VERSUS NARRATOR

It is an important principle of narratology that the narrator cannot automatically be equated with the author; rather, it is a creation of that author, like the characters. This is evident in example (1).

(1) Sir Arthur Conan Doyle, *The Five Orange Pips:*[1]

> When I glance over my records and notes of the Sherlock Holmes cases between the years '82 and '90, I am faced by so many which present strange and interesting features that it is no easy matter to know which to choose and which to leave.

The narrating 'I' is Dr Watson, while the author is Arthur Conan Doyle. But even when we are dealing with an anonymous voice telling us the story or with a narrator who has the same name as the author, this anonymous or homonymous narrator is not simply to be identified with the author. Some authors explicitly warn their readers, as in (2).

(2) Christopher Isherwood, *Goodbye to Berlin*, preface:

> If I have given my own name to the 'I' of this narrative, readers are certainly not entitled to assume that its pages are purely autobiographical, or that its characters are libellously exact portraits of living persons. 'Christopher Isherwood' is a convenient ventriloquist's dummy, nothing more.

Such warnings are lacking in ancient texts and this, together with an almost complete absence of theorizing on the notion of poetic persona in antiquity, has led to an all too easy biographical interpretation of passages like (3).

(3) Hesiod, *Theogony* 22–3:

> αἵ νύ ποθ' Ἡσίοδον καλὴν ἐδίδαξαν ἀοιδήν,
> ἄρνας ποιμαίνονθ' Ἑλικῶνος ὕπο ζαθέοιο.

They [the Muses] one day taught Hesiod fine singing as he was shepherding his lambs below holy Helicon.

Should we really believe that the historical poet Hesiod had an encounter with the Muses? It seems more likely that he is creating a narrator-figure of himself inside the text, who as a textual creature can experience more miraculous things than real persons of flesh and blood. The distinction is also valid in the many instances of what has been called the oral subterfuge: Latin authors, like Virgil (*arma*

---

[1] References for the example passages are mainly to chapters, as numerous editions to these works are available. Where there are no chapters, as in this example, I have provided a page number. In rare instances, when the passage is from a short story for example, I have provided neither page nor chapter number.

virumque cano) or Ovid (*ad mea perpetuum deducite tempora carmen*), posing in their texts as singing narrators.

Some narratologists, starting with Wayne Booth, have posited the need for the concept of an *implied author* between author and narrator. This is the author's second self in the text. It embodies the norms and choices of that text (or a reconstruction of those norms by readers) and provides the standard against which to gauge the narrator's reliability or explain cases of irony at the narrator's expense. The concept is heavily debated, and it is questionable whether we really need this extra entity.[2] In this book, the concept will not be used.

2.2. THE IDENTITY OF THE NARRATOR

Given that every narrative text has a narrator, the next step is to define that narrator. There are, in fact, many types. The first thing to ask oneself is whether the narrator is a character in his own story: if he is, we speak of an *internal* narrator; if not, of an *external* narrator.[3] Internal narrators are often called 'first-person narrators', but this is a less fortunate term, since external narrators can also refer to themselves as 'I', as does for example the Homeric narrator in 'tell *me*, Muse, of the man' (*Odyssey* 1.1). In fact, all narratives are in principle recounted by a narrating subject, even if this narrating 'I' never refers to itself. So the use of the 'I' form is not a watertight criterion for distinguishing narrators. Internal narrators may be the protagonist of their own story (Pip in *Great Expectations* or Odysseus in *Odyssey* 9–12) or a mere witness (Nick Carraway in Scott Fitzgerald's *The Great Gatsby* or the messenger of Attic drama), as well as everything that lies in between.

Narratives usually have more than one narrator, acting on different levels. The narrator who recounts the main story, and whose voice is usually the first we hear when the story begins, is the *primary*

---

[2] A clear overview of the debate is given by Ansgar Nünning in the *Routledge Encyclopedia of Narrative Theory*, s.v. implied author.

[3] One also often finds the terminology of Genette: homodiegetic (internal) versus heterodiegetic (external). Note that many incorrectly use the term 'internal narrator' when they actually mean text-internal narrator (as opposed to the author).

narrator. This primary narrator may hand over the presentation of events to a character who recounts a story in direct speech, in which case we speak of a *secondary* narrator.[4] When this character in turn embeds another narrative in his or her own narrative, we are dealing with a *tertiary* narrator, and so on. A celebrated classical example of the nesting of narratives is Ovid *Metamorphoses* 5.341–661, where a Muse tells about a song the Muse Calliope sang about the nymph Arethusa, who tells the story of her life.

Between them, the criteria internal–external and primary–secondary suffice to describe most narrators in world literature. For an *external primary narrator* we may turn to (4) and (5).

(4) Jane Austen, *Pride and Prejudice*, chapter 1:

> It is a truth universally acknowledged, that a single man in possession of a good fortune must be in want of a wife. However little known the feelings or views of such a man may be on his first entering a neighbourhood, this truth is so well fixed in the minds of the surrounding families, that he is considered as the rightful property of some one or other of their daughters.

(5) Apollonius of Rhodes, *Argonautica* 1.1–4:

> ἀρχόμενος σέο, Φοῖβε, παλαιγενέων κλέα φωτῶν
> μνήσομαι, οἳ Πόντοιο κατὰ στόμα καὶ διὰ πέτρας
> Κυανέας βασιλῆος ἐφημοσύνῃ Πελίαο
> χρύσειον μετὰ κῶας ἐύζυγον ἤλασαν Ἀργώ.

> Beginning with you, Phoebus, I will recount the famous deeds of men of old, who sped well-benched Argo down through the mouth of Pontus and between the Cyanean rocks at the behest of King Pelias in quest of the Golden Fleece.

The famously ironic narrator of (4) does not participate in the world of Elizabeth Bennet and Mr Darcy, the heroes of the novel, and in (5) the narrator, like all epic narrators, tells about events from a distant past ('deeds of men of old') and hence is not a character in his own story.

An *internal primary narrator* is to be found in (6).

(6) Charles Dickens, *Great Expectations*, chapter 1:

> Ours was the marsh country, down by the river, within, as the river wound, twenty miles of the sea. My first most vivid and broad

---

[4] In Genette's terminology: extradiegetic (primary) versus intradiegetic (secondary).

impression of the identity of things, seems to me to have been gained on a memorable raw afternoon towards evening.

(7) Apuleius, *The Golden Ass* 3.24–5:

nec ullae plumulae nec usquam pinnulae, sed plane pili mei crassantur in setas et cutis tenella duratur in corium et in extimis palmulis perdito numero toti digiti coguntur in singulas ungulas et de spinae meae termino grandis cauda procedit. [...] ac dum salutis inopia cuncta corporis mei considerans, non avem me, sed asinum video [...]

no feathers, no wings [appear] anywhere, but my hairs turn rugged, my soft skin hardened into hide; and at the end of my palms my fingers, losing their number, all grow together into single hooves and from the end of my back grows a great tail. [...] And while I, helplessly, inspect every part of my body, I see that I am no bird but an ass [...]

In (6) the narrator is Pip, who in the novel to follow looks back on his life, starting with the 'memorable' encounter he had as a six-year-old with the escaped convict Magwitch on the marsh. In (7) Lucius describes the moment when, anointing himself with a magic unguent, he does not turn into a bird, as he had intended, but an ass. The story of how he regained his human shape will take up the next eight books. For an *external secondary narrator* we may think of (8) and (9).

(8) *Tales from the Thousand and One Nights*, chapter 1:

Then Dunyazad said to Scheherazade: 'Tell us, my sister, a tale of marvel, so that the night may pass pleasantly.' 'Gladly', she answered, 'if the King permits.' And the King, who was troubled with sleeplessness, eagerly listened to the tale of Scheherazade: 'Once upon a time, in the city of Basrah, there lived a prosperous tailor [...]'

(9) Plato, *Gorgias* 522e–3a:

(ΣΩ.) 'εἰ δὲ βούλει, σοὶ ἐγώ, ὡς τοῦτο οὕτως ἔχει, ἐθέλω λόγον λέξαι.'
(ΚΑΛ.) 'Ἀλλ' ἐπείπερ γε καὶ τ'ἄλλα ἐπέρανας, καὶ τοῦτο πέρανον.' (ΣΩ.)
'Ἄκουε δή, φασί, μάλα καλοῦ λόγου, ὃν σὺ μὲν ἡγήσῃ μῦθον, ὡς ἐγὼ
οἶμαι, ἐγὼ δὲ λόγον· [...] ἦν οὖν νόμος ὅδε περὶ ἀνθρώπων ἐπὶ Κρόνου
[...] τῶν ἀνθρώπων τὸν μὲν δικαίως τὸν βίον διελθόντα καὶ ὁσίως,
ἐπειδὰν τελευτήσῃ, εἰς μακάρων νήσους ἀπιόντα οἰκεῖν ἐν πάσῃ
εὐδαιμονίᾳ ἐκτὸς κακῶν [...]'

[Socrates:] 'If you want, I will tell you a story, to show you that the case is so.' [Callias:] 'Well, as you have completed the rest of the business, complete this also.' [Socrates:] 'Give ear then, as they say, to a very fine story, which you will regard as a myth, I think, but I as a true story.

[. . .] Now in the time of Cronus there was the following law concerning mankind [. . .] that every man who has lived a just and pious life departs after his decease to the Isles of the Blest and lives in total bliss without ill [. . .]'

In (8) the primary narrative is that about Scheherazade, who must tell a sultan stories in order to save her life. In the stories she tells him as a secondary narrator she plays no role, as is immediately made clear by her opening formula ('once upon a time'), which indicates that the events took place in an indefinite past. Scheherazade's primary narrative is a *frame narrative*, a vehicle for telling a great deal of other narratives. Other famous frame narratives are Boccaccio's *Decameron* and Chaucer's *Canterbury Tales*, while Ovid's *Metamorphoses* is a possible (or at least very special) case. In (9) Socrates, a character in the dialogue narrated by the primary narrator 'Plato', himself turns (secondary) narrator in order to tell a 'myth' from the remote past ('the time of Cronus').

Finally, examples of *internal secondary narrators* include (10) and (11).

(10) Emily Brontë, *Wuthering Heights*, chapter 4:

[Mr Lockwood:] 'Well, Mrs. Dean, it will be a charitable deed to tell me something of my neighbours—I feel I shall not rest, if I go to bed; so be good enough to sit and chat an hour.' [Nelly Dean:] 'Oh, certainly, sir! [. . .] Before I came to live here', she commenced, waiting no further invitation to her story, 'I was almost always at Wuthering Heights.'

(11) Virgil, *Aeneid* 2.10–16:

'sed si tantus amor casus cognoscere nostros
et breviter Troiae supremum audire laborem,
quamquam animus meminisse horret luctuque refugit,
incipiam. fracti bello fatisque repulsi
ductores Danaum tot iam labentibus annis
instar montis equum divina Palladis arte
aedificant [. . .]'

'But if there is so much desire to learn our vicissitudes and briefly hear about Troy's last agony, although my mind shudders to remember and has taken refuge in sorrow, I will make the attempt. Broken by the war and thrust back by fate, the Greek leaders, seeing that the years were passing by, build with the help of Pallas' divine art a horse high as a mountain [. . .]'

In (10) the primary narrator, Mr Lockwood, is informed about the inhabitants of the neighbouring house, Wuthering Heights, by his housekeeper, Nelly Dean, who knows its inhabitants well and therefore can function as an internal secondary narrator; in (11) Aeneas, at the behest of his host Dido, tells the sad story of the fall of Troy and his ensuing wanderings ('our vicissitudes').

A hybrid form between primary and secondary narrator that is important for ancient literature but only rarely crops up in modern novels is the *reported narrator*, when a primary narrator presents a story in indirect speech and ascribes it to (an often anonymous) 'they', who are not characters in the story (12–13).

(12) Herodotus, *Histories* 1.24.1:

> τοῦτον τὸν Ἀρίονα λέγουσι, τὸν πολλὸν τοῦ χρόνου διατρίβοντα παρὰ
> Περιάνδρῳ, ἐπιθυμῆσαι πλῶσαι ἐς Ἰταλίην τε καὶ Σικελίην [. . .]

> They [the Corinthians and Lesbians] say that this Arion lived for most
> of the time at the court of Periander and then conceived the desire to
> sail to Italy and Sicily [. . .]

(13) Catullus, *Carmen* 64.1–3:

> Peliaco quondam prognatae vertice pinus
> dicuntur liquidas Neptuni nasse per undas
> Phasidos ad fluctus et fines Aeeteos [. . .]

> Pine-trees, born on the top of the mountains of Pelion, are said once to
> have swum through the clear waters of Neptune to the waves of Phasis
> and the realm of Aeetes [. . .]

In (12) the Herodotean narrator employs reported narrators to acknowledge the oral sources on which he bases his tale. By the time of Catullus (13), this device has acquired the function of the 'Alexandrian footnote', that is, it flags the dependence on literary tradition. Thus *dicuntur*, 'are said', here points to the earlier versions of the tale of the Argonauts in Euripides, Apollonius of Rhodes, and Ennius.

A special phenomenon is *second-person narration*, which means that a narrator recounts the acts of a character in 'you' form. In antiquity this form of narration is typically found in combination with the device of the apostrophe, a narrator no longer talking *about* a character but, 'turning away' from his narratees, directly addressing that character and recounting his or her deeds in the 'you' form (14–15).

(14) *Homeric Hymn to Apollo* 124–9:

> ἀλλὰ Θέμις νέκταρ τε καὶ ἀμβροσίην ἐρατεινήν
> ἀθανάτῃσιν χερσὶν ἐπήρξατο· χαῖρε δὲ Λητώ
> οὕνεκα τοξοφόρον καὶ καρτερὸν υἱὸν ἔτικτεν.
> αὐτὰρ ἐπεὶ δή, Φοῖβε, κατέβρως ἄμβροτον εἶδαρ,
> οὔ σέ γ᾽ ἔπειτ᾽ ἴσχον χρύσεοι στρόφοι ἀσπαίροντα,
> οὐδ᾽ ἔτι δεσμά σ᾽ ἔρυκε, λύοντο δὲ πείρατα πάντα.

And Themis served him [the baby Apollo] nectar and lovely ambrosia with her immortal hands, and Leto rejoiced, because she had borne a bow-bearing and forceful son. But after you ate the divine food, Phoebus Apollo, the golden cords no longer restrained you, wriggling, and the fastenings no longer held you, but all the ties became undone.

(15) Ovid, *Metamorphoses* 1.717–21:

> nec mora, falcato nutantem vulnerat ense,
> qua collo est confine caput, saxoque cruentem
> deicit et maculat praeruptam sanguine rupem.
> Arge, iaces, quodque in tot lumina lumen habebas
> extinctum est centumque oculos nox occupat una.

And without delay he [Mercury] smites him [Argus], while nodding, with his crooked sword where the head joins the neck and sends it bleeding down the rocks and defiles the rugged cliff with blood. Argus, you lie dead; and that light which you used to have for so many eyes has been extinguished, and one night fills a hundred eyes.

Example (14) illustrates the origin of the apostrophe and concomitant you-narration: cult hymns typically start with an invocation of the god that is hymned, and this cultic *Du-Stil* occasionally crops up in literary hymns (like the Homeric hymns) too, either at the end or, as here, in the course of the narrative. By the time of Ovid (15), the apostrophe had become a purely literary device. Here it is employed to arouse sympathy for Argus, the hundred-eyed giant appointed to guard Io, after he is beheaded by Mercury.

Modern novels employ second-person narration only rarely and by way of narrative experiment. A celebrated example is Michel Butor's *Second Thoughts*, which describes a train trip from Paris to Rome during which a man changes his mind about giving up his marriage and starting a new life with his mistress (16).

(16) Michel Butor, *Second Thoughts* (*La modification*), chapter 1:

> Standing with your left foot on the grooved brass sill, you try in vain with your right shoulder to push the sliding door a little wider open. You edge your way in through the narrow opening, then you lift up your suitcase of bottle-green grained leather, the smallish suitcase of a man used to making long journeys, grasping the sticky handle with fingers that are hot from having carried even so light a weight so far, and you feel the muscles and tendons tense not only in your finger-joints, the palm of your hand, your wrist and your arm, but in your shoulder too, all down one side of your back along your vertebrae from neck to loins.

The narrator refers to his main character (himself) in you-form, the result being that the narratees feel directly involved in the process of taking stock of his life and thus question their own life and decisions alongside him. It is interesting to realize that what surely is intended as the height of modernist experimentation is prefigured in classical literature.

The same observation can be made about another less common type of narrator: the *we-narrator*. This type is only occasionally found in modernist novels (17) but was used more regularly in Greek and Latin literature (18).

(17) John Barth, *Sabbatical*, chapter 1:

> Nineteen Sixty we declared our *Wanderjahr*; one might even say our sabbatical. It was also a test. We sold our car, withdrew our savings, subleased our apartment, took Oroonoko out of school, and went off to spend the winter in the south of Spain, where I was to get a real novel written at last. Neither of us had been out of the country before; the plan was to live cheaply till spring somewhere along the Costa del Sol, which hadn't been turned into Miami Beach; then to make a camping reconnaissance of Western Europe, whereof I would keep a useful writerly notebook for future reference.

(18) Virgil, *Aeneid* 2.21–5:

> 'est in conspectu Tenedos, notissima fama
> insula [. . .]
> huc se provecti deserto in litore condunt;
> nos abiisse rati et vento petiisse Mycenas.'

'There lies in sight Tenedos, an island of great fame [. . .] To this island they [the Greeks] sail and hide themselves on its uninhabited shore. We thought they had left and before the wind had gone for Mycenae.'

In (17) the internal narrator often talks in 'we' form, to refer to herself, a female professor on sabbatical, and her husband, an ex-CIA officer, who undertake a journey on which they sum up their years together and try to make important decisions about the years ahead. In (18) the internal narrator Aeneas uses the 'we' form in the first part of his account of the fall of Troy, to make clear how the Trojans collectively were fooled by the treacherous Greeks and their Wooden Horse.

2.3. THE ROLE OF THE NARRATOR

Having established the identity of the narrator, we may go on to investigate his role. It is easiest to start with an *overt narrator*, that is, a narrator who clearly manifests himself as narrator throughout the text. His presence can take various forms: he may be dramatized (given a life and personality of his own), comment on the events he relates, or be self-conscious (showing awareness of and thematizing his role as narrator). It will be readily understood that internal primary narrators tend to be overt. They are by definition dramatized, since they are characters in their own stories, and will often be self-conscious, as in example (1), in which Dr Watson refers to the act of writing down his memories of Sherlock Holmes. Likewise, secondary narrators will be more often overt, as in (8–11), where there are regular references to the telling of a story. But external primary narrators may also be overt, as in (19) and (20).

(19) William Thackeray, *Vanity Fair*, chapter 8:

> And, as we bring our characters forward, I will ask leave [. . .] not only to introduce them, but occasionally to step down from the platform, and talk about them [. . .]

(20) Virgil, *Aeneid* 9.446–9:

> fortunati ambo! si quid mea carmina possunt,
> nulla dies umquam memori vos eximet aevo,
> dum domus Aeneae Capitoli immobile saxum
> accolet imperiumque pater Romanus habebit.

> Happy pair! If my poetry has any power, no day shall ever blot you from time's memory, so long as Aeneas' house shall stand on the Capitol's immovable rock, and the Roman father rule supreme.

In (19) the narrator draws attention to himself *qua* narrator. In (20) the Virgilian narrator interrupts his account of the death of two Trojans, the friends Nisus and Euryalus, and, stepping forward very prominently as person and narrator, promises them eternal fame. Other narrators do their work in a more implicit way, without commenting or reflecting. In this case we speak of a *covert narrator*, as in (21) and (22).

(21) Ernest Hemingway, *For Whom the Bell Tolls*, chapter 1:

> He lay flat on the brown, pine-needled floor of the forest, his chin on his folded arms, and high overhead the wind blew in the tops of the pine trees. The mountainside sloped gently where he lay; but below it was steep and he could see the dark of the oiled road winding through the pass. There was a stream alongside the road and far down the pass he saw a mill beside the stream and the falling water of the dam, white in the sunlight. 'Is that the mill?' he asked. 'Yes.' 'I do not remember it.' 'It was built since you were here. The old mill is farther down; much below the pass.' He spread the photo-stated military map out on the forest floor and looked at it carefully. The old man looked over his shoulder.

(22) Homer, *Iliad* 1.48–52:

> ἕζετ' ἔπειτ' ἀπάνευθε νεῶν, μετὰ δ' ἰὸν ἕηκε·
> δεινὴ δὲ κλαγγὴ γένετ' ἀργυρέοιο βιοῖο·
> οὐρῆας μὲν πρῶτον ἐπῴχετο καὶ κύνας ἀργούς,
> αὐτὰρ ἔπειτ' αὐτοῖσι βέλος ἐχεπευκὲς ἐφιεὶς
> βάλλ'· αἰεὶ δὲ πυραὶ νεκύων καίοντο θαμειαί.

He [Apollo] then settled at a distance from the ships and let an arrow fly. Terrible was the twang from his silver bow. The mules he attacked first and quick dogs, but then he sent his sharp arrow at the men themselves. And constantly burned the close-packed pyres of the dead.

In (21) the narrating voice from beginning to end is anonymous and disembodied, while the Homeric narrator (22) is famous for his invisibility, except for an occasional Muse-invocation.

The distinction between a covert and an overt narrative style is often referred to as 'showing' (letting the tales tell themselves) versus 'telling' (letting the presence of a narrator between ourselves and the recounted events transpire). It should be noted, however, that even covert narrators employ 'the rhetoric of fiction', that is, guide the emotions and reception of their narratees in myriad subtle ways, and that tales never really tell themselves.

2.4. NARRATEES

Storytelling is an act of communication, and every narrator presupposes a narratee or narratees. More specifically, for every primary narrator there is a corresponding primary narratee, for every secondary narrator, a secondary narratee, and so on. When we turn to the question of whether the narratees are characters in the story told, that is, whether they are external or internal, many combinations are possible.

To an external primary narrator may correspond *external primary narratees* (23–4).

(23) George Eliot, *The Mill on the Floss*, book 5, chapter 2:

> From what you have seen of Tom, I think he is not a youth of whom you would prophesy failure in anything he had thoroughly wished.

(24) Chariton, *Callirhoe* 8.1.4:

> νομίζω δὲ καὶ τὸ τελευταῖον τοῦτο σύγγραμμα τοῖς ἀναγινώσκουσιν ἥδιστον γενήσεσθαι· καθάρσιον γάρ ἐστι τῶν ἐν τοῖς πρώτοις σκυθρωπῶν.

> And I think that this last book will prove to be the most enjoyable for the readers, too. For it is an antidote to the grim events of the first ones.

The 'you' in (23) and even more clearly 'the readers' in (24) are no characters in the story but the addressees of the external narrator.

An internal primary narrator usually has no corresponding internal primary narratee, but tells his story either to no one in particular or to an external primary narratee (25–6).

(25) J.D. Salinger, *The Catcher in the Rye*, chapter 26:

> That's all I'm going to tell about. I could probably tell you what I did after I went home, and how I got sick and all, and what school I'm supposed to go to next fall, after I get out of here, but I don't feel like it. I really don't. That stuff doesn't interest me too much right now. A lot of people, especially this one psychoanalyst guy they have here, keeps asking me if I'm going to apply myself when I go back to school next

September. It's such a stupid question, in my opinion. I mean how do you know what you're going to do till you do it? The answer is, you don't. I think I am, but how do I know? I swear it's a stupid question.

(26) Achilles Tatius, *Leucippe and Clitophon* 1.1–2:

Σιδὼν ἐπὶ θαλάσσῃ πόλις·[...] ἐνταῦθα ἥκων ἐκ πολλοῦ χειμῶνος σῶστρα ἔθυον ἐμαυτοῦ τῇ τῶν Φοινίκων θεᾷ·

Sidon is a city on the board of the sea. [. . .] Having arrived there after a severe storm, I went to make votive offerings for my safe arrival to the Phoenicians' goddess.

In (25) the internal narrator of *The Catcher in the Rye*, seventeen-year-old Holden Caulfield, tells 'you' while in hospital about the events leading to his mental breakdown. Is this 'you' the external narratee, as in examples (23–24), or is it one of the doctors (an internal narratee)? The anonymous narrator in (26) tells about his arrival in Sidon without any acknowledgement of an addressee. Soon he will get into conversation with a young man, Clitophon, while standing in front of a painting of Europe and the bull, and then become himself a (secondary) narratee.

As in the case of the narrator and the author, it is tempting simply to equate the external narratees with the historical readers of flesh and blood, not least because they are often referred to as 'readers', as happens in (24). But we only have to think of examples (27–28) to realize that here again (as in the case of the narrator) we are dealing with a product of the author's imagination.

(27) Laurence Sterne, *Tristram Shandy*, book 6, chapter 33:

I told the Christian reader—I say *Christian*—hoping he is one—and if he is not, I am sorry for it—and only beg he will consider the matter with himself, and not lay the blame entirely on the book.

(28) Apuleius, *The Golden Ass* 9.30:

sed forsitan lector scrupulosus reprehendens narratum meum sic argumentaberis: 'Unde autem tu, astutule asine, intra terminos pistrini contentus, quid secreto, ut adfirmas, mulieres gesserint, scire potuisti?'

But perhaps as a careful reader you will find fault with what I tell and will reason as follows: 'How could you, clever ass, shut up within the walls of the mill-house, know what the women did in secret, as you affirm?'

Not all actual readers of *Tristram Shandy* will be Christians (27), just as they will not feel inclined to identify with the 'careful reader' conjured up by Apuleius in (28), who comes up with an irrelevant question that will never be answered.

Like primary narrators, primary narratees can be overt, as in examples (27) and (28), or covert, as in (25), where we hear nothing specific about the 'you'. But even when narratees are covert, we may still sense their presence, for example, in explanations that the narrator inserts on their behalf, or in negated passages that contradict their expectations, as in (29) and (30).

(29) Virginia Woolf, *Mrs Dalloway*:

> And as she began to go with Miss Pym from jar to jar, choosing, nonsense, nonsense, she said to herself, more and more gently, as if this beauty, this scent, this colour, and Miss Pym liking her, trusting her, were a wave which she let flow over her and surmount that hatred, that monster, surmount it all; and it lifted her up and up when—oh! a pistol shot in the street outside! 'Dear, those motor cars', said Miss Pym, going to the window to look [...] The violent explosion which made Mrs Dalloway jump and Miss Pym go to the window and apologise came from a motor car which had drawn to the side of the pavement precisely opposite Mulberry's shop window.

(30) Homer, *Iliad* 16.140–1:

> ἔγχος δ' οὐχ ἔλετ' οἶον ἀμύμονος Αἰακίδαο,
> βριθὺ μέγα στιβαρόν·

The spear of the blameless son of Aeacus [Achilles] alone he [Patroclus] did not take, heavy, big, massive.

In (29) the narrator explains to the narratees the noise that the two characters have been hearing: it is not a pistol shot, as Mrs Dalloway thinks at first, but it comes from a motor car, as the flower seller Miss Pym had already rightly guessed. In (30) the Homeric narrator contradicts the expectation of his narratees, based on other arming scenes, that Patroclus will take Achilles' spear while putting on his armour. At the same time he creates suspense for them: what is the role of this spear *not* taken by Patroclus going to be?

Turning to secondary narratees, a first situation is when character A informs character B about something A has experienced or witnessed (*internal* secondary narrator–*external* secondary narratee), as in (31) and (32).

(31) Emily Brontë, *Wuthering Heights*, chapter 7:

> 'But, Mr Lockwood, I forgot these tales cannot divert you. I'm annoyed how I should dream of chattering on at such a rate; and your gruel cold, and you nodding for bed! I could have told Heathcliff's history, all that you need hear, in half a dozen words.' Thus interrupting herself, the housekeeper rose, and proceeded to lay aside her sewing; but I felt incapable of moving from the hearth, and I was very far from nodding.

(32) Ovid, *Metamorphoses* 4.695–701:

> 'lacrimarum longa manere
> tempora vos poterunt, ad opem brevis hora ferendam est.
> hanc ego si peterem Perseus Iove natus et illa,
> quam clausam implevit fecundo Iuppiter auro,
> Gorgonis anguicomae Perseus superator et alis
> aetherias ausus iactatis ire per auras,
> praeferrer cunctis certe gener.'

> 'There will rest much time later for your tears, but time for helping is very short. If I sought this girl [Andromeda] as Perseus, son of Jove and her, whom, imprisoned, Jove filled with his fertile shower of gold, as Perseus, victor of the Gorgo, and as the one who dared to ride the breezes of the air on fluttering wings, surely I should be preferred to all as your son-in-law.'

In (31) Mr Lockwood is the external secondary narratee of his housekeeper Nelly Dean, who as internal secondary narrator informs him about his mysterious neighbours at Wuthering Heights. In (32) Perseus recounts his semi-divine descent and previous glorious adventures to the parents of Andromeda, in order to gain her hand when he will have saved her.

Next, in (33–34), we have character A telling character B about events in which neither has participated (*external* secondary narrator–*external* secondary narratee).

(33) Miguel de Cervantes, *Don Quixote*, book 1, chapter 32:

> The innkeeper was just taking away the trunk and the books when the priest said to him: 'Wait. I would like to see what is in those papers that are written in such a good hand.' The landlord took them out, and handed them to the priest who found about eight sheets of manuscript, and at the beginning a title in large letter: *The Tale of Foolish Curiosity* [. . .] Whilst the two of them were talking, Cardenio had picked up the tale and began to read it. He formed the same opinion of it as the priest had done, and begged him to read it aloud so that they could all hear it.

[. . .] So seeing that it would give them all pleasure, and himself as well, the priest began. 'Well, well! Listen to me, all of you, for this is how the tale begins: *Chapter XXXIII. The tale of Foolish Curiosity.* In Florence, a wealthy and famous Italian city in the province called Tuscany, lived Anselmo and Lothario, two rich and noble gentlemen [. . .]'

(34) Herodotus, *Histories* 1.31.1–2:

ἐπειρώτα τίνα δεύτερον μετʼ ἐκεῖνον ἴδοι, δοκέων πάγχυ δευτερεῖα γῶν οἴσεσθαι. ὁ δὲ εἶπε· 'Κλέοβίν τε καὶ Βίτωνα. τούτοισι γὰρ ἐοῦσι γένος Ἀργείοισι βίος τε ἀρκέων ὑπῆν καὶ πρὸς τούτῳ ῥώμη σώματος τοιήδε· ἀεθλοφόροι τε ἀμφότεροι ὁμοίως ἦσαν, καὶ δὴ καὶ λέγεται ὅδε [ὁ] λόγος· ἐούσης ὁρτῆς τῇ Ἥρῃ τοῖσι Ἀργείοισι [. . .]'

He [Croesus] asked whom he [Solon] saw second after him [Tellus the Athenian], being assured that he would at least gain second prize. But he said: 'Cleobis and Biton. These were Argives, had sufficient means, and next to that such bodily strength as I will show. Both were prize-winning athletes and the following story is told about them. The Argives were celebrating the festival of Hera [. . .]'

In (33) the tale read by the priest introduces an external secondary narrator, to whom Don Quixote and the other guests function as external secondary narratees, since the tale is located at a different place and time and none of them take part in it. In (34) Solon tells his Lydian narratee Croesus the story of two Greek athletes from the past, Cleobis and Biton, who to him are a paragon of happiness.

Then, there is character A recalling in the presence of character B something they have both experienced (*internal* secondary narrator–*internal* secondary narratee), as in (35–36).

(35) Virginia Woolf, *Mrs Dalloway*:

'Do you remember', she said, 'how the blinds used to flap at Bourton?' 'They did', he said; and he remembered breakfasting alone, very awkwardly, with her father; who had died; and he had not written to Clarissa. But he had never got on well with old Parry, that querulous, weak-kneed old man, Clarissa's father, Justin Parry. 'I often wish I'd got on better with your father', he said. 'But he never liked any one who—our friends', said Clarissa; and could have bitten her tongue for thus reminding Peter that he had wanted to marry her.

(36) Catullus, *Carmen* 64.132–42:

'sicine me patriis avectam, perfide, ab aris, perfide, deserto liquisti in litore, Theseu? [. . .]

at non haec quondam blanda promissa dedisti
voce mihi, non haec miserae sperare iubebas,
sed coniubia laeta, sed optatas hymenaeos.'

'In this way, having taken me away from my father's altars, have you left
me on the lonely shore, faithless, faithless Theseus? [. . .] But not such
were the promises that you made me once with sweet voice; not such
were the hopes that you encouraged me to entertain, no, happy mar-
riages and much desired for weddings.'

In (35) Mrs Dalloway (Clarissa) stirs up memories of a shared past in
her old friend Peter Walsh. In (36) Ariadne apostrophizes her lover
Theseus, who has deserted her, and reminds him of his promises.

Narratees, both primary and secondary, are a powerful instrument
for influencing the reception of a text, in that they provide the readers
figures with whom to identify or from whom to distance themselves.

2.5. SOME SPECIAL CASES

Some genres of ancient Greek and Latin literature ask for special
consideration. To start with there are the narratives inserted in non-
narrative genres. A lyric poem often has a mythical or historical
section and an oration has an account of what has happened (the
so-called *narratio*). It is most logical to say that the lyric or oratorical
'I' becomes a primary narrator at the moment he turns to the
mythical or historical part of the poem or *narratio*, just as his
addressees become primary narratees. The transition can be marked
explicitly (37) or take place smoothly (38).

(37) Lysias, *Oration* 1.5:

ἐγὼ τοίνυν ἐξ ἀρχῆς ὑμῖν ἅπαντα ἐπιδείξω τὰ ἐμαυτοῦ πράγματα, οὐδὲν
παραλείπων, ἀλλὰ λέγων τἀληθῆ· ταύτην γὰρ ἐμουτῷ μόνην ἡγοῦμαι
σωτηρίαν, ἐὰν ὑμῖν ἅπαντα δυνηθῶ τὰ πεπραγμένα.

I shall therefore tell you from the beginning my whole story, leaving out
nothing but telling the truth. For I consider that my sole rescue, when
I am able to tell you all that has happened.

(38) Propertius, *Elegy* 2.8.29–36:

ille etiam abrepta desertus coniuge Achilles
cessare in tectis pertulit arma sua.

> viderat ille fugam et stratos in litore Achivos
> feruere et Hectorea Dorica castra face;
> viderat informem multa Patroclon harena
> porrectum et sparsas caede iacere comas,
> omnia formosam propter Briseida passus:
> tantus in erepto saevit amore dolor.

Even famous Achilles, deserted when his wife was taken from him, let his arms rest in his tent. He had seen the Greeks fleeing and then stretched on the beach and the Dorian camp ablaze with Hector's torch; he had seen Patroclus, deformed with much sand and his hair stained with blood, lie outstretched, suffering all that for beautiful Briseis: so deep is grief when love is torn away.

In (37) the narrator emphatically marks his role as narrator by a transitional formula which recalls the oath required in modern American law courts to tell 'the truth, the whole truth, and nothing but the truth', while in (38) the elegiac voice smoothly (via the word *etiam*, 'even') moves from his own situation of deserted lover to the Iliadic tale of Achilles loosing Patroclus and killing Hector because of his love for Briseis.

In the case of philosophical dialogues and mimetic idylls or eclogues, we are dealing with a suppressed primary narrator, and hence when characters in those poems start narrating they should be considered secondary narrators.

In the case of drama, the messengers, chorus, or characters telling a story are best seen as secondary narrators although there is no primary narrator. The reason for this is that they tell their story to other characters, who are secondary narratees, since they are to be distinguished from the spectators in the theatre (acting the part of primary narratees), if we want to explain, for example, the working of dramatic irony. To these secondary narratees only secondary narrators can correspond.

2.6. EMBEDDED NARRATIVES (TALE WITHIN A TALE)

We have already seen in Section 2.2 how primary narrators may give the floor to secondary narrators, both internal and external; the result is an embedded narrative or tale within a tale. Such embedded narratives can fulfil various functions in relation to the main narrative. First, they are *explanatory* when, by way of flashback or analepsis (see §4.3), they recount how the present of the main narrative has come to be. Well-known examples include the tales in which Odysseus and Aeneas recount their adventures on their way home/to Italy after the fall of Troy and thus explain how they have landed on Scheria/in Carthage. Second, embedded narratives are *predictive* when they take the form of a flash-forward or prolepsis that announces what will happen in the main narrative. Gods like Zeus or Jove typically are the tellers of such predictive narratives. Third, they can have a *thematic* function when the embedded narrative and main narrative share a common theme. A famous example is the tale of Cupid and Psyche, which is placed at the midpoint of Apuleius' *Metamorphoses* and shares with the main narrative the themes of dangerous curiosity, punishment and trials, and redemption through divine favour. Fourth, they can have a *persuasive* function when the embedded narrative is intended to influence the course of events in the main narrative. Characters in classical literature typically use mythological or historical paradigms for this purpose. Finally, embedded narratives are *distractive* when the embedded narrative is primarily told to entertain. Frame narratives like the *Canterbury Tales* or *Tales from the Thousand and One Nights* typically present the telling of stories as a pleasant way to pass the time.

Needless to say, an embedded narrative can fulfil more than one function at the same time. In particular, it may have a persuasive function on the level of the communication between the narrating character and his secondary narratees, while the primary narratees may detect in it a thematic or predictive relevance for the main narrative. In such cases, we speak of an embedded narrative's *key function* (for the primary narratees) and its *argument function* (for the secondary narratees). A well-known example is the paradigm of Meleager, as told by Phoenix to Achilles in *Iliad* book 9 (529–99). The hero Meleager retires from the fight between the citizens of his hometown Calydon and the Curetes. The city's elders and his father and dearest friends beg him to re-enter battle, promising him many gifts, but he adamantly refuses. Only when the city is in great peril is he moved by his wife Cleopatra to take up arms again. He saves the city but no longer receives the promised gifts. Phoenix tells the story to persuade Achilles to end his wrath, accept Agamemnon's conciliatory gifts, and help his friends (argument function), but the primary narratees may hear in it a prefiguration of the *Iliad* itself (key function). Since 8.474–6, they have known that Achilles will only re-enter battle after, and on account of, the death of his friend Patroclus, and they sense that, as in the case of Meleager, his return will bring the hero no joy.

An embedded narrative that reflects the main narrative, as flash-back/flash-forward or thematically, is also called a *mirror-story*. A famous modern example is found in a short story by Edgar Allan Poe in which the internal narrator reads to another character a novel involving a knight called Ethelred, which uncannily mirrors what happens in the main narrative itself (39).

(39) Edgar Allan Poe, *The Fall of the House of Usher*:

'Ethelred uplifted his mace, and struck upon the head of the dragon, which fell before him, and gave up his pesty breath, with a shriek so horrid and harsh, and withal so piercing, that Ethelred had fain to close his ears with his hands against the dreadful noise of it, the like whereof was never before heard.' Here again I paused abruptly, and now with a feeling of wild amazement—for there could be no doubt whatever that, in this instance, I did actually hear (although from what direction it proceeded I found it impossible to say) a low and apparently distant, but harsh, protracted, and most unusual screaming or grating sound—the exact counterpart of what my fancy had already conjured up for the dragon's unnatural shriek as described by the romancer.

In this case, the mirror-story creates suspense: the screaming heard in the main narrative will turn out to be produced by the sister of the narratee, who in the end will kill him. Mirror-stories may also look back on what has been told in the main narrative. Thus, on the verge of dying, the Persian King Cambyses ruefully recounts how he killed his own brother (40).

(40) Herodotus, *Histories* 3.65.2–3:

'ἐγὼ γὰρ ἐὼν ἐν Αἰγύπτῳ εἶδον ὄψιν ἐν τῷ ὕπνῳ, τὴν μηδαμὰ ὤφελον ἰδεῖν· ἐδόκεον δέ μοι ἄγγελον ἐλθόντα ἐξ οἴκου ἀγγέλλειν ὡς Σμέρδις ἱζόμενος ἐς τὸν βασιλήιον θρόνον ψαύσειε τῇ κεφαλῇ τοῦ οὐρανοῦ. δείσας δὲ μὴ ἀπαιρεθέω τὴν ἀρχὴν πρὸς τοῦ ἀδελφεοῦ, ἐποίησα ταχύτερα ἢ σοφώτερα· ἐν τῇ γὰρ ἀνθρωπηίῃ φύσι οὐκ ἐνῆν ἄρα τὸ μέλλον γίνεσθαι ἀποτρέπειν, ἐγὼ δὲ ὁ μάταιος Πρηξάσπεα ἀποπέμπω ἐς Σοῦσα ἀποκτενέοντα Σμέρδιν.'

'When in Egypt I [Cambyses] had a dream, which I would I had never seen: it seemed that a messenger came from my palace and reported that

Smerdis was sitting on the royal throne and that his head touched the heavens. Fearing that my power would be taken over by my brother, I acted with more haste than wisdom; for, as I now understand, no human power can avert what is fated to happen. But I, fool, send Prexaspes to Susa to kill Smerdis.'

Earlier, the primary narrator had narrated the same event as follows (30.2–3):

ὄψιν εἶδε ὁ Καμβύσης ἐν τῷ ὕπνῳ τοιήνδε· ἐδόκεέ οἱ ἄγγελον ἐλθόντα ἐκ Περσέων ἀγγέλλειν ὡς ἐν τῷ θρόνῳ τῷ βασιληίῳ ἱζόμενος Σμέρδις τῇ κεφαλῇ τοῦ οὐρανοῦ ψαύσειε. πρὸς ὧν ταῦτα δείσας περὶ ἑωυτῷ μή μιν ἀποκτείνας ὁ ἀδελφεὸς ἄρχῃ, πέμπει Πρηξάσπεα ἐς Πέρσας, ὃς ἦν οἱ ἀνὴρ Περσέων πιστότατος, ἀποκτενέοντά μιν. ὁ δὲ ἀναβὰς ἐς Σοῦσα ἀπέκτεινε Σμέρδιν [. . .]

Cambyses had the following dream: he saw a messenger coming from Persia who reported that Smerdis was sitting on the royal throne and with his head touched the heavens. Fearing on the basis of that dream for himself, that his brother would kill him, he sends Prexaspes to Persia, who was the man most trusted by him, to kill him. And having gone up to Susa, he killed Smerdis [. . .]

Comparison of the mirror-story told by Cambyses with the narrator's version reveals his emotions: 'which I would I had never seen', 'I acted with more haste than wisdom', and 'fool'. He now understands the true meaning of the dream (it was not his brother Smerdis but an impostor with the name Smerdis who was sitting on his throne) and realizes that he has himself made the dream come true by having his brother killed (and thus allowing the false Smerdis to take his place). Mirror-stories are a subtype of the device of *mise en abyme*: the situation when a part of a work resembles the larger work in which it occurs. The device is also used in visual art (Jan van Eyck's *The Arnolfini Portrait*, in which a mirror in the painting reflects the painted scene and the painter himself) or drama (the play 'The Murder of Gonzago' in Shakespeare's *Hamlet*).

2.7. THE VERTICAL STRUCTURE OF NARRATIVE

Narratologists have long realized that a narrative consists of two layers: the level of the world and events represented and the level of representation. The theories of Bal and Genette even distinguish three levels. When we read or hear a narrative we read or hear words that together form a *text*. This text contains a *story*, told to narratees by a narrator. The story he tells contains his version or focalization of a series of events that are either supposed to have taken place (the 'suspension of disbelief' characteristic of fiction) or that really have taken place (historiographical or biographical narratives), and that together form the *fabula*. The fabula does not exist in and of itself but is a reconstruction by the narratees. The notion of story in this technical sense can be equated with that of plot: a story does not deal with a random set of events but with events that are somehow causally related to each other, and have, as Aristotle famously put it in his *Poetics* 7, a beginning, middle, and end. A plot usually starts with the disruption of an equilibrium and ends with some form of closure. More will be said about this in Section 4.4. The three layers of text–story–fabula form the vertical structure of narrative, in that a reader gets from the words on a page (the text) into a story, from which he or she may reconstruct the fabula.

Narratologists have argued that in some categories of narrative, it is appropriate to add a fourth level, which Dorrit Cohn calls the referential level or the *material*. A good example is historiography. Before writing a history, a historian will read or listen to the histories of others and use them as sources, as in (41–42).

(41) Alphonse de Lamartine, *History of the Girondists* (*Histoire des Girondins*) I.i–ii:

> I began writing only after a scrupulous investigation into facts and characters. I am not asking to be taken at my word. Even though I have not encumbered the narrative with notes, quotations, and supporting documents, there is not one of my assertions which is not authorized by authentic memoirs, by unpublished memoirs [. . .] or by the reliable information taken directly from the mouths of the last survivors of that great age.

(42) Livy, *History of Rome* 22.7.3–4:

> multiplex caedes utrimque facta traditur ab aliis; ego praeterquam quod nihil auctum ex uano uelim, quo nimis inclinant ferme scribentium animi, Fabium, aequalem temporibus huiusce belli, potissimum auctorem habui.

Some writers have estimated the casualties, both our own and the enemy's, at many times the number; I myself, apart from my unwillingness to exaggerate on insufficient evidence, that all too common vice of historians, have based my account on Fabius, a contemporary witness of these events.

The narrating 'I' in (41) explicitly refers to the fact that his history is based on written memoirs and oral testimonies of witnesses. This example, incidentally, once more proves the validity of distinguishing between author and narrator, in that scholars agree that although the author de Lamartine will undoubtedly have investigated 'facts and characters' before starting to write, the narrator's claim to have *always* done so and his request *not* to be taken at his word is a rhetorical pose. Latin historians like Livy in (42) regularly refer to the writings of predecessors.

The fourth level of the material is particularly relevant for ancient narrative texts, which deal with the same myths over and over again. Earlier versions of myths are the material or intertexts (as intertextual theory calls it) from which later authors draw. When interpreting a given version of a myth, it can be rewarding to compare the fabulae, stories, and texts of this and of the earlier versions: which details are included or excluded (level of fabula), how does the choice for an external or internal narrator affect the emotional colouring of the narrative (level of story), and how do words echo each other (level of text)? Narratology thus can be a useful instrument in intertextual research.

2.8. THE HORIZONTAL STRUCTURE OF NARRATIVE

It was first observed by the sociolinguist William Labov that natural narratives, that is, narratives spontaneously told by real speakers verbalizing their own experiences or those of others that they witnessed, tend to display the same global structure: they start with an *abstract* (a summary of the outcome) and continue with the *orientation* (an indication of place and time), *complication* (the event that triggers a chain of events), *peak* (the climax of the story), *resolution* (a release of tension and indication of what finally happened), and *coda* (an indication that the story is over and/or its moral). This structure is found in many classical narratives, for example the messenger-speeches of ancient drama (43).

(43) Euripides, *Hippolytus* 1162–1254:

summary (1162–3)	Ἱππόλυτος οὐκέτ᾽ ἔστιν, ὡς εἰπεῖν ἔπος· δέδορκε μέντοι φῶς ἐπὶ σμικρᾶς ῥοπῆς. [...] Hippolytus is no more, as good as no more: he still sees the daylight but by a slender thread. [...]
orientation (1173–4)	ἡμεῖς μὲν ἀκτῆς κυμοδέγμονος πέλας ψήκτραισιν ἵππων ἐκτενίζομεν τρίχας [...] We were grooming the horses' hair with combs near the wave-beaten shore [...] (*Hippolytus who has been sent into exile mounts his chariot and drives along the coast*)
complication (1198–1202)	ἐπεὶ δ᾽ ἔρημον χῶρον εἰσεβάλλομεν [...] ἔνθεν τις ἠχὼ χθόνιος, ὡς βροντὴ Διός, βαρὺν βρόμον μεθῆκε, φρικώδη κλύειν· And when we were coming into desolate territory [...] From there an echo from the earth, like Zeus' thunder, let forth a deep roar, hair-raising to hear. (*A bull appears from the sea and drives the horses into panic. Hippolytus' chariot crashes*)
peak (1236–9)	αὐτὸς δ᾽ ὁ τλήμων ἡνίαισιν ἐμπλακεὶς δεσμὸν δυσεξέλικτον ἕλκεται δεθείς, σποδούμενος μὲν πρὸς πέτραις φίλον κάρα θραύων τε σάρκας, δεινὰ δ᾽ ἐξαυδῶν κλύειν· [...] And the wretch himself, entangled in the reins' bonds in an inextricable knot, is being dragged, smashing his head against the rocks, his flesh being torn, and letting out shrieks terrible to hear. [...]
resolution (1246–8)	πίπτει, βραχὺν δὴ βίοτον ἐμπνέων ἔτι· ἵπποι δ᾽ ἔκρυφθεν καὶ τὸ δύστηνον τέρας ταύρου λεπαίας οὐ κάτοιδ᾽ ὅποι χθονός. He falls upon the ground, still breathing a little; and the horses and monstrous bull disappeared I don't know where in the rocky land.
coda (1249–51)	δοῦλος μὲν οὖν ἔγωγε σῶν δόμων, ἄναξ, ἀτὰρ τοσοῦτόν γ᾽ οὐ δυνήσομαί ποτε, τὸν σὸν πιθέσθαι παῖδ᾽ ὅπως ἐστὶν κακός [...]

> I'm only a slave in your house, lord,
> but I will never be able to do this,
> to believe that your son is evil [...]

It is interesting to see the order of natural storytelling that Labov identified on the basis of stories from twentieth-century youths in New York already employed by Attic playwrights of the fifth century BC! Narrative texts hardly ever are purely narrative but usually include non-narrative elements. Thus there is the dramatic element of the speeches of characters, what Plato called *mimēsis* (see §1.1). There is also description, which usually involves the present tense and may temporarily bring the story to a standstill. More will be said about description in Section 5.2. Discourse linguists divide up narrative texts into even smaller units or narrative modes: narrative (in the strict sense, i.e. the account of events in the past), description, report (when the narrator comments on events, rather than merely recounts them), and speech.

2.9. METALEPSIS

This chapter has been devoted to the careful setting up of distinctions and levels of analysis. In principle the world of the events narrated and the world of the narrator are separate and stand in a hierarchical relation to each other: a narrator tells about something that has happened, without the characters in that story being aware that they are part of a story. But occasionally the principal distinction between, or hierarchy of, levels is broken down or violated. The narrator enters the universe of the characters or, conversely, a character enters the universe of the narrator. This device is called *metalepsis* (lit. 'sharing'), as in (44–46).

(44) Charlotte Brontë, *Shirley*, chapter 1:

> You shall see them, reader. Step into this neat garden-house on the skirts of Whinbury, walk into the little parlour—there they are at dinner [...] You and I will join the party, see what is to be seen, and hear what is to be heard. At present, however, they are only eating; and while they eat we will talk aside.

(45) Spike Milligan, *Puckoon*, chapter 1:

> He eyed them [his legs] with obvious dissatisfaction. After examining them he spoke aloud: 'Holy God! Wot are these den? Eh?' He looked

around for an answer. 'Wot are dey?' he repeated angrily. 'Legs.' 'Legs? LEGS? Whose legs?' 'Yours.' 'Mine? And who are you?' 'The Author.' 'Author? Author? Did you write these legs?' 'Yes.' 'Well, I don't like dem. I don't like 'em at all at all . . .'

(46) Homer, *Iliad* 6.357–8:

'οἷσιν ἐπὶ Ζεὺς θῆκε κακὸν μόρον, ὡς καὶ ὀπίσσω
ἀνθρώποισι πελώμεθ' ἀοίδιμοι ἐσσομένοισι.'

'(Hector, you have to fight hard because of Paris and myself), on whom Zeus set a vile destiny, so that even hereafter we shall be subjects of song for men of future generations.'

In (44) the external narrator and his narratees 'enter' the world of the story; in (45), conversely, a character shows an awareness of having an author, while in (46) a character, Helen, herself announces the 'song' of which it forms a part, the *Iliad*. The device of metalepsis has been heralded as a typically postmodern phenomenon, but it in fact can be traced to ancient literature.

Narrators and narratees are crucial factors in every narrative. They represent the communication in a narrative text, the giving and receiving of a message. While modern novelists since Gustave Flaubert have tended to minimize the presence of a narrating voice as much as possible, in classical antiquity narrators were often endowed with numinous authority, or claimed authority on the basis of their status as eyewitness, their research, or force of argumentation. Investigating the narrators of classical texts, therefore, always is a fascinating and rewarding activity.

FURTHER READING

Narratology

Bal, M., *Narratology: Introduction to the Theory of Narrative* (Toronto and London 1997; first published 1985).

Bonheim, H., *The Narrative Modes: Techniques of the Short Story* (Woodbridge, Suffolk and Rochester, NY 1982).

Booth, W.C., *The Rhetoric of Fiction* (Chicago 1983; first published 1961).

Chatman, S., *Story and Discourse: Narrative Structure in Fiction and Film* (Ithaca, NY 1978).

Dällenbach, L., *The Mirror in the Text* (Chicago 1989; first published in French 1977).

Fludernik, M., 'Introduction: Second-Person Narrative and Related Issues', *Style* 28, 1994, 281–328.

Fludernik, M., 'Second-Person Narrative as a Test-Case for Narratology: The Limits of Realism', *Style* 28, 1994, 445–79.

Fludernik, M., *Towards a 'Natural' Narratology* (London 1996).

Fludernik, M., 'Scene Shift, Metalepsis, and the Metaleptic Mode', *Style* 37, 2003, 382–400.

Fludernik, M., *An Introduction to Narratology* (London and New York 2009; first published in German 2006).

Genette, G., *Narrative Discourse: An Essay in Method* (Ithaca, NY and London 1980; first published in French 1972).

Genette, G., *Narrative Discourse Revisited* (Ithaca, NY and London 1988; first published in French 1983).

Genette, G., *Métalepse: de la figure à la fiction* (Paris 2004).

Herman, D., 'Toward a Formal Description of Narrative Metalepsis', *Journal of Literary Semantics* 26, 1997, 132–52.

Herman, D., *Basic Elements of Narrative* (Malden, Oxford, and Chicester 2009).

Kacandes, I., 'Narrative Apostrophe: Reading, Rhetoric, Resistance in Michel Butor's *La modification* and Julio Cortazar's *Graffiti*', *Style* 28, 1994, 329–49.

Kearns, M., *Rhetorical Narratology* (Lincoln, NE 1999).

Korthals, H., *Zwischen Drama und Erzählung: Ein Beitrag zur Theorie geschehensdarstellender Literatur* (Berlin 2003).

Labov, W., *Language in the Inner City: Studies in the Black English Vernacular* (Philadelphia 1972).

Marcus, A., 'A Contextual View of Narrative Fiction in the First Person Plural', *Narrative* 16, 2008, 46–64.

Margolin, U., 'Telling Our Story: On "We" Literary Narratives', *Language and Literature* 5, 1996, 115–33.

Montalbetti, C., 'Autarcie du narrataire', *Poétique* 122, 2000, 243–52.

Nelles, W., *Frameworks: Narrative Levels and Embedded Narrative* (New York 1997).

Prince, G., 'Introduction to the Study of the Narratee', in J.P. Tompkins (ed.), *Reader-Response Criticism: From Formalism to Post-Structuralism* (London 1980), 7–25.

Rabinowitz, P.J., *Before Reading: Narrative Conventions and the Politics of Interpretation* (Columbus 1997).

Richardson, B., 'The Poetics and Politics of Second Person Narrative', *Genre* 24, 1991, 309–30.

Richardson, B., 'I etcetera: On the Poetics and Ideology of Multipersoned Narratives', *Style* 28, 1994, 312–29.

Romberg, B., *Studies in the Narrative Technique of the First-Person Novel* (Stockholm 1962).

Scheffel, M., *Formen selbstreflexiver Erzählung: Ein Typologie und exemplarische Analysen* (Tübingen 1997).

Schmid, W., *Narratologia: Elemente der Narratologie* (Berlin 2008; first published 2005).

Smith, C.S., *Modes of Discourse: The Local Structure of Texts* (Cambridge 2003).

Stanzel, F., *A Theory of Narrative* (Cambridge and New York 1984; first published in German 1979).

Stewart, G., *Dear Reader: The Conscripted Audience in Nineteenth-Century British Fiction* (Baltimore 1996).

Sturrock, J., *The Language of Autobiography: Studies in the First Person Singular* (Cambridge 1993).

Narratology and classics

Allan, R.J., 'Towards a Typology of the Narrative Modes in Ancient Greek: Text Types and Narrative Structure in Euripidean Messenger Speeches', in S. Bakker and G. Wakker (eds), *Discourse Cohesion in Ancient Greek* (Leiden and Boston 2009), 171–203.

Barchiesi, A., 'Voci e istanze narrative nelle Metamorfosi di Ovidio', *Materiali e Discussioni* 23, 1989, 55–97.

Behr, F.D., 'The Narrator's Voice: A Narratological Reappraisal of Apostrophe in Virgil's *Aeneid*', *Arethusa* 38, 2005, 189–221.

Berger, D., *Cicero als Erzähler: forensische und literarische Strategien in den Gerichtsreden* (Frankfurt 1978).

Block, E., 'The Narrator Speaks: Apostrophe in Homer and Vergil', *Transactions of the American Philological Association* 112, 1982, 7–22.

Byre, C.S., 'The Narrator's Address to the Narratee in Apollonius Rhodius' *Argonautica*', *Transactions of the American Philological Association* 121, 1991, 215–28.

Doherty, L.E., *Siren Songs: Gender, Audiences, and Narrators in the Odyssey* (Ann Arbor 1995).

Georgacopulou, S., *Aux frontières du récit épique: l'emploi de l'apostrophe du narrateur dans la Thébaide de Stace* (Brussels 2005).

Jong, I.J.F. de, '*Iliad* 1.366–392: A Mirror Story', reprinted (with revisions) in D.L. Cairns (ed.), *Oxford Readings in Homer's Iliad* (Oxford 2001), 478–95 (first published 1985).

Jong, I.J.F. de, *Narrators and Focalizers: The Presentation of the Story in the Iliad* (London 2004; first published 1987).

Jong, I.J.F. de, 'Metalepsis in Ancient Greek Literature', in J. Grethlein and
A. Rengakos (eds), *Narratology and Interpretation: The Content of Narrative Form in Ancient Literature* (Berlin 2009), 87–115.

Jong, I.J.F. de, R. Nünlist, and A. Bowie (eds), *Narrators, Narratees, and Narratives in Ancient Greek Literature*. Studies in Ancient Greek Narrative 1 (Leiden 2004).

Konstan, D., 'The Death of Argus, or What Stories Do: Audience Response in Ancient Fiction and Theory', *Helios* 18, 1991, 15–30.

Kroon, C.H.M., 'Discourse Modes and the Use of Tenses in Ovid's *Metamorphoses*', in R.J. Allan and M. Buijs (eds), *The Language of Literature: Linguistic Approaches to Classical Texts* (Leiden 2007), 65–92.

Morrison, A.D., *The Narrator in Archaic Greek and Hellenistic Poetry* (Cambridge 2007).

Richardson, S., *The Homeric Narrator* (Nashville 1990).

Schlonski, F., *Studien zum Erzählerstandort bei Lucan* (Trier 1995).

Stoddard, K., *The Narrative Voice in the Theogony of Hesiod* (Leiden 2004).

Wheeler, S.M., *A Discourse of Wonders: Audiences and Performances in Ovid's Metamorphoses* (Philadelphia 1999).

Winkler, J.J., *Auctor and Actor: A Narratological Reading of Apuleius's The Golden Ass* (Berkeley and Oxford 1985).

Zimmerman, M., '*Quis ille . . . lector*: Addressees(s) in the Prologue and throughout the *Metamorphoses*', in A. Kahane and A. Laird (eds), *A Companion to the Prologue of Apuleius' Metamorphoses* (Oxford 2001), 245–55.

3

Focalization

In this book we start from the following analysis of how a narrative 'works': when we read or hear a narrative we read or hear words which together form a *text*. This text contains a *story*, told to narratees by a narrator. The story he tells contains his view on a series of events that are either supposed to have taken place (the suspension of disbelief characteristic of fiction) or that really have taken place (historiographical or biographical narratives), and that together form the *fabula*. The viewing of the events of the fabula is called focalization: there is the seeing or recalling of events, their emotional filtering and temporal ordering, and the fleshing out of space into scenery and persons into characters.[1] It should be understood that the fabula always is a reconstruction, made by the narratees on the basis of the story and the text in order to provide a standard against which to gauge the alterations in the story as a result of the presence of a focalizer: from a chronological order to *in medias res*, from a wood to a *locus horridus*, from a person to a lovable character.

According to some narratologists, narratives without focalization can exist. Events would be merely 'filmed', without the presence of someone who sees. As the metaphor of the film makes clear, however, this claim cannot be true: even 'filming' always implies a camera angle and distance, in other words a form of mediation and hence filtering of events. Thus it is the assumption of this book that narration always entails focalization.

---

[1] The word 'focalization' is often used incorrectly in the sense of 'the giving of emphasis'.

3.1. PRIMARY AND SECONDARY NARRATOR-FOCALIZERS

Since narration entails focalization, the primary narrator of a narrative is always a primary narrator-focalizer. Let us start with the type of the *overt external primary narrator-focalizer* in (1–2).

(1) Jane Austen, *Emma*, chapter 1:

Emma Woodhouse, handsome, clever, and rich, with a comfortable home and happy disposition, seemed to unite some of the best blessings of existence [. . .] The real evils indeed of Emma's situation were the power of having rather too much her own way, and a disposition to think a little too well of herself [. . .]

(2) Apollonius Rhodius, *Argonautica* 3.275–9:

τόφρα δ' Ἔρως πολιοῖο δι' ἠέρος ἷξεν ἄφαντος,
τετρηχὼς οἷόν τε νέαις ἐπὶ φορβάσιν οἶστρος
τέλλεται, ὅν τε μύωπα βοῶν κλείουσι νομῆες.
ὦκα δ' ὑπὸ φλιὴν προδόμῳ ἔνι τόξα τανύσσας
ἰοδόκης ἀβλῆτα πολύστονον ἐξέλετ' ἰόν.

Meanwhile Eros came unseen through the bright air busily like the gadfly which attacks young heifers and which the herdsmen call myops. Quickly he reached the foot of the doorpost in the vestibule and strung his bow and selected from his quiver a new arrow bringing much sorrow.

In (1) the external primary narrator-focalizer starts off with a fairly objective description of her protagonist, but soon evaluative elements ('seemed', 'too much', 'too well') and an attitudinal particle ('indeed') creep in, indicating an overt focalizer. In (2) the focalization of the narrator-focalizer transpires from the simile, which casts Medea in the role of young heifer soon to be 'bitten' by the frenzy of love, and from the epithet 'bringing much sorrow' of the arrow.

But careful reading may reveal traces of the focalization even of a *covert* external narrator-focalizer, as in (3–4).

(3) Ernest Hemingway, *For Whom the Bell Tolls*, chapter 1:

He [Robert Jones] lay flat on the brown, pine-needled floor of the forest, his chin on his folded arms, and high overhead the wind blew in the tops of the pine trees. [. . .] The young man, who was studying the country, took his glasses from the pocket of his faded, khaki flannel

shirt, wiped the lenses with a handkerchief. [...] They were all eating
out of the platter, not speaking, as is the Spanish custom.

(4) Homer, *Iliad* 6.482–5:

> ὣς εἰπὼν ἀλόχοιο φίλης ἐν χερσὶν ἔθηκε
> παῖδ᾽ ἑόν· ἡ δ᾽ ἄρα μιν κηώδεϊ δέξατο κόλπῳ
> δακρυόεν γελάσασα· πόσις δ᾽ ἐλέησε νοήσας,
> χειρί τέ μιν κατέρεξεν ἔπος τ᾽ ἔφατ᾽ ἔκ τ᾽ ὀνόμαζε·

> Having spoken thus he [Hector] put his child into the hands of his wife.
> She took him to her scented breast smiling through her tears. And her
> husband saw it and took pity, and stroked her with his hand and said.

In (3) the narrator is looking at the protagonist of the novel, the
young American Robert Jones, and seems to recount his movements
neutrally. However, his focalizing presence is revealed by the comment 'as is the Spanish custom'. The Homeric narrator is a paragon of
covert narration, but in (4) the mere substitution of 'child', 'wife', and
'husband' for the proper names Astyanax, Andromache, and Hector
reveals his focalization: the narrator looks at his characters in terms of
prototypes of a family of which the father leaves for war, and thereby
turns the scene into a profoundly sad one.

The focalization of an *internal primary narrator-focalizer* is by
definition overt, as in (5–6).

(5) J.D. Salinger, *The Catcher in the Rye*, chapter 2:

> The minute I went in, I was sorry I'd come. He was reading the *Atlantic
> Monthly*, and there were pills and medicine all over the place, and
> everything smelled like Vick's Nose Drops. It was pretty depressing.

(6) Apuleius, *The Golden Ass* 11.12:

> et ecce praesentissimi numinis promissa nobis accedunt beneficia et fata
> salutemque ipsam meam gerens sacerdos adpropinquat [...]

> And behold, there come to me the benefits promised by the most
> powerful goddess, there approaches the priest bringing me my fated
> rescue [...]

In (5) the narrator, the hero of the story, Holden Caulfield, recounts a
visit to his father and his focalization transpires from 'it was pretty
depressing'. In (6) the narrator, Lucius (who has changed into an ass),
thankfully focalizes the goddess who will give him back his human
shape in superlative terms ('the most powerful goddess').

When characters act as *secondary narrator-focalizers*, their focalization will usually also be overt, as in (7–8).

(7) Jane Austen, *Emma*, chapter 1:

> 'Well', said Emma [...] 'you want to hear about the wedding, and I shall be happy to tell you, for we all behaved charmingly. Every body was punctual, every body in their best looks. Not a tear, and hardly a long face to be seen. Oh! no, we all felt that we were going to be only half a mile apart, and were sure of meeting every day.'

(8) Ovid, *Metamorphoses* 1.218–21:

> 'Arcadis hinc sedes at inhospita tecta tyranni
> ingredior, traherent cum sera crepuscula noctem.
> signa dedi venisse deum, vulgusque precari
> coeperat; inridet primo pia vota Lycaon [...]'

'From there I approach the seat and inhospitable abode of the Arcadian king, just when late shades were ushering in the night. I indicated that a god had arrived and the common folk began to pray; Lycaon first mocked their pious prayers [...]'

In (7) Emma gives a report on the marriage of her governess, Miss Taylor, and her focalization transpires from qualifications like 'we all behaved charmingly' and 'not a tear', which suggest her emotions (and efforts to restrain them) in seeing her dear friend go. In (8) Jove tells about the impious behaviour of a king belonging to the iron race, Lycaon, and the critical focalization of the supreme god follows from 'inhospitable' and the contrast between 'pious' and 'mocked'.

3.2. EMBEDDED FOCALIZATION

It is one of the special characteristics of narrative texts that a primary narrator-focalizer can *embed* the focalization of a character in his narrator-text, recounting what that character is seeing, feeling, or thinking, without turning him into a secondary narrator-focalizer (who would voice his own focalization in a speech).

Such embedding of focalization is *explicit* when it is marked by a verb of seeing, feeling, or thinking, and so on, as in (9–10).

(9) E.M. Forster, *A Room with a View*, chapter 1:

> Miss Bartlett was startled. Generally at a pension people looked them
> over for a day or two before speaking [...] She knew that the intruder
> was ill-bred, even before she glanced at him. He was an old man, of
> heavy build, with a fair, shaven face and large eyes. There was some-
> thing childish in those eyes, though it was not the childishness of
> senility. What exactly it was Miss Bartlett did not stop to consider, for
> her glance passed on to his clothes.

(10) Livy, *History of Rome* 21.32.7:

> [...] ex propinquo visa montium altitudo nivesque caelo prope in-
> mixtae, tecta informia inposita rupibus, pecora iumentaque torrida
> frigore, homines intonsi et inculti, animalia inanimaque omnia rigentia
> gelu, cetera visu quam dictu foediora terrorem renovarunt.
>
> [...] the height of the mountains when viewed so near, and the masses
> of snow almost mingling with the sky, the shapeless huts situated on the
> cliffs, the cattle and beasts of burden withered by the cold, the men
> unshorn and wildly dressed, all things, animate and inanimate, stiff
> because of the frost, and other objects more terrible when seen than
> described, renewed their alarm.

In (9) we enter Miss Bartlett's mind from 'was startled', her focalizing
being advertised further in 'she knew', 'she glanced at him', and 'her
glance passed on'. The content of her focalization appears from words
like 'the intruder' or 'ill-bred', which show her disapproval of another
English tourist, Mr Emerson, who is behaving unconventionally and
spontaneously (but sympathetically in the eyes of the primary narrator-
focalizer 'Forster'!). Passage (10) presents the first, terrified focalization
of the Alps by Hannibal and his men, their act of viewing being noted
twice ('viewed', 'when seen').

The embedding of focalization may, however, also remain implicit,
when verbs of seeing and so on are lacking. Here we must look for
other signs, such as evaluative words, interactional particles, moods,
or deictics that reveal a character's focalization, as in (11–12).

(11) E.M. Forster, *A Passage to India*, chapter 2:

> She [the mother of Ronny] went back into the billiard-room, where she
> was greeted by 'I want to see the real India', and her appropriate life
> came back with a rush. This was Adela Quested, the queer, cautious girl
> whom Ronny had commissioned her to bring from England.

52   *Narratology and Classics*

(12) Homer, *Iliad* 24.478–9:

> χερσὶν Ἀχιλλῆος λάβε γούνατα καὶ κύσε χεῖρας
> δεινὰς ἀνδροφόνους, αἵ οἱ πολέας κτάνον υἷας.

He [Priam] took the knees of Achilles and kissed his hands, the terrible ones, man-killing, that had killed many of his sons.

In (11) the presence of 'this', 'her', and the name 'Ronny' (for the City Magistrate Mr Heaslop) indicates that the 'This was...' sentence contains the focalization of the 'she', the mother of Ronny, and hence that the qualification 'the queer, cautious girl' of the character Adela Quested, her son's fiancée, derives from her (and not from the primary narrator-focalizer). In (12) Achilles' hands are focalized by Priam, as transpires from the epithets 'terrible' and 'man-killing' and, in the relative clause, from the possessive dative οἱ, 'his'. Indeed, in this case we can 'prove' our analysis by comparing two passages where Priam himself speaks about Achilles: 'For he killed so many of my sons in their bloom' (*Iliad* 22.423) and 'I dared to bring to my lips the hand of a child-killing man' (*Iliad* 24.505–6). These parallels confirm that Priam sees Achilles foremost as the killer of his sons and that in (12) line 479 represents his focalization, that is, the thoughts that run through his mind when kissing Achilles' hands.

But not all cases of embedded focalization, whether explicit and implicit, are so clear-cut. Embedded focalization in principle entails ambiguity: what is to be ascribed to the primary narrator-focalizer and what to the secondary focalizer? After all, it is the primary narrator-focalizer who is verbalizing the focalization of the character. And where does the embedding stop or (in the case of implicit embedded focalization) begin? Some examples are seen in (13) and (14).

(13) E.M. Forster, *A Passage to India*, chapter 24:

> While thinking of Mrs. Moore she [Adela Quested] heard sounds, which gradually grew more distinct. The epoch-making trial had started, and the Superintendent of Police was opening the case for the prosecution.

(14) Virgil, *Aeneid* 10.565–70:

> Aegaeon qualis, centum cui bracchia dicunt
> centenasque manus, quinquaginta oribus ignem
> pectoribusque arsisse, Iovis cum fulmina contra

Focalization

53

tot paribus streperet clipeis, tot stringeret ensis.
sic toto Aeneas desaevit in aequore victor [...]

Even as Aegaeon, who, they say, had a hundred arms, a hundred hands,
and belched fire from fifty mouths and chests, when against Jupiter's
lightnings he clang with as many identical shields, bared as many identical swords. Thus did Aeneas rage over the whole field, victorious [...]

In (13) the focalizer is Adela Quested ('thinking of', 'heard'), a young
English woman who had a mysterious encounter with an Indian
doctor inside the Marabar caves and is now on trial. But does she
qualify the trial as 'epoch-making', or does the primary narrator-
focalizer? And in (14) is it the primary narrator-focalizer 'Virgil' who
comments via the simile on Aeneas' violent nature at this stage of the
narrative, or does it represent the frightened focalization of his
opponents on the battlefield?

A narrator can also *intrude upon* the focalization of a character,
adding information which that character cannot know (a form of
paralepsis—see §3.3), as in (15–16).

(15) Thomas Hardy, *Tess of the D'Urbervilles*, chapter 16:

These myriads of cows stretching under her [Tess's] eyes from the far
east to the far west outnumbered any she had ever seen at a glance
before. The green lea was speckled as thickly with them as a canvas by
Van Alsloot or Sallaert with burghers.

(16) Virgil, *Aeneid* 1.421–2:

miratur molem Aeneas, magalia quondam,
miratur portas strepitumque et strata viarum.

Aeneas marvels at the solid bulk of the buildings, once shepherd huts,
marvels at the gates, the din, and the paved streets.

In (15) it is highly unlikely that the focalizing Tess, an uneducated
farm girl, would think of paintings when looking at hills with cows on
them; rather it is the narrator who takes over and inserts the comparison of the paintings. In (16) Aeneas looks at Carthage from a
distance; all elements mentioned are discernible to him, but the
ancient commentator Servius already noted that the detail 'once
shepherd huts', with the Punic word *magalia*, could only derive
from the primary narrator.

Finally, a narrator may describe what a character does *not* see,
completely taking over his or her focalization, as in (17–18).

(17) W. Somerset Maugham, *The Force of Circumstances*:

> If Doris had not been so absorbed she might have noticed that there was a change in Guy. She would have found it hard to describe and harder still to explain. There was in his eyes a sort of watchfulness and in his mouth a slight droop of anxiety.

(18) Homer, *Iliad* 22.445–6:

> νηπίη, οὐδ᾽ ἐνόησεν ὅ μιν μάλα τῆλε λοετρῶν
> χερσὶν Ἀχιλλῆος δάμασε γλαυκῶπις Ἀθήνη.

Poor woman, for she [Andromache] was not aware that, far from his bath, owl-eyed Athena had made him [Hector] perish through the hands of Achilles.

Passage (17) belongs to a short story about the eventual splitting up of a married couple after the wife found out that her husband had had an affair, and the negated focalization contains a first hint of their loss of contact. In (18) the narrator emphatically notes that Andromache is the only Trojan who does not know that her husband has died, building to the dramatic moment when she finds out.

Because of the inherent ambiguity of embedded focalization and the possibility of intrusion, it could be argued that embedded focalization should be restricted to those cases where the focalization by a character is without question, for instance because the views expressed or the language used can be shown to be typical of that character. This would considerably reduce the amount of embedded focalization in a narrative text and increase the presence and dominance of the primary narrator-focalizer. It seems therefore more enriching to operate the other way around and assume that the presence of a verb of seeing and so on *always* indicates that an embedding of focalization takes place, keeping open the possibility of ambiguity or intrusion. One more example may prove the heuristic values of the concept of focalization (19).

(19) Virgil, *Aeneid* 1.422–6:

> miratur portas strepitumque et strata viarum.
> instant ardentes Tyrii: pars ducere muros
> molirique arcem [. . .]
> iura magistratusque legunt sanctumque senatum.

He [Aeneas] marvels at the gates, the din, and paved streets. The Tyrians eagerly press on: some to build walls and to construct a citadel [. . .] Laws and magistrates they ordain, and a venerable senate.

The Virgilian narrator recounts Aeneas' admiring focalization of the Carthaginians building their new city, but the last line, according to some scholars, does not fit this context, since strictly speaking it does not describe something that Aeneas can see. However, realizing that we are dealing with his focalization makes the line acceptable: he is looking at the founding of a city, a task also awaiting himself, with the eyes of a Roman. Constructing a city inevitably brings with it the introduction of the societal instruments, laws, magistrates, and senate needed to manage it.

The ability to look into another person's head is a typically literary device, not to be found in real life. Some narrators thematize this point, as in (20).

(20) Henry James, *The Bostonians*, chapter 32:

> If we were at this moment to take an inside view of Mrs. Burrage (a liberty we have not yet ventured on), I suspect we should find [. . .]

The device offers many possibilities of exploitation, one of which is the juxtaposition of what a character says and what he or she really thinks.

(21) Virginia Woolf, *Mrs Dalloway*:

> 'And how are you?' said Peter Walsh, positively trembling; taking both her hands; kissing both her hands. She's grown older, he thought, sitting down. I shan't tell her anything about it, he thought, for she's grown older.

(22) Herodotus, *Histories* 7.5.2–6.1:

> '[. . .] στρατηλάτεε ἐπὶ τὰς Ἀθήνας, ἵνα λόγος τέ σε ἔχῃ πρὸς ἀνθρώπων ἀγαθὸς καί τις ὕστερον φυλάσσηται ἐπὶ γῆν τὴν σὴν στρατεύεσθαι.' [. . .] ταῦτα δὲ ἔλεγε οἷα νεωτέρων ἔργων ἐπιθυμητὴς ἐὼν καὶ θέλων αὐτὸς τῆς Ἑλλάδος ὕπαρχος εἶναι.

> '[. . .] lead your armies against Athens in order that you [Xerxes] may have a good reputation among men and that everyone in future should beware of marching against your country.' [. . .] He [Mardonius] said these things because he desired adventures and wanted himself to be viceroy of Greece.

In (21) we have a confrontation between Mrs Dalloway and an old friend. They hold a polite conversation, but inwardly the man hesitates whether to tell her that he has married ('it'). In (22) the Persian general Mardonius delivers a speech to Xerxes that appeals to the king's desire for glory, but his unspoken thoughts reveal him to be driven by personal motives.

3.3. FOCALIZATION AND INFORMATION

Focalization also has a cognitive aspect: the less restricted the focalization of a narrator, the more the narratees are allowed to know. As of old, narratology knows the concept of 'omniscience', which means that an undramatized and hence bodiless external primary narrator-focalizer (not impaired by any anthropomorphical restrictions) has access to his characters' inner thoughts (23–24), is present at all settings (25–26), and knows the future (27–28).

(23) E.M. Forster, *A Room with a View*, chapter 1:

> Miss Bartlett, though skilled in the delicacies of conversation, was powerless in the presence of brutality. It was impossible to snub anyone so gross. Her face reddened with displeasure. She looked around as much as to say, 'Are you all like this?' And two little old ladies, who were sitting further up the table, with shawls hanging over the backs of the chairs, looked back, clearly indicating, 'We are not; we are genteel.'

(24) Apollonius Rhodius, *Argonautica* 3.422–5:

> ὁ δέ σῖγα ποδῶν πάρος ὄμματα πήξας,
> ἧστ' αὔτως ἄφθογγος, ἀμηχανέων κακότητι·
> βουλὴν δ' ἀμφὶ πολὺν στρώφα χρόνον, οὐδέ πῃ εἶχε
> θαρσαλέως ὑποδέχθαι, ἐπεὶ μέγα φαίνετο ἔργον.

And he [Jason] sat silent where he was, his eyes fixed on the ground before his feet, unable to speak, at a loss as to how to deal with his wretched situation. For a long time he turned over and over what he should do: it was impossible to accept with confidence, as the challenge seemed overwhelming.

In (23) we find an effective combination of the omniscient narrator first telling us what goes on in Miss Bartlett's mind (finding herself rendered speechless by her male interlocutor's grossness) and then showing how the characters, like all human beings, can only infer thoughts from facial expressions. In (24) the narrator can probe Jason's mind and tell us what the hero is loath to say in public, namely that he is afraid to accept the trial King Aeetes set him to get the Golden Fleece.

(25) William Thackeray, *Vanity Fair*, chapter 12:

> We must now take our leave of Arcadia, and those amiable people practising the rural virtues there, and travel back to London, to inquire what has become of Miss Amelia.

(26) Chariton, *Callirhoe* 4.2:

> Καλλιρόη μὲν οὖν ἐν Μιλήτῳ Χαιρέαν ἔθαπτε, Χαιρέας δὲ ἐν Καρίᾳ δεδεμένος εἰργάζετο.

> While Callirhoe was burying Chaereas in Miletus, Chaereas himself was working in chains in Caria.

The external narrators of (25) and (26) effortlessly and in the course of one sentence move from the one setting of their story to the other, whereby the first narrator, somewhat metaleptically, pretends to be physically on the set and to 'travel' from the countryside to the city.

(27) W.M. Thackeray, *Vanity Fair*, chapter 14:

> For as Rebecca was shawling her in an upper apartment, where these two friends had an opportunity for a little of that secret talking and conspiring which form the delight of female life, Amelia, coming up to Rebecca, and taking her two little hands in hers, said, 'Rebecca, I see it all.' Rebecca kissed her. And regarding this delightful secret, not one syllable was said by either of the young women. But it was destined to come out before long.

(28) Virgil, *Aeneid* 4.169–70:

> ille dies primus leti primusque malorum
> causa fuit.

> That day was the first day of her death, the first cause of her woe.

In (27) the omniscient narrator can announce that the 'delightful secret', Rebecca Sharp's engagement to Rawdon Crawley, will come out soon, while in (28) the Virgilian narrator reveals, at the moment of Dido's 'marriage' to Aeneas in the cave, that this liaison will eventually bring her nothing but ill, namely her death (suicide) after Aeneas has left her.

Internal narrators, always characters in the story, lack the special facilities of the bodiless external narrator, and their focalization is more restricted, as in (29–30).

(29) Emily Brontë, *Wuthering Heights*, chapter 1:

> Before passing the threshold, I paused to admire a quantity of grotesque
> carving lavished over the front, and especially about the principal door,
> above which [...] I detected the date '1500' and the name 'Hareton
> Earnshaw'. I would have made a few comments, and requested a short
> history of the place, from the surly owner, but his attitude at the door
> appeared to demand my speedy entrance [...]

(30) Sophocles, *Oedipus Coloneus* 1656–62:

> μόρῳ δ' ὁποίῳ κεῖνος ὤλετ' οὐδ' ἂν εἷς
> θνητῶν φράσειε πλὴν τὸ Θησέως κάρα.
> οὐ γάρ τις αὐτὸν οὔτε πυρφόρος θεοῦ
> κεραυνὸς ἐξέπραξεν οὔτε ποντία
> θύελλα κινηθεῖσα τῷ τότ' ἐν χρόνῳ,
> ἀλλ' ἤ τις ἐκ θεῶν πομπός, ἢ τὸ νερτέρων
> εὔνουν διαστὰν γῆς ἀλάμπετον βάθρον.

> But by what death that man [Oedipus] perished, none among mor-
> tals could tell except Theseus. For no fiery thunderbolt of the god
> put an end to him at that moment, nor a whirlwind suddenly rising
> from the sea, but either an escort from the gods, or the dark nether
> world on which the ground is based split open for him in friendly
> fashion.

In (29) the internal primary narrator, Mr Lockwood, visits Wuthering
Heights for the first time, and the house and its inhabitants at this
stage are unknown to him. Much of the ensuing novel will be devoted
to filling him (and the narratees) in. In (30) the internal secondary
narrator, a messenger, for once can *not* do what his theatrical role
demands of him, namely tell his narratees (and the spectators) about
offstage events. Oedipus himself had earlier ordained his death to
remain a secret to all, except Theseus, probably in order for him to
function maximally as a *heros* after his death.

It is one of the perennial themes of narrative to contrast the more
restricted focalization of the characters entangled in the action with
the superior understanding of the primary narrator-focalizer recounting it, as in (31–32).

(31) George Eliot, *Middlemarch*, chapter 16:

> Poor Lydgate! or shall I say, Poor Rosamond! Each lived in a world of
> which the other knew nothing. It had not occurred to Lydgate that he
> had been a subject of eager meditation to Rosamond [...]

(32) Virgil, *Aeneid* 10.500–5:

> quo nunc Turnus ovat spolio gaudetque potitus.
> nescia mens hominum fati sortisque futurae
> et servare modum rebus sublata secundis!
> Turno tempus erit magno cum optaverit emptum
> intactum Pallanta, et cum spolia ista diemque
> oderit.

In that spoil Turnus now exults and rejoices over its acquisition. O mind of men, which does not know fate or destiny to come or how to keep within bounds when uplifted by success! A time will come for Turnus when he would wish at any price to have bought Pallas intact and when he will hate those spoils and that day.

In (31) the narrator reflects on the first meeting between Lydgate, Middlemarch's idealistic young doctor, and the beautiful but self-centred Rosamond, whose marriage will become a failure. In (32) the narrator contrasts his own knowledge of what the killing of Pallas will bring Turnus (death at the hands of Aeneas, avenging Pallas) with the latter's joy at the moment of despoiling his opponent; this emphatic narratorial intervention both marks the event that will eventually precipitate Turnus' own death, one of the climactic scenes of the *Aeneid*, and characterizes Turnus as a tragic hero in the Greek vein, prematurely elated by success.

Narrators, of course, can play with focalization as the regulator of information. Thus occasionally less information is given by a narrator than is strictly speaking compatible with his, or a character's, focalization (*paralipsis*) or more (*paralepsis*). As examples of paralipsis, we may think of (33) and (34).

(33) Thomas Hardy, *Tess of the D'Urbervilles*, chapter 39:

Nobody ever knew how Izz spent the dark hours that intervened between Angel Clare's parting from her and her arrival home.

(34) Herodotus, *Histories* 1.51.3–4:

καὶ περιρραντήρια δύο ἀνέθηκε, χρύσεόν τε καὶ ἀργύρεον, τῶν τῷ χρυσέῳ ἐπιγέγραπται Λακεδαιμονίων φάμενων εἶναι ἀνάθημα, οὐκ ὀρθῶς λέγοντες· ἔστι γὰρ καὶ τοῦτο Κροίσου, ἐπέγραψε δὲ τῶν τις Δελφῶν Λακεδαιμονίοισι βουλόμενος χαρίζεσθαι, τοῦ ἐπιστάμενος τὸ οὔνομα οὐκ ἐπιμνήσομαι.

Croesus also dedicated two sprinkling-vessels, one of gold, one of silver, of which the golden one bears an inscription saying that it was a dedication of the Lacedaemonians, falsely: for that vessel is Croesus' too, but the inscription derives from a Delphian, who wanted to please the Lacedaemonians; though I know his name, I will not mention it.

In (33) the external, omniscient narrator shares in the general ignorance, of course for rhetorical purposes; it suggests the extent of the milkmaid Izz's confusion after her meeting with the attractive Angel. In (34) the Herodotean narrator apparently does not wish to bring a Delphian into discredit.

Turning to paralepsis, we have already come across examples in passages (15) and (16), the narrator intruding upon a character's focalization. Another form paralepsis can take is when a character acting as secondary narrator is able to tell more than his or her focalization would, strictly speaking, allow (35).

(35) Homer, *Iliad* 16.844–6:

> ʽσοὶ γὰρ ἔδωκε
> νίκην Ζεὺς Κρονίδης καὶ Ἀπόλλων, οἵ με δάμασσαν
> ῥηιδίως· αὐτοὶ γὰρ ἀπ' ὤμων τεύχε' ἕλοντο.ʼ

'For Zeus, Cronus' son, and Apollo gave you [Hector] victory, who easily overpowered me. For they themselves took of my armour from my shoulders.'

Patroclus here recounts something that he cannot know: when Apollo came up to him to knock off his armour, Patroclus 'did not see him moving though the rout' because he came from behind, hidden in mist (16.789–90). Scholars have wanted to strike the lines as illogical, but the ancient scholia understood that the narrator here has endowed his character with the knowledge of the primary narratees, a phenomenon to be observed often in Homer.

3.4. SPATIAL STANDPOINT

Focalization means a narrator or character looking at, and thereby emotionally colouring and filtering, the events of the fabula. The concept partly replaces the older, more general term of 'perspective' or 'point of view'. That all-embracing term also included an aspect of the presentation of a story that is here called the spatial standpoint.

From what position does a narrator-focalizer look at events, charac-
ters, objects, or settings? A first possibility is the *narratorial panoramic* standpoint, as in
(36–37).

(36) Virginia Woolf, *The Years*, chapter 1:

> The autumn wind blew over England [. . .] The streets were crowded.
> Upon the sloping desks of the offices near St. Paul's, clerks paused with
> their pens on the ruled page [. . .] But in England, in the North it was
> cold [. . .] In Devonshire where the round red hills and the steep valleys
> hoarded the sea air leaves were still thick on the trees [. . .] The smoke
> hung in veils over the spires and domes of the University cities [. . .]

(37) Homer, *Iliad* 2.459–68:

> τῶν δ', ὥς τ' ὀρνίθων πετεηνῶν ἔθνεα πολλὰ [. . .]
> ὣς τῶν ἔθνεα πολλὰ νεῶν ἄπο καὶ κλισιάων
> ἐς πεδίον προχέοντο Σκαμάνδριον· αὐτὰρ ὑπὸ χθὼν
> σμερδαλέον κονάβιζε ποδῶν αὐτῶν τε καὶ ἵππων.
> ἔσταν δ' ἐν λειμῶνι Σκαμανδρίῳ ἀνθεμόεντι
> μυρίοι, ὅσσά τε φύλλα καὶ ἄνθεα γίγνεται ὥρῃ.

> Like the numerous flocks of flying birds [. . .], so the many companies
> of men poured out from their ships and tents on to the plain of the
> Scamander. And the earth rang fearfully under the feet of men and
> horses. They came to a stand in the flowering meadow by Scamander, in
> their tens of thousands, as many as the leaves and flowers that grow in
> springtime.

In (36) and (37) external narrator-focalizers are able to oversee large
parts of England and the Trojan plain, respectively.

The panoramic standpoint can also be that of one of the characters,
acting as secondary focalizer (*actorial panoramic* standpoint), as in
(38–39).

(38) Thomas Hardy, *Tess of the D'Urbervilles*, chapter 16:

> These myriads of cows stretching under her [Tess's] eyes from the far
> east to the far west outnumbered any she had ever seen at a glance
> before. [. . .] The ripe hue of the red and dun kine absorbed the evening
> sunlight, which the white-coated animals returned to the eye in rays
> almost dazzling, even at the distant elevation on which she stood. The
> bird's-eye perspective before her was not so luxuriantly beautiful per-
> haps, as that other one which she knew so well; yet it was more cheering.

(39) Valerius Flaccus, *Argonautica* 6.575–9:

> ecce autem muris residens Medea paternis
> singula dum magni lustrat certamina belli
> atque hos ipsa procul densa in caligine reges
> agnoscit quaeritque alios Iunone magistra
> conspicit Aesonium longe caput [...]

But there sitting on her father's walls Medea at first scans the individual battles of the mighty conflict and herself recognizes from afar some leaders in the clouds of dust and asks about others, but then, at Juno's prompting, perceives in the distance the head of Jason [...]

In (38) the narrator makes Tess focalize her surroundings and for this purpose puts her on a hill, which allows her a 'bird's-eye perspective'. In (39) we are dealing with a *teichoskopia* ('view from the walls'), a narrative device that is utilized regularly in classical literature after it was introduced by Homer in *Iliad* 3 (when Helen looks at the Greek warriors from the walls of Troy).

A second, very common, spatial standpoint is the *narratorial scenic* one, which means that a narrator positions himself at the scene, as in (40–41).

(40) Charles Dickens, *Little Dorrit*, chapter 1:

> In Marseilles that day there was a villainous prison. In one of its chambers [...] were two men. Besides the two men, a notched and disfigured bench, immovable from the wall, with a draught-board rudely hacked upon it with a knife, a set of draughts, made of old buttons and soup bones, a set of dominoes, two mats, and two or three wine bottles [...] It received such light as it got through the grating of iron bars fashioned like a pretty large window, by means of which it could be always inspected from the gloomy staircase on which the grating gave.

(41) Virgil, *Aeneid* 1.159–68:

> est in secessu longo locus: insula portum
> efficit obiectu laterum, quibus omnis ab alto
> frangitur inque sinus scindit sese unda reductos. [...]
> fronte sub adversa scopulis pendentibus antrum;
> intus aquae dulces vivoque sedilia saxo,
> Nympharum domus.

There is a spot in a deep inlet: an island forms a harbour with the barrier of its coasts, on which every wave from the open sea is broken and splits up in quiet ripples. [...] Under the cliff-face straight ahead is a cave formed of hanging rocks, within are fresh water and seats of living rock, a haunt of Nymphs.

In (40) the external narrator gives an ample description of the interior of a prison cell, as it were walking around in it; in (41) the Virgilian narrator takes stock of the place where the Trojans will land after the storm, as it were visiting it before them.

A narrator may also position itself next to one of the characters on the scene and as it were accompany him or her (*actorial scenic standpoint*), which may, but need not, entail the embedding of that character's focalization, as in (42–43).

(42) Jane Austen, *Emma*, chapter 10:

> Emma had a charitable visit to pay to a poor sick family, who lived a little way out of Highbury. Their road to this detached cottage was down Vicarage-lane, a lane leading at right-angles from the broad [...] and, as may be inferred, containing the blessed abode of Mr. Elton. A few inferior dwellings were first to be seen, and then, about a quarter of a mile down the lane rose the Vicarage; an old and not very good house, almost as close to the road as could be. It had no advantage of situation; but had been very much smartened up by the present proprietor; and, such as it was, there could be no possibility of the two friends passing it without a slackened pace and observing eyes.—Emma's remark was— 'There it is. There go you and your riddle-book one of these days.'— Harriet's was—'Oh! What a sweet house!—How very beautiful!'

(43) Sophocles, *Antigone* 1196–1209:

> ἐγὼ δὲ σῷ ποδαγὸς ἑσπόμην πόσει
> πεδίον ἐπ᾽ ἄκρον, ἔνθ᾽ ἔκειτο νηλεὲς
> κυνοσπάρακτον σῶμα Πολυνείκους ἔτι· [...]
> χώσαντες αὖθις πρὸς λιθόστρωτον κόρης
> νυμφεῖον Ἅιδου κοῖλον εἰσεβαίνομεν.
> φωνῆς δ᾽ ἄπωθεν ὀρθίων κωκυμάτων
> κλύει τις ἀκτέριστον ἀμφὶ παστάδα, [...]
> τῷ δ᾽ ἀθλίας ἄσημα περιβαίνει βοῆς [...]

I accompanied your husband [Creon] as a guide to the furthest part of the plain, where Polynices' unpitied body, torn by dogs, still lay. [...] We next went towards the maiden's [Antigone's] stone-floored hollow bridal room of death. From a distance one of us heard the sound of shrill wailing near the unhallowed portico [...] And he [Creon] perceived an indistinct noise of pitiful shouting [...]

In (42) the external narrator accompanies Emma and her friend Harriet, who is interested in the local vicar Mr Elton, on their stroll through the village. It is not easy to make out whether the actorial scenic standpoint of the narrator also entails the embedding of focalization: it would seem to be the ironic narrator who calls the Vicarage 'the blessed abode of Mr. Elton', but is it the narrator or Emma who qualifies it as 'old and not very good' and with 'no advantage of situation'? In (43) the messenger accompanies Creon on his hurried—and doomed—mission to bury Polynices and release Antigone from the cave in which she has been locked to starve to death. He recounts events from his master's spatial position, and at least from 1209 ('he perceived') onwards largely via his focalization. But how about 'unpitied' and 'unhallowed'? Is this the focalization of the messenger and the other servants or are we to suppose that Creon had already come to see things differently? As so often, the focalization is ambiguous but thereby forces us to reflect more deeply on what is going on.

A third type of standpoint is the *close-up*, when events, characters, objects, and so on are looked at from nearby, as in (44–45).

(44) Virginia Woolf, *To the Lighthouse*, part 1, chapter 17:

> Now eight candles were stood down the table, and after the first stoop the flames stood upright and drew with them into visibility the long table entire, and in the middle a yellow and purple dish of fruit. What had she done with it, Mrs. Ramsay wondered, for Rose's arrangement of the grapes and pears, of the horny pinked-lined shell, of the bananas, made her think of a trophy fetched from the bottom of the sea [. . .]

(45) Catullus, *Carmen* 64.43–51:

> ipsius at sedes, quacumque opulenta recessit
> regia, fulgenti splendent auro atque argento. [. . .]
> pulvinar vero divae geniale locatur
> sedibus in mediis, Indo quod dente politum
> tincta tegit roseo conchyli purpura fuco.
> Haec vestis priscis hominum variata figuris
> heroum mira virtutes indicat arte.

But the house of the bridegroom [Peleus], as far as the sumptuous palace stretched out, shines with glittering gold and silver. [. . .] The marriage-bed of the goddess is being positioned in the middle of the house, which, smoothly fashioned of Indian tusk, is covered by a purple coverlet steeped in the rosy dye of the purple shell. This coverlet, embroidered with figures of men of old, shows with stunning art the feats of heroes.

In (44) we look through the eyes of Mrs Ramsay at the 'long table' and together with the flaming up of the candles are allowed gradually to discern the details of what is on it: a dish of fruits, and then different pieces of fruit and a shell. In (45) the external narrator gradually zooms in from the palace as a whole via the marriage bed in its middle to the coverlet on that bed in order to prepare for the detailed description that narrator will give of the 'figures' embroidered on it.

There is often a connection between spatial standpoint and temporal rhythm: a panoramic standpoint tends to involve a summary, a scenic standpoint a scenic rhythm, and a close-up a retardation. The topic of rhythm will be discussed in Section 4.5.

3.5. NARRATING AND EXPERIENCING FOCALIZATION

In the case of internal narration, that is, when a narrator tells about events he himself has experienced, it is customary to distinguish between the narrator's experiencing focalization ('erlebendes Ich') and narrating focalization ('erzählendes Ich'). *Experiencing focalization* means that the narrator-focalizer recounts events exactly as he saw and (mis)understood them at the time of experiencing them, while *narrating focalization* means that he draws on the understanding possessed at the moment of narration, which is often that of a wiser but sadder person. Let us start with some examples of experiencing focalization (46–7).

(46) Charlotte Brontë, *Jane Eyre*, chapter 10:

> I mounted the vehicle which was to bear me to new duties and a new life in the unknown environs of Millcote.

(47) Homer, *Odyssey* 10.100–2:

> δὴ τότ᾽ ἐγὼν ἑτάρους προΐειν πεύθεσθαι ἰόντας
> οἵ τινες ἀνέρες εἶεν ἐπὶ χθονὶ σῖτον ἔδοντες [. . .]

> Then I [Odysseus] sent out companions to go and find out what sort of bread-eating men lived in that country [. . .]

In (46) the internal primary narrator Jane Eyre leaves school to become a governess in the house of the man who will become her husband. Of course, at this stage she has no idea about this; for her, everything is 'new' and the area to which she is travelling 'unknown'. In (47) the internal secondary narrator Odysseus actually knows at the moment of narration that the men he will meet are the cannibalistic Laestrygonians, but he suppresses his hindsight knowledge and recounts this adventure from his unknowing perspective at that time, when he was still thinking in terms of normal 'bread-eating' men. As a result, he increases the excitement of his narrative, as the revelation of the cannibalism also comes as a shock to the narratees, and excuses his failing as a leader who unwittingly sends some of his men to their deaths.

Now we turn to some examples of narrating focalization (48–9).

(48) Charles Dickens, *David Copperfield*, chapter 11:

> I know enough of the world now, to have almost lost the capacity of being much surprised by anything; but it is a matter of some surprise to me, even now, that I can have been so easily thrown away at such an age. A child of excellent abilities, and with strong powers of observation, quick, eager, delicate, and soon hurt bodily or mentally, it seems wonderful to me that nobody should have made any sign in my behalf. But none was made; and I became, at ten years old, a little labouring hand in the service of Murdstone and Grinby.

(49) Lysias, *Oration* 1.7–10:

> ἐπειδὴ δέ μοι ἡ μήτηρ ἐτελεύτησεν, ἣ πάντων τῶν κακῶν ἀποθανοῦσα αἰτία μοι γεγένηται. ἐπ᾽ ἐκφορὰν γὰρ αὐτῇ ἀκολουθήσασα ἡ ἐμὴ γυνὴ ὑπὸ τούτου τοῦ ἀνθρώπου ὀφθεῖσα χρόνῳ διαφθείρεται· ἐπιτηρῶν γὰρ τὴν θεράπαιναν τὴν εἰς τὴν ἀγορὰν βαδίζουσαν καὶ λόγους προσφέρων ἀπώλεσεν αὐτήν. [...] καὶ ταῦτα πολὺν χρόνον οὕτως ἐγίγνετο, καὶ ἐγὼ οὐδέποτε ὑπώπτευσα [...]

> But after my mother died, her death became the cause of all my troubles. For it was when attending her funeral that my wife was seen by that man and eventually was corrupted. For looking out for the servant who went to the market and getting into contact via her he corrupted her. [...] And this went on for a long time, while I never suspected anything [...]

In (48) the internal primary narrator David Copperfield looks back bitterly at the events of his childhood from his present position as an adult ('now', 'even now'). In (49) the internal narrator has to defend himself against a charge of killing the man who had an affair with his wife ('that man'), and hence his interest is to lay bare in his narrative the incriminating facts from the beginning, even though he found out about them only much later.

Though originally devised for *internal* narrators, it makes sense to apply the distinction 'narrating' versus 'experiencing' focalization to *external* narrators as well. They usually tell stories according to a narrating focalization, which means using their omniscient knowledge and inserting prolepses. But at times they may opt for a kind of eyewitness style, using historic presents, adopting a scenic standpoint, and abstaining from prolepses. Examples of external narrators using an experiencing focalization can be observed in examples (50) and (51).

(50) Ernest Hemingway, *For Whom the Bell Tolls*, chapter 1:

They were all eating out of the platter, not speaking, as is the Spanish custom. It was rabbit cooked with onions and green peppers and there were chick peas in the red wine sauce. It was well cooked, the rabbit meat flaked off the bones, and the sauce was delicious. Robert Jordan drank another cup of wine while he ate. The girl watched him all through the meal. Everyone else was watching his food and eating.

(51) Thucydides, *Histories* 8.34:

ἐν τούτῳ δὲ καὶ ἡ τῶν Ἀθηναίων στρατιὰ ταῖς ναυσὶν ἐκ τοῦ Κωρύκου περιπλέουσα κατ' Ἀργῖνον ἐπιτυγχάνει τρισὶ ναυσὶ τῶν Χίων μακραῖς, καὶ ὡς εἶδον, ἐδίωκον· καὶ χειμών τε μέγας ἐπιγίγνεται καὶ αἱ μὲν τῶν Χίων μόλις καταφεύγουσιν ἐς τὸν λιμένα, αἱ δὲ τῶν Ἀθηναίων αἱ μὲν μάλιστα ὁρμήσασαι τρεῖς διαφθείρονται καὶ ἐκπίπτουσι πρὸς τὴν πόλιν τῶν Χίων, καὶ ἄνδρες οἱ μὲν ἁλίσκονται, οἱ δ' ἀποθνῄσκουσιν, αἱ δ' ἄλλαι καταφεύγουσιν ἐς τὸν ὑπὸ τῷ Μίμαντι λιμένα Φοινικοῦντα καλούμενον.

Meanwhile the Athenian ships also left Corcyrus and, as they were rounding the point of Arginum, they chance upon three Chian warships, and as soon as they saw them, went after them. And a great storm comes up, and the Chian ships barely make it to the harbour, but the three Athenian ships that had pursued most hotly are wrecked and driven ashore to the city of Chios, and the crews are taken prisoner or killed; the other ships flee to the harbour called Phoenicus at the foot of Mount Mimas.

In (50) the external narrator describes the way in which a group of people eat graphically and without temporal deviations. In (51) the external narrator recounts the vicissitudes of the Athenian fleet, first clashing with Chian ships and then suffering from a heavy storm. Using historic presents almost throughout ('chance upon', 'comes up', 'make it', 'are wrecked and driven ashore', 'are taken prisoner or killed', 'flee') the narrator creates an eyewitness effect and increases the emotional effect of this fatal episode on the narratees.

3.6. SOME SPECIAL TYPES OF FOCALIZERS

Up to now this chapter has dealt with the focalization by the primary narrator-focalizer, by characters acting as secondary focalizers (embedded focalization), or by secondary narrator-focalizers (direct speech). But there can, in fact, be other focalizers at work in a narrative text. One age-old device consists in turning a 'you', that is, the narratee, into a *hypothetical focalizer* (52–3).

(52) W. Somerset Maugham, *Lord Mountdrago*:

> His eyes remained fixed on the other's face, but they were so empty of expression that you might have thought he did not even see him.

(53) Ovid, *Metamorphoses* 5.429–37:

>   'molliri membras videres,
> ossa pati flexus, ungues posuisse rigorem;
> primaque de tota tenuissima quaeque liquescunt,
> caerulei crines [. . .];
> denique pro vivo vitiatas sanguine venas
> lympha subit, restatque nihil quod prendere possis.'

> 'you would have seen her limbs soften, her bones becoming flexible, her nails losing their hardness. And first of all melt the slenderest parts, her dark hair [. . .] And finally, in place of living blood, clear water flows through her weakened veins, and nothing remained, which you could grasp.'

Employing this device a narrator draws his narratees more forcefully into his narrative, in that he makes them, through an effort of the imagination, place themselves into the situation recounted. Thus, in (52) the external narrator asks the narratees to visualize the empty gaze of one of the characters; in (53) the internal tertiary narrator Calliope describes in detail how the nymph Cyane dissolves into tears and appeals both at the beginning and end of her description to her (internal secondary) narratees, to visualize the liquefaction and feel its final result.

Another device, which likewise serves to engage the narratees, is that of introducing a 'man', 'traveller', or mere 'someone' and having that person wander through the setting of the story or witness an event as an *anonymous focalizer* (54–5).

(54) George Eliot, *Scenes of Clerical Life*, chapter 2:

> More than a quarter of a century has slipped by since then, and in the interval Milby has advanced at as rapid a pace as other market-towns in her Majesty's dominions. By this time it has a handsome railway station, where the drowsy London traveller may look out by the brilliant gas-light and see perfectly sober papas and husbands alighting with their leather bags after transacting their day's business at the county town.

(55) Homer, *Iliad* 4.539–42:

> ἔνθα κεν οὐκέτι ἔργον ἀνὴρ ὀνόσαιτο μετελθών,
> ὅς τις ἔτ᾽ ἄβλητος καὶ ἀνούτατος ὀξέϊ χαλκῷ
> δινεύοι κατὰ μέσσον, ἄγοι δέ ἑ Παλλὰς Ἀθήνη
> χειρὸς ἑλοῦσ᾽, αὐτὰρ βελέων ἀπερύκοι ἐρωήν·

> There no longer would a man who came at the scene make light of the battle, whoever still unscathed by throw or stab of sharp bronze would wander around at its centre, and Athena would lead him, having taken his hand, and shield him against the onslaught of missiles.

The anonymous focalizer is an expedient device to enliven a narrative and draw in the narratees, in that they can identify with 'the drowsy London traveller' looking out of the train (54) or the 'man' walking like an embedded war reporter over the Iliadic battlefield (55).

Focalization is arguably the most important new analytical tool that narratology has brought classics. The analysis of the focalization in a given passage is usually complex, not least because of its inherent ambiguity (is it the focalizer or verbalizing narrator who is responsible for a certain word?), but always leads to the heart of the emotional or ideological force of that passage. The simple question of 'who sees', as Genette famously defined focalization, is, thus, always a crucial one to ask when reading an ancient narrative text.

FURTHER READING

Narratology

Bal, M., *Narratology: Introduction to the Theory of Narrative* (Toronto 1997; first published 1988).

Cohn, D., *Transparent Minds: Narrative Modes for Presenting Consciousness in Fiction* (Princeton 1978).

Cordessse, G., 'Narration et focalisation', *Poétique* 76, 1988, 487–98.

Culler, J.D., 'Omniscience', *Narrative* 12, 2004, 22–34.

Edmiston, W.F., *Hindsight and Insight: Focalization in Four Eighteenth-Century French Novels* (University Park 1991).

Fludernik, M., *An Introduction to Narratology* (London and New York 2009; first published in German 2006).

Friedman, N., 'Point of View in Fiction: The Development of a Critical Concept', *Publications of the Modern Language Association* 70, 1955, 1160–84.

Genette, G., *Narrative Discourse: An Essay in Method* (Ithaca, NY 1980; first published in French 1972).

Genette, G., *Narrative Discourse Revisited* (Ithaca, NY 1988; first published in French 1983).

Herman, D., 'Hypothetical Focalisation', *Narrative* 2, 1994, 230–53.

Herman, D., *Basic Elements of Narrative* (Malden, Oxford, and Chicester 2009).

Herman, L., and D. Vervaeck, 'Focalization between Classical and Postclassical Narratology', in J. Pier (ed.), *The Dynamics of Narrative Form: Studies in Anglo-American Narratology* (Berlin 2004), 115–38.

Hühn, P., W. Schmid, and J. Schönert (eds), *Point of View, Perspective, and Focalization: Modeling Mediation in Narrative* (Berlin 2009).

Jahn, M., 'Windows of Focalization: Deconstructing and Reconstructing a Narratological Concept', *Style* 30, 1996, 241–67.

Kablitz, A., 'Erzählperspektive—Point of View—Focalisation', *Zeitschrift für französische Sprache und Literatur* 98, 1988, 237–55.

Nelles, W., 'Getting Focalization into Focus', *Poetics Today* 11, 1990, 365–82.

Rabatel, A., *La construction textuelle du point de vue* (Lausanne 1998).

Ronen, R., 'La focalisation dans les mondes fictionnels', *Poétique* 83, 1990, 305–22.

Schmid, W., *Narratologia: Elemente der Narratologie* (Berlin 2008; first published 2005).

Stanzel, F., *A Theory of Narrative* (Cambridge and New York 1984; first published in German 1979).

Sternberg, M., 'Omniscience in Narrative Construction: Old Challenges and New', *Poetics Today* 28, 2007, 683–794.

Narratology and classics

Allan, R.J., 'Towards a Typology of the Narrative Modes in Ancient Greek: Text Types and Narrative Structure in Euripidean Messenger Speeches', in S. Bakker and G. Wakker (eds), *Discourse Cohesion in Ancient Greek* (Leiden and Boston 2009), 171–203.

Bonfanti, M., *Punto di vista e modi della narrazione nell' Eneide* (Pisa 1985).

Byre, C.S., 'The Narrator's Addresses to the Narratee in Apollonius Rhodius' *Argonautica*', *Transactions of the American Philological Association* 121, 1991, 215–27.

Dewald, C., 'The Figured Stage: Focalizing the Initial Narratives of Herodotus and Thucydides', in T.M. Falkner, N. Felson, and D. Konstan (eds), *Contextualizing Classics: Ideology, Performance, Dialogue: Essays in Honor of John Peradotto* (Lanham 1999), 221–52.

Fowler, D.P., 'Deviant Focalisation in Vergil's *Aeneid*', *Proceedings of the Cambridge Philological Society* 36, 1990, 42–63 (reprinted in *Roman Constructions: Readings in Postmodern Latin* (Oxford 2000), 40–63).

Gilmartin, K., 'A Rhetorical Figure in Latin Historical Style: The Imaginary Second Person Singular', *Transactions of the American Philological Association* 105, 1975, 99–121.

Jong, I.J.F. de, 'Between Word and Deed: Hidden Thoughts in the *Odyssey*', in I.J.F. de Jong and J.P. Sullivan (eds), *Modern Critical Theory and Classical Literature* (Leiden 1994), 27–50 (reprinted in L.E. Doherty (ed.), *Oxford Readings in Classical Studies: Homer's Odyssey* (Oxford 2009), 62–90).

Jong, I.J.F. de, 'The Origins of Figural Narration in Antiquity', in W. van Peer and S. Chatman (eds), *New Perspectives on Narrative Perspective* (New York 2001), 67–81.

Jong, I.J.F. de, *Narrators and Focalizers. The Presentation of the Story in the Iliad* (London 2004; first published 1987).

Jong, I.J.F. de, and R. Nünlist, 'From Bird's Eye View to Close Up: The Standpoint of the Narrator in the Homeric Epics', in A. Bierl, A. Schmitt, and A. Willi (eds), *Antike Literatur in neuer Deutung* (Leipzig 2004), 63–83.

Kraus, C.S., 'Caesar's Account of the Battle of Massilia (*Bellum Gallicum* 1.34–2.22): Some Historiographical and Narratological Approaches', in J. Marincola (ed.), *A Companion to Greek and Roman Historiography*, vol. 2 (Malden 2007), 371–8.

Kullmann, W., 'Die Darstellung verborgener Gedanken in der antiken Literatur', in *Realität, Imagination, und Theorie* (Stuttgart 2002), 177–205.

Pelling, C.B.R., 'Seeing through Caesar's Eyes: Focalisation and Interpretation', in J. Grethlein and A. Rengakos (eds), *Narratology and*

Interpretation: The Content of Narrative Form in Ancient Literature (Berlin 2009), 507–26.

Wheeler, S.M., *A Discourse of Wonders: Audiences and Performances in Ovid's Metamorphoses* (Philadelphia 1999).

Winkler, J.J., *Auctor and Actor: A Narratological Reading of Apuleius's The Golden Ass* (Berkeley and London 1985).

4

Time

In this chapter we turn to what after the narrator and focalizer is perhaps the most defining element of a narrative: time. A narrative deals with events caused or experienced by characters; these events take up time and they are connected to each other in some form of temporal order.

When discussing time in a narrative text, it may be instructive to start by considering its time awareness: does the narrator provide us with a precise schedule, marking the years, months, days, and hours, or is the chronology vague? Examples of the former include Virginia Woolf's *The Years*, in which the titles of chapters are in the form of years (1880, 1891, etc.) and each chapter opens with an elaborate description of a season ('It was an uncertain spring...', 'The autumn wind blew over England...'), and the Homeric epics, which likewise specify almost every day of the story. In Marguerite Duras's *L'après-midi de Monsieur Andesmas*, conversely, we are confronted with snippets from a man's life without any precise temporal anchoring, just as the ancient Greek novels of Chariton or Xenophon of Ephesus are rather vague in their temporal structure (they abound in formulas such as 'some time later'). When it is impossible to determine the temporal relationship between the various events, we are dealing with an *achronical* narrative.

4.1. RELATION BETWEEN NARRATION AND EVENTS NARRATED

A basic feature to be determined concerns the relation between the moment of narration and the events that are recounted: the narration can be *subsequent* (the events have already taken place), *simultaneous* (the events are taking place at the moment of narration), or *prior* (the events have yet to take place). In all ages and all literatures, subsequent narration is the default form, whereby narrators occasionally may explicitly stress the difference in time between themselves and the events they relate (1–2).

(1) Elizabeth Gaskell, *Wives and Daughters*, chapter 1:

> This was no unusual instance of the influence of the great landowners over humble neighbours in those days before railways [. . .]

(2) Ovid, *Metamorphoses* 10.152–6:

> 'nunc opus est leviore lyra; puerosque canamus
> dilectos superis [. . .]
> rex superum Phrygii quondam Ganymedis amore
> arsit [. . .]'

> 'Now there is need for a lighter touch, and let me sing of boys loved by gods [. . .] The king of the gods once burned with love for the Phrygian Ganymede [. . .]'

In (1) the narrator herself clearly belongs to a time when there *are* railways, while the secondary narrator Orpheus signals the beginning of a story from the mythical past with *quondam*, 'once', in (2).

Simultaneous narration is very rare. Some modernist novelists have, by way of experiment, adopted it for entire novels (3), while brief stretches are found in ancient drama to narrate events that take place inside the *skēnē*-building (4).

(3) Michel Butor, *Second Thoughts* (*La modification*), chapter 1:

> Standing with your left foot on the grooved brass sill, you try in vain with your right shoulder to push the sliding door a little wider open. You edge your way in through the narrow opening, then you lift up your suitcase of bottle-green grained leather, the smallish suitcase of a man used to making long journeys, grasping the sticky handle with fingers that are hot from having carried even so light a weight so far, and you feel the muscles and tendons tense not only in your finger-joints, the palm of your hand, your wrist and your arm, but in your shoulder too, all down one side of your back along your vertebrae from neck to loins.

(4) Euripides, *Heracles Furens* 867–70:

καὶ δὴ τινάσσει κρᾶτα βαλβίδων ἄπο
καὶ διαστρόφους ἑλίσσει σῖγα γοργωποὺς κόρας,
ἀμπνοὰς δ' οὐ σωφρονίζει, ταῦρος ὣς ἐς ἐμβολήν,
δεινὰ μυκᾶται δέ.

See, he [Heracles] has left the starting-posts and is already tossing his head
and not speaking a word and is rolling his fierce eyes; he does not temper
his breathing, like a bull about to charge, and he is bellowing frightfully.

The modernist novel of Michel Butor (3) is revolutionary in its sustained use not only of the second person (see §2.2), but also of the
present tense. In (4) the goddess Lyssa, who has just struck Heracles
with madness, recounts his wild and frightening behaviour inside the
palace to the chorus and Iris on stage (and the spectators in the theatre).

Prior narration, finally, is regularly used in prolepses (these may
also be in the past tense) and only rarely for the narration of a whole
narrative (5–6).

(5) Michael Frayn, *A Very Private Life*, chapter 1:

Once upon a time there will be a little girl called Uncumber. Uncumber
will have a younger brother called Sulpice, and they will live with their
parents in the middle of the woods. There will be no windows in the
house, because there will be nothing to see outside except the forest.
[...] For this will be in the good new days a long, long while ahead, and
it will be like that in people's houses then.

(6) Sophocles, *Oedipus Tyrannus* 449–56:

'λέγω δέ σοι· τὸν ἄνδρα τοῦτον, ὃν πάλαι
ζητεῖς [...] οὗτός ἐστιν ἐνθάδε,
ξένος λόγῳ μέτοικος· εἶτα δ' ἐγγενὴς
φανήσεται Θηβαῖος, οὐδ' ἡσθήσεται
τῇ ξυμφορᾷ· τυφλὸς γὰρ ἐκ δεδορκότος
καὶ πτωχὸς ἀντὶ πλουσίου ξένην ἔπι
σκήπτρῳ προδεικνὺς γαῖαν ἐμπορεύσεται.'

'And I [Tiresias] tell you [Oedipus] this: that man you have been long
looking for [...] that man is here. He is thought to be a stranger who
has migrated here, but later he will be revealed to be a native Theban,
and he will not take pleasure in the turn out. For blind instead of seeing,
and poor instead of rich, he shall travel over strange land, feeling his
way with a stick.'

The postmodernist novel of (5) starts with a protracted piece of prior narration, the common 'once upon a time' surprisingly being combined with a future rather than a past tense. In (6) the seer Tiresias reveals the future to Oedipus in a prophecy that functions as an internal prolepsis for the spectators, who in the course of the play will see Oedipus being revealed to be a Theban, blinding himself, and leaving his country.

There is a final category of narration that merits mention: what might have happened (but did not). This may be called *hypothetical narration* or, in Gerald Prince's terms, the 'disnarrated' (7–8).

(7) Virginia Woolf, *Mrs Dalloway*:

> Gliding across Piccadilly, the car turned down St. James's Street. [. . .]
> Shawled Moll Pratt with her flowers on the pavement wished the dear
> boy well (it was the Prince of Wales for certain) and would have tossed
> the price of a pot of beer—a bunch of roses—into St. James's Street out
> of sheer light-heartedness and contempt of poverty had she not seen the
> constable's eye upon her, discouraging an old Irishwoman's loyalty.

(8) Livy, *History of Rome* 36.18.8:

> et aut incepto inrito recessissent aut plures cecidissent, ni M. Porcius ab
> iugo Callidromi deiectis inde Aetolis et magna ex parte caesis [. . .]
> super imminentem castris collem apparuisset.

> And they [the Roman troops] would either have been forced to with-
> draw, their plan having misfired, or more men would have fallen, if
> M. Porcius had not appeared on a hill which commanded the camp. He
> had thrown the Aetolians from the flanks of Mount Callidromus and
> killed the greater part of them [. . .]

In (7) we hear about what a character, the old Irishwoman Moll Pratt, considers doing for a moment but eventually does not do, so the disnarrated has a characterizing function. In (8) the narrator uses a particular form of hypothetical narration, the 'if not' situation (some-thing terrible would have happened, if X had not done Y), to highlight the decisive role of the Roman general (M. Porcius) Cato.

4.2. FABULA—STORY—TEXT

In order to describe in more detail the many forms of temporal relationships between narrative and events recounted, the distinctions between fabula, story, and text are important (see §2.7). The reconstructed fabula consists of the events in their full form in chronological order. When a focalizer looks at or remembers these events, they are turned into a story, which means that events may be presented in a different order, left out, told more than once, or reported at greater or lesser length. A narrator, finally, puts the story into a text, and this text is the practical yardstick by which all these temporal effects can be measured: how many words or pages are spent on an event? Schematically, we may represent the three levels of a narrative as follows:

Fabula	A–B–C–D–E
Story	B–Cccc–A–C–B′–D–Ee
	(the order is no longer chronological; some events are told in greater detail: Cccc and Ee; and some are told more than once: B and B').
Text	B (100 words)–Cccc (400)–A (100)–B′ (75)–D (50)–Ee (150)

It is customary to speak of 'story' versus 'fabula', but in fact the 'story' usually consists of a main story and many secondary stories or embedded narratives. Thus the (reconstructed) fabula of the *Odyssey* consists of Odysseus' ten-year journey home from Troy. To this fabula corresponds both the main story told by the primary narrator, which starts with the divine council in which Odysseus' return is set in motion (book 1) and ends with Athena as a kind of *deus ex machina* reconciling Odysseus with the families of the killed suitors (book 24), and the long embedded story of his adventures on his way home which Odysseus tells at the court of the Phaeacians (books 9–12).

In the case of an overt external narrator who has a great deal to say about himself, his act of narration, or his own time, the text may undergo considerable expansion (9–10).

(9) George Eliot, *The Mill on the Floss*, book 4, chapter 1:

But these dead-tinted, hollow-eyed, angular skeletons of villages on the Rhône, oppress me with the feeling that human life—very much of it— is a narrow, ugly, grovelling existence which even calamity does not elevate [...] Perhaps, something akin to this oppressive feeling may have weighed upon you in watching the old-fashioned family life on the banks of the Floss, which even sorrow hardly suffices to lift above the level of the tragi-comic. [...] I share with you this sense of oppressive narrowness; but it is necessary that we should feel it, if we care to understand how it acted in the lives of Tom and Maggie.

(10) Herodotus, *Histories* 2.44.1–2:

θέλων δὲ τούτων πέρι σαφές τι εἰδέναι ἐξ ὧν οἷόν τε ἦν, ἔπλευσα καὶ ἐς τύρον τῆς Φοινίκης, πυνθανόμενος αὐτόθι εἶναι ἱρὸν Ἡρακλέος ἅγιον. καὶ εἶδον πλουσίως κατεσκευασμένον ἄλλοισί τε πολλοῖσι ἀναθήμασι [...] ἐς λόγους δὲ ἐλθὼν τοῖσι ἱρεῦσι τοῦ θεοῦ εἰρόμην ὁκόσος χρόνος εἴη ἐξ οὗ σφι τὸ ἱρὸν ἵδρυται·

Wishing to get clear knowledge of this matter from a place where it was possible to do so, I also sailed to Tyre in Phoenicia, since I had heard that there was a holy sanctuary of Heracles there. And I observed that it was richly appointed with a large number of dedicatory offerings [...] Having entered into a conversation with the priests I asked them how long ago the sanctuary was founded.

The narrator in George Eliot's novels takes her time to express her opinions on all kind of matters related to the story, often engaging in some sort of conversation with her narratees, as happens in (9). The Herodotean narrator regularly refers to his travels and enquiries, sometimes even embarking on a mini-narrative, as in (10).

In what follows three temporal procedures which narrator-focalizers have at their disposal will be discussed: they can change the sequence of events (order), they can spend more or less time on recounting events (rhythm), and they can recount events more than once (frequency).

4.3. ORDER: ANALEPSES AND PROLEPSES

One of the oldest and best-known temporal procedures is to present the story in a different *order* than the (reconstructed) chronological one of the fabula. Gérard Genette speaks of *anachrony*. We can distinguish between *prolepsis* (flash-forward), the narration of an event that has not yet taken place at the point in the story where we find ourselves, and *analepsis* (flashback), the narration of an event that has already taken place by the point in the story where we find ourselves.

We have already come across prolepses in Section 3.3, since they are, in fact, one of the hallmarks of omniscient narration. Some more examples follow (11–12).

(11) Marcel Proust, *Remembrance of Things Past* (*A la recherche du temps perdu*), volume 1, part 1:

> We shall see, in due course, that for quite another reason, the memory of this impression was to play an important part in my life.

(12) Valerius Flaccus, *Argonautica* 5.338–40:

> mox stare paventes
> viderat intenta pueros nece seque trementum
> spargere caede manus et lumina rumpere fletu.

> Soon she [Medea] had seen her children standing in fear of threatening murder and herself, trembling, stain her hands with their blood and burst her eyes with tears.

In (11) the narrator has watched a meeting between Albertine, his future beloved, and another woman ('this impression'), which will later spawn his jealousy. In (12) Medea has a dream in which she sees events the narratees know will really take place.

For analepses we may think of (13) and (14).

(13) George Eliot, *Middlemarch*, chapter 15:

> At present I have to make the new settler Lydgate better known to any one interested in him than he could possibly be even to those who had seen the most of him since his arrival in Middlemarch [. . .] He had been left an orphan when he was fresh from a public school. His father, a military man, had made but little provision for three children [. . .]

(14) Apollonius Rhodius, *Argonautica* 1.524–7:

> σμερδαλέον δὲ λιμὴν Παγασήιος ἠδὲ καὶ αὐτή
> Πηλιὰς ἴαχεν Ἀργὼ ἐπισπέρχουσα νέεσθαι·
> ἐν γάρ οἱ δόρυ θεῖον ἐλήλατο, τό ῥ᾽ ἀνὰ μέσσην
> στεῖραν Ἀθηναίη Δωδωνίδος ἥρμοσε φηγοῦ.

> The harbour of Pagasae and Pelian Argo itself gave a terrible shout, eager to be under way. For in the ship a divine beam made of Dodonian oak was fitted, which Athena had placed in the middle of the keel.

In (13) the narrator interrupts her story about the arrival of the idealistic young doctor Lydgate in Middlemarch to sketch his earlier life. The 'novelistic' nature of the analepsis is indicated by her remark that it makes him 'better known [...] than he could possibly be even to those who had seen the most of him since his arrival in Middlemarch'. In (14) the narrator recounts how the ship the Argo shouts and thereby urges the men to depart. An analepsis informs the narratees that Athena had placed a divine beam in the ship, which explains why the ship can shout.

The scale of prolepses and analepses may vary. Some are brief, so as not to disrupt the flow of events in the main story. But they can also get the upper hand, as in Thornton Wilder's *The Bridge of San Luis Rey*, where the analeptic narrations of the lives of five people who die when a bridge collapses take up a large part of the novel. Prolepses are often used to create suspense or tension among the narratees about how things are going to develop, while analepses often fill them in on the background of characters or the 'prehistory' of the narrative they are reading. Just as prolepses heighten the narratees' expectation of what is to come, analepses may cause them to revise their previous interpretations. There seem to be no narratives that are totally devoid of anachronies, and the presence of analepses and prolepses is one of the major points in which the story differs from the fabula.

Narratologists, mainly Genette, have proposed several subtypes of analepses and prolepses. In the first place, we can distinguish between *internal* analepses/prolepses, which concern events that take place *within* the time span of the main story, and *external* analepses/prolepses, which fall *outside* this time span. For instance, the main story of the *Iliad* consists of a period of fifty-one days, starting with the arrival of Chryses on day one and ending with the burial of Hector on day 51. Achilles' account of the quarrel with Agamemnon that he gives his mother Thetis (1.370–92) is an internal analepsis, Odysseus' recollection of the gathering of the Greeks at Aulis (2.299–330) an external analepsis, the narrator's announcement that Hector was destined to be 'short-lived' (15.612–14) an internal prolepsis, and Priam's depiction of the fall of Troy (22.59–76) an external prolepsis. The main story of fifty-one days and all external analepses and prolepses together make up the fabula of the *Iliad*, the ten years of the Trojan War.

Analepses that do not form part of the fabula at all, that is, those that recount events that belong to a different storyline altogether, are called *heterodiegetic* analepses. Examples are the story of Niobe that

Achilles tells Priam in *Iliad* 24.602–17 and the story of Cupid and
Psyche embedded in Apuleius' *Metamorphoses* 4.28–6.25.

Within the group of analepses we can further distinguish between
completing analepses, which fill in events that had been passed over in
the main story, and *repeating* analepses, which cover the same ground
as the main story. Some examples of completing analepses follow
(15–16).

(15) Charles Dickens, *Great Expectations*, chapter 2:

> My sister, Mrs. Joe Gargary, was more than twenty years older than I,
> and had established a great reputation with herself and the neighbours
> because she had brought me up 'by hand'. Having at that time to find
> out for myself what that expression meant, and knowing her to have a
> hard and heavy hand, and to be much in the habit of laying it upon her
> husband as well as upon me, I supposed that Joe Gargary and I were
> both brought up by hand.

(16) Thucydides, *Peleponnesian War* 1.50.5–51.1:

> ἤδη δὲ ἦν ὀψὲ καὶ ἐπεπαιάνιστο αὐτοῖς ὡς ἐς ἐπίπλουν, καὶ οἱ Κορίνθιοι
> ἐξαπίνης πρύμναν ἐκρούοντο κατιδόντες εἴκοσι ναῦς Ἀθηναίων
> προσπλεούσας, ἃς ὕστερον τῶν δέκα βοηθοὺς ἐξέπεμψαν οἱ Ἀθηναῖοι,
> δείσαντες, ὅ περ ἐγένετο, μὴ νικηθῶσιν οἱ Κερκυραῖοι καὶ αἱ σφέτεραι
> δέκα νῆες ὀλίγαι ἀμύνειν ὦσιν.

> It was already late and the Athenians had already sung the paean to
> attack, when all of a sudden the Corinthians started to back water,
> having seen twenty ships of the Athenians approaching, which the
> Athenians had sent out after the original ten by way of reinforcement,
> since they feared, exactly as happened, that the Corcyreans might be
> defeated and that their own ten ships would be not enough to give
> support.

In (15) the internal narrator Pip returns in time and fills in the
narratees about his life up until the moment of the start of the main
story, which is his eventful meeting with the escaped convict Magwitch. In (16) the external narrator 'Thucydides' only now tells his
narratees that the Athenians had sent twenty more ships to reinforce
their original ten. The completing analepsis here, as often, has a
surprise effect and goes hand in hand with narrative delay, which
means that a narrator withholds crucial information at its proper
chronological place in the story in order to release it later to greater
effect (a form of paralipsis). Thus it is more effective to tell about the

twenty extra Athenian ships when the Corinthians all of a sudden detect them than at the moment of their departure from Athens. For repeating analepses we may think of (17) and (18).

(17) Charlotte Brontë, *Jane Eyre*, chapter 13:

> 'You [Jane Eyre] have been resident in my [Mr Rochester's] house three months?' 'Yes, sir.' 'And you come from—?' 'From Lowood school in—shire.' 'Ah! a charitable concern. How long were you there?' 'Eight years' 'Eight years! [. . .] Who are your parents?' 'I have none.'

(18) Ovid, *Metamorphoses* 2.748–51:

> aspicit hunc oculis isdem quibus abdita nuper
> viderat Aglauros flavae secreta Minervae,
> proque ministerio magni sibi ponderis aurum
> postulat.

> Aglauros looks at him [Mercury] with the same eyes with which she had lately peeped at the things hidden by fair Minerva, and asks for her service a mighty weight of gold.

In (17) Jane Eyre fills in her new master, Mr Rochester, about herself, information that the narratees had already received in earlier chapters of the novel; the function of the analepsis is to show the reaction of Mr Rochester, who eventually will become Jane's husband. In (18) the Ovidian narrator recalls how Aglauros had opened the secret chest of Minerva in which Erichthonius was hidden. He had recounted these events shortly before at 2.552–61 (as the *nuper*, 'lately', seems to remind the narratees). Aglauros arguably opened the chest because she expected it to contain a treasure, and the analepsis prepares for the sequel, when Minerva, also recalling Aglauros' earlier deed (755–7), punishes her for her greed, both present and past.

When analysing analepses and prolepses, it is important to realize who is making them: the narrator (in which case we speak of *narratorial* analepses and prolepses) or a character, in embedded focalization or a speech (*actorial* analepses and prolepses). Clear examples of *narratorial analepses* include (19) and (20).

(19) Lawrence Sterne, *Tristram Shandy*, volume 2, chapter 19:

> I have dropped the curtain over this scene for a minute,—to remind you of one thing,—and to inform you of another. What I have to inform you, comes, I own, a little out of its due course; for it should have been told a hundred and fifty pages ago [. . .]

(20) Polybius, *Histories* 5.40.3–5:

τοῦ δ᾽ ἀσμένως δεξαμένου τὴν ἐλπίδα, ταχεῖαν ἐλάμβανε τὸ πρᾶγμα
τὴν οἰκονομίαν. ἵνα δὲ καὶ περὶ ταύτης τῆς οἰκίας τὸ παραπλήσιον
ποιήσωμεν, ἀναδραμόντες ἐπὶ τὴν παράληψιν τῆς Ἀντιόχου δυναστείας
ἀπὸ τούτων τῶν καιρῶν ποιησόμεθα κεφαλαιώδη τὴν ἔφοδον ἐπὶ τὴν
ἀρχὴν τοῦ μέλλοντος λέγεσθαι πολέμου. Ἀντίοχος γὰρ ἦν μὲν υἱὸς
νεώτερος Σελεύκου τοῦ Καλλινίκου προσαγορευθέντος [...]

Antiochus gladly grasped at the proposal and the matter was quickly
arranged. In order that I may perform for this royal family the same [as
I did for the Egyptian one], I will go back to Antiochus' succession to
the throne and give a summary of events between that date and the war
I am about to describe. Antiochus was the younger son of Seleucus
Callinicus [...]

In both these examples we have a (primary external) narrator who
explicitly marks that he is going back in time.

Examples of *actorial analepses* include (21) and (22).

(21) Virginia Woolf, *Mrs Dalloway*:

'That is all', she [Mrs Dalloway] said, looking at the fishmonger's. 'That
is all,' she repeated, pausing for a moment at the window of a glove shop
where, before the War, you could buy almost perfect gloves. And her old
Uncle William used to say a lady is known by her shoes and her gloves.
He had turned on his bed one morning in the middle of the War. He
had said, 'I have had enough.'

(22) Ovid, *Metamorphoses* 13.159–64:

'ergo operum quoniam nudum certamen habetur,
plura quidem feci quam quae comprendere dictis
in promptu mihi sit, rerum tamen ordine ducar.
Praescia venturi genetrix Nereia leti
dissimulat cultu natum, et deceperat omnes,
in quibus Aiacem, sumptae fallacia vestis.'

'So, since the contest is merely about deeds, and I have done more
than I can convey briefly in words, I will nevertheless tell all in order.
His Nereid mother, foreseeing his death, disguises her son [Achilles]
with clothing, and the trick of the assumed clothing deceived all,
including Ajax.'

In (21) Mrs Dalloway recalls the death of an uncle after seeing gloves
in a shop; in (22) Odysseus, engaged in a contest with Ajax over
Achilles' armour, gives an account of the many deeds that, he claims,

entitle him to that armour. The first was that he alone saw through Thetis' trick of dressing up Achilles in female clothing. Examples of *narratorial prolepses* include (23) and (24).

(23) Gabriel García Márquez, *Chronicle of a Death Foretold*:

> On the day they were going to kill him, Santiago Nasar woke up at five-thirty in the morning to wait for the boat the bishop was coming on.

(24) Ovid, *Metamorphoses* 15.875–9:

> parte tamen meliore mei super alta perennis
> astra ferar, nomenque erit indelebile nostrum;
> quaque patet domitis Romana potentia terris
> ore legar populi, perque omnia saecula fama
> (si quid habent veri vatum praesagia) vivam.

Yet with the best part of me I shall be borne, immortal, beyond the lofty stars, and my name will be imperishable; and wherever Rome's power extends over the countries conquered by it, I will be spoken about by people's lips, and (if there is any truth in the prophecies of poets) I shall live in fame through all the ages.

Passage (23) is the spectacular opening sentence of a novella in which the protagonist, Santiago Nasar, is killed by two brothers to avenge a crime he did not commit (deflowering their sister). Passage (24) is the conclusion of the *Metamorphoses*, and the Ovidian narrator self-consciously proclaims his eternal literary fame.

Examples of *actorial prolepses* include (25) and (26).

(25) William Thackeray, *Vanity Fair*, chapter 6:

> 'He must propose to-morrow,' thought Rebecca. 'He called me his soul's darling, four times; he squeezed my hand in Amelia's presence. He must propose to-morrow.' And so thought Amelia, too [. . .] Oh ignorant young creatures! How little do you know the effect of rack punch! [. . .] There is no headache in the world like that caused by Vauxhall punch. [. . .] and Joseph Sedly, who had a liver complaint, had swallowed at least a quart of the abominable mixture.

(26) Euripides, *Medea* 1386–8:

> ʻσὺ δ᾽, ὥσπερ εἰκός, κατθανῆι κακὸς κακῶς,
> Ἀργοῦς κάρα σὸν λειψάνωι πεπληγμένος,
> πικρὰς τελευτὰς τῶν ἐμῶν γάμων ἰδών.ʼ

'And you [Jason], as is fitting, shall die the miserable death of a coward, struck on the head by a piece of the Argo, having seen the bitter result of your marriage to me [Medea].'

In (25) a character speculates about the future, but the marriage between Rebecca and Joseph Sedly is never to take place, as the narrator immediately reveals to his narratees. In (26) Medea, functioning as *deus ex machina*, gives a reliable prolepsis of Jason's death. Example (25) makes clear that not all prolepses are certain. There is even the well-known type of the *false prolepsis* or *misdirection*, when the narratees are given a false impression that events are going to take place (27–8).

(27) Ambrose Bierce, *An Occurrence at Owl Creek Bridge*, chapter 1:

> He unclosed his eyes and saw again the water below him. 'If I could free my hands,' he thought, 'I might throw off the noose and spring into the stream. By diving I could evade the bullets and, swimming vigorously, reach the bank, take to the woods and get away home.'

(28) Virgil, *Aeneid* 12.402–4:

> multa manu medica Phoebique potentibus herbis
> nequiquam trepidat, nequiquam spicula dextra
> sollicitat prensatque tenaci forcipe ferrum.

> with healing hand and strong herbs of Phoebus, he [the doctor Iapyx] anxiously tries many remedies, in vain; in vain he pulls with his right hand at the spear-point and with a gripping fork tugs at the steel.

In (27) a man has been sentenced to death by hanging and just prior to his execution contemplates escape. The remainder of the short story seems to recount his escape, until the last sentences make clear that it was merely the thoughts running through his head during the time between falling and the noose breaking his neck. In (28) the Virgilian narrator twice uses the ominous *nequiquam*, 'in vain', which always announces doom (e.g. 7.652–3), and the narratees are thus led to believe, against their better knowledge, that Aeneas is not going to survive the wounding by a spear.

In addition to prolepses, which are usually *explicitly* marked as such one way or another (through the use of a future tense, through a comment of the type 'little could I know that this would turn out very differently', or through the use of verbs which concern the future, such as 'hope', 'fear', 'expect', etc.), narratives often feature forms of *implicit foreshadowing* (29–30).

(29) John Steinbeck, *Of Mice and Men*, chapter 1:

> Lennie sat down on the ground and hung his head dejectedly. 'I don't know where there is no other mouse. I remember a lady used to give 'em

to me- ever' one she got. But that lady ain't here.' George scoffed. 'Lady, huh? Don't even remember who that lady was. That was your own Aunt Clara. An' she stopped givin' 'em to ya. You always killed 'em.' Lennie looked sadly up at him. 'They was so little', he said, apologetically. 'I'd pet 'em, and pretty soon they bit my fingers and I pinched their heads a little and then they was dead—because they was so little.'

(30) Homer, *Odyssey* 12.166-9:

> τόφρα δὲ καρπαλίμως ἐξίκετο νηῦς εὐεργὴς
> νῆσον Σειρήνοιϊν· ἔπειγε γὰρ οὖρος ἀπήμων.
> αὐτίκ᾽ ἔπειτ᾽ ἄνεμος μὲν ἐπαύσατο ἠδὲ γαλήνη
> ἔπλετο νηνεμίη, κοίμησε δὲ κύματα δαίμων.

Meanwhile the well-made ship came quickly to the Sirens' island, sped by a safe wind. But then immediately the wind dropped and there came a windless calm, and a god stilled the waves.

In (29) the inadvertent killing of mice by the mentally disabled Lennie anticipates his unintentionally breaking the neck of a woman later on in the narrative. In (30), as Odysseus approaches the island of the Sirens, about whom he has been warned by Circe, the sudden silence of nature is ominous and announces that something is going to happen.

A special type of foreshadowing is the *seed* (hint or advance mention), the insertion of a piece of information of which the relevance will only later become clear (31-2).

(31) E.M. Forster, *A Passage To India*, chapter 1:

> Except for the Marabar Caves—and they are twenty miles off—the city of Chandrapore presents nothing extraordinary.

(32) Virgil, *Aeneid* 1.647-52:

> munera praeterea, Iliacis erepta ruinis,
> ferre iubet [...]
>   circumtextum croceo velamen acantho,
> ornatus Argivae Helenae, quos illa Mycenis,
> Pergama cum peteret inconcessosque hymenaeos,
> extulerat [...]

He [Aeneas] also orders to bring presents, snatched from the ruins of Troy [...] a veil fringed with yellow acanthus, attire of Argive Helen, which she had taken with her from Mycene, when she sailed for Troy and her unlawful marriage [...]

Example (31) forms the opening of the novel. The narrator will go on to describe the city of Chandrapore, the setting of the narrative to follow. But, mentioned in passing, the Marabar caves will soon become the scene of the central event of that narrative: the joint visit to these caves by the Indian Aziz and the young English woman Adela Quested. In (32) the veil given Dido by Aeneas is ominous: it is associated with an unlawful marriage and therefore casts a shadow over their upcoming affair, whose status as marriage the two partners will bitterly debate.

4.4. BEGINNINGS, ENDS, AND MULTIPLE STORYLINES

The narratological category of 'order' is also relevant to the beginning and end of narratives. By its very nature the *beginning* of a narrative (opening, *incipit*) is an element to which narrators devote much attention, invoking the Muses to authenticate their narrative or indicating time or space to ease their narratees into the world of the characters (33–4).

(33) William Thackeray, *Vanity Fair*, chapter 1:

> While the present century was in its teens, and on one sunshiny morning in June, there drove up to the great iron gate of Miss Pinkerton's academy for young ladies, on Chiswick Mall, a large family coach [...]

(34) Euripides, *Bacchae* 677–80:

> ἀγελαῖα μὲν βοσκήματ' ἄρτι πρὸς λέπας
> μόσχων ὑπεξήκριζον, ἡνίχ' ἥλιος
> ἀκτῖνας ἐξίησι θερμαίνων χθόνα.
> ὁρῶ δὲ θιάσους τρεῖς γυναικείων χορῶν [...]

> The grazing herds of cattle were just moving up towards the slopes at the time when the sun emits rays warming the earth. And I see three groups consisting of female choruses [...]

While the external narrator in (33) indicates the year, month, and time of the day and the precise address, the internal narrator in (34), a herdsman acting as messenger, takes recourse to the one temporal marker he has, the sun, and speaks about 'the slopes' (of Mount Cithaeron). After such indications of temporal or spatial setting, opening *topoi*, such as arrival, departure, meeting, or awaking, often follow to set the action going.

Stories may start at the beginning of the fabula or *in medias res*, that is, at some point further on in the fabula. Narrative texts where the beginning of story and fabula coincide are rare, since few narrators would pass up the opportunity to add a 'prehistory' to their main story by means of external analepses. The *in medias res* opening is famously exemplified by the *Odyssey*, which starts in the tenth year of Odysseus' return and only fills in the preceding years through a four-book-long embedded narrative by the hero himself halfway through (books 9–12). A modern example is Graham Greene's *The End of the Affair*, which starts near the end of a love affair and fills in the early and middle phases by means of analepses, for instance the diary of the woman the male narrator has fallen in love with.

It should be noted that in its original definition by Horace in his *Ars Poetica* 147–8, the concept of *in medias res* also refers to a narrator selecting only the most interesting period in a character's life for his narrative, as against starting *ab ovo* (lit. 'from the egg', from which Helen was born, i.e. from the very beginning) and including everything. Here Horace is adopting ideas of Aristotle, who in chapter 8 of his *Poetics* praises Homer for not including in his *Odyssey* everything that ever happened to Odysseus but focusing on the ten years of the hero's return from Troy. Gradually, *in medias res* became exclusively associated with the choice of the beginning of the story as compared to the (chronological) fabula.

Narrators may thematize finding the right point to start their narrative (35–6).

(35) Graham Greene, *The End of the Affair*, chapter 1:

> A story has no beginning or end: arbitrarily one chooses that moment of experience from which to look back or from which to look ahead. I say 'one chooses' with the inaccurate pride of a professional writer who has been praised for his technical ability, but did I in fact of my own will choose that black wet January night on the Common, in 1946, the sight of Henry Miles slanting across the wide river of rain, or did these images choose me?

(36) Statius, *Thebaid* 1.1–17:

> fraternas acies alternaque regna profanis
> decertata odiis sontisque evolvere Thebas,
> Pierius menti calor incidit. unde iubetis
> ire, deae? gentisne canam primordia dirae,
> Sidonios raptus et inexorabile pactum
> legis Agenoreae scrutantemque aequora Cadmum? [...]
> atque adeo iam nunc gemitus et prospera Cadmi
> praeteriisse sinam: limes mihi carminis esto
> Oedipodae confusa domus [...]

Pierian fire takes hold of my mind, to unfold fraternal fights, and alternate reigns fought for in impious hatred, and guilty Thebes. Where do you command me to begin, goddesses? Shall I sing of the origins of that disastrous race, Europa's rape, the strictness of Agenor's ordinance, and Cadmus' searching quest across the sea? [...] No; I will already let the agonies and joys of Cadmus be bygones. Let the troubled house of Oedipus set the limit to my song [...]

In (35) the internal narrator, having the persona of a 'professional writer', alludes to the Aristotelian notion that a narrative is defined by having a beginning, middle, and end, and remarks that these are, in fact, the choice of the narrator/writer. The external narrator in (36) has decided to recount the story of the sons of Oedipus, Eteocles and Polynices, but discusses how far to go back in Theban mythology for his starting point with the Muse.

Turning now to the *end* (*excipit*) of narratives, we may note that less attention was paid to ends than to beginnings in antiquity. Epilogues are much less common than proems. This is often explained as the result of the oral nature of early Greek narrative. Since singers could always be interrupted by their narratees, as we see happening several times in *Odyssey* 8, they did not spend their energy on developing the art of the epilogue. Hence Homer bequeathed the proem but not the epilogue to later narratives. Be this as it may, there is a repertoire of ending *topoi*, like death, return, reunion, and marriage, and of other formal devices that may mark the end of a narrative, such as ring-composition, *sphragis* (lit. 'seal', a personal reference by the narrator to himself and his work), and recapitulation. We came across a *sphragis* in example (24), and some more examples follow (37–8).

(37) Jane Austen, *Emma*, chapter 54:

> The wedding was very much like other weddings, where the parties have
> no taste for finery or parade [...] But in spite of these deficiencies, the
> wishes, the hopes, the confidence, the predictions of the small band of
> true friends who witnessed the ceremony, were fully answered in the
> perfect happiness of the union.

(38) Apollonius Rhodius, *Argonautica* 4.1773–80:

> ἵλατ᾽ ἀριστῆες, μακάρων γένος, αἵδε δ᾽ ἀοιδαὶ
> εἰς ἔτος ἐξ ἔτεος γλυκερώτεραι εἶεν ἀείδειν
> ἀνθρώποις. ἤδη γὰρ ἐπὶ κλυτὰ πείραθ᾽ ἱκάνω
> ὑμετέρων καμάτων, ἐπεὶ [...]
> ἀσπασίως ἀκτὰς Παγασηίδας εἰσαπέβητε.

> Be gracious heroes, race of blessed men, and may these songs be from
> year to year ever sweeter to sing for men. For now I have reached the
> glorious end of tour toils, since [...] you gladly disembarked on the
> shores of Pagasae.

In (37) the narrator uses the wedding of the protagonist Emma as
end-point, the final words perhaps (ironically?) echoing the stock
phrasing with which folktales end ('and they lived happily ever after').
In (38) the narrator emphatically marks the end of his narrative by
saying farewell to his heroes in hymnic style, inserting the ending
topos of the return, using the word 'end', and including a *sphragis*
('may these songs ... ').

While the end simply is the concluding section of a narrative,
closure is the degree to which narratees come to see that end as
satisfyingly final, answering any remaining questions and resolving
any tensions. Thus the end of the *Iliad* is marked by the ending *topos*
of the burial of Hector and the formal device of the ring-composition
of a father coming to hostile territory to reclaim his child (book 1:
Chryses–Chryseis; book 24: Priam–Hector), while closure is effected
through the conversation between Achilles and Priam, sworn enemies
who for a brief moment are reunited in their predicament of being
mortals.

Just as the beginning of a story need not coincide with the beginning of the fabula, the end need not be the end of the fabula. The
Odyssey concludes with Odysseus' reunion with his wife and coun-
trymen, but the remainder of his life was announced by Tiresias in an
external prolepsis at 11.134–7. The forthcoming tragedy of Medea

looms over the apparent happy end of the *Argonautica*. This device, when a narrative somehow acknowledges a future not part of the narrative proper, is called 'aftermath' by Deborah Roberts. It can take the form of external prolepses made in the course of the narrative (as in the *Odyssey*), a summary prolepsis at the very end of the narrative (of the type 'and they lived happily ever after' or the *sphragis* of example (24)), or be left implicit, the narrator counting on his narratees' historical or intertextual knowledge (as in the *Argonautica*). A modern example is (39).

(39) Charles Dickens, *The Pickwick Papers*, chapter 57:

> It is the fate of all authors or chroniclers to create imaginary friends, and lose them in the course of art. Nor is this the full extent of their misfortunes; for they are required to furnish an account of them besides. In compliance with this custom—unquestionably a bad one—we subjoin a few biographical words, in relation to the party at Mr. Pickwick's assembled. Mr. and Mrs. Winkle, being fully received into favour by the old gentleman, were shortly afterwards installed in a newly-built house [. . .] Mr. Pickwick himself continued to reside in his new house, employing his leisure hours in arranging the memoranda which he afterwards presented to the secretary of the once famous club [. . .]

Here the narrator, providing a summary prolepsis about all of his characters, pokes fun at readers' habit of believing in literary characters as real people and hence wondering about their life after the novel. Because Dickens wrote his novels in feuilleton form, he may well have been literally confronted with this habit in his career.

Many narratives, in particular (post)modern ones, lack a clear ending or closure altogether, that is, they are open-ended. The narratees are not sure how the life of the protagonist will continue. The term 'open-endedness' is also used to refer to narratives of which the interpretation is ambiguous, such as Virgil's *Aeneid*: is it propaganda for Augustus or subtle criticism of his rise to power and reign?

A last aspect of narration that involves order is the device of the *multiple storylines*, which means that a narrative follows the vicissitudes of different characters at different places. When a narrator switches from storyline A to storyline B, he may return in time to fill in what happened with B while the situation in A was evolving (40), or he may let time tick on and proceed with B at the point where he left A (41).

(40) William Thackeray, *Vanity Fair*, chapter 12:

> We must now take our leave of Arcadia, and those amiable people practising the rural virtues there, and travel back to London, to inquire what has become of Miss Amelia.

(41) Homer, *Odyssey* 14.523 and 15.1–5:

> ὣς ὁ μὲν ἔνθ᾽ Ὀδυσεὺς κοιμήσατο [. . .]
> ἡ δ᾽ εἰς εὐρύχορον Λακεδαίμονα Παλλὰς Ἀθήνη
> ᾤχετ᾽, Ὀδυσσῆος μεγαθύμου φαίδιμον υἱὸν
> νόστου ὑπομνήσουσα καὶ ὀτρυνέουσα νέεσθαι.
> εὗρε δὲ Τηλέμαχον καὶ Νέστορος ἀγλαὸν υἱὸν
> εὕδοντ᾽ ἐν προδόμῳ Μενελάου κυδαλίμοιο [. . .]

> Thus Odysseus slept there [. . .] But Pallas Athena went to Lacedaemon with broad dancing places in order to remind the son of great-hearted Odysseus of his return home and to urge him to go. She found Telemachus and the splendid son of Nestor asleep in the portico of famous Menelaus' house [. . .]

In (40) the narrator turns from the vicissitudes of one of his female protagonists in the country to those of Amelia in London, and in so doing also returns in time. In (41) the narrator switches to Telemachus after ten books (covering 31 days) but does not go back in time to recount what the youth had been doing those days. Instead, he seamlessly turns from sleeping father to sleeping son.

4.5. RHYTHM

A second important difference between fabula and story concerns their speed. While in the fabula events can be assumed to take up the same amount of time they would in real life, their duration in the story may differ: narrator-focalizers may spend more or less or no time at all on events. Narratologists use the term *rhythm* (duration, speed) to refer to the amount of time that is devoted to an event in the story (story time: ST) as compared to that in the fabula (fabula time: FT). In practice ST is often determined on the basis of the amount of text devoted to events.

Theoretically, there are an infinite number of possibilities when it comes to rhythm. In practice, however, narratives typically modulate between *scenes*, in which events are told in great detail (often including the words spoken by a character) and come close to—but of course never really match—their real-time duration (ST≈FT), and *summaries*, where events are dealt with quickly and in broad strokes (ST<FT). Some examples follow (42–3).

(42) John Galsworthy, *The Man of Property*, part 2, chapter 1:

> The winter had been an open one. Things in the trade were slack; and as Soames had reflected before making up his mind, it had been a good time for building. The shell of the house at Robin Hill was thus completed by the end of April. [...] On April 30 he had an appointment with Bosinney to go over the accounts, and five minutes before the proper time he entered the tent which the architect had pitched for himself close to the old oak tree. The accounts were already prepared on a folding table, and with a nod Soames sat down to study them. It was some time before he raised his head. 'I can't make them out,' he said at last [...]

(43) Virgil, *Aeneid* 4.189–94:

> haec tum multiplici populos sermone replebat
> gaudens, et pariter facta atque infecta canebat:
> venisse Aenean [...]
> nunc hiemem inter se luxu, quam longa, fovere
> regnorum immemores turpique cupidine captos.

> This Rumour then, rejoicing in all kind of gossip, filled the various peoples, and sang alike of fact and falsehood: that a certain Aeneas had come [...] and that they now snugly spend the winter together, all its length, in dalliance, forgetful of their realms and enthralled by shameless passion.

In (42) we start with a summary, which turns into a scene halfway through (from 'On April 30' onwards). In (43) the Virgilian narrator uses the event of Rumour spreading the news of Dido's affair with Aeneas as a summary to suggest the passing of a considerable amount of time ('the winter', 'all its length').

The choice of a particular rhythm can be highly effective. Telling examples include (44) and (45).

(44) D.H. Lawrence, *Sons and Lovers*, chapter 1:

> The next Christmas they were married, and for three months she was perfectly happy: for six months she was very happy.

94   *Narratology and Classics*

(45) Thucydides, *Peloponnesian War* 5.116.4:

οἱ δὲ ἀπέκτειναν Μηλίων ὅσους ἡβῶντας ἔλαβον, παῖδας δὲ καὶ
γυναῖκας ἠνδραπόδισαν· τὸ δὲ χωρίον αὐτοὶ ᾤκισαν, ἀποίκους ὕστερον
πεντακοσίους πέμψαντες.

They [the Athenians] killed all the grown men of Melos they captured,
enslaved the children and women, and settled the place themselves by
sending out five hundred colonists later.

In (44) the summary makes clear the brevity of the happiness of Paul
Morel's parents, which was soon to be followed by years of fighting
and estrangement. In (45) the Athenian annihilation of the Melians is
presented in an extreme summary, following a seven-page account of
negotiations between Athenians and Melians, and is open for different interpretations: is it a signal that the narrator Thucydides con-
dones the Athenian act, considering the Melians foolish in resisting
the Athenian arguments to surrender? Or is it a way of bringing out
the Athenians' ruthless brutality?

Other types of rhythm are the *retardation* or slowing down
(ST>FT) and *acceleration* or speeding up (ST<FT). First let us consider some examples of retardation (46–7).

(46) Thomas Hardy, *Tess of the D'Urbervilles*, chapter 7:

On the morning appointed for her departure Tess was awake before
dawn—at the marginal minute of the dark when the grove is still mute
save for one prophetic bird, who sings with a clear-voiced conviction
that he at least knows the correct time of day, the rest preserving silence,
as if equally convinced that he is mistaken. She remained upstairs
packing [. . .]

(47) Homer, *Iliad* 4.134–8:

ἐν δ' ἔπεσε ζωστῆρι ἀρηρότι πικρὸς ὀϊστός·
διὰ μὲν ἂρ ζωστῆρος ἐλήλατο δαιδαλέοιο,
καὶ διὰ θώρηκος πολυδαιδάλου ἠρήρειστο
μίτρης θ', ἣν ἐφόρει ἔρυμα χροός, ἕρκος ἀκόντων,
ἥ οἱ πλεῖστον ἔρυτο· διαπρὸ δὲ εἴσατο καὶ τῆς.

The bitter arrow hit home in the belt's fastening. And it passed through
the elaborately made belt, and through the richly adorned corselet it
forced its way, and the skirt-piece, which he wore to guard his body,
protection against spears, and it was his greatest defence. But it went
even through that.

In (46) the narrator marks the momentous day of Tess leaving home by slowing down his speed and inserting an extensive description of an early bird singing, arguably focalized by Tess herself. It is a general principle of ancient storytelling that at moments of crisis, as in (47), where Pandarus wounds Menelaus and hence breaks the truce between the Greeks and Trojans, the rhythm will invariably slow down. Or, to put it differently, a moment of crisis is marked by a retardation of the narrative speed. We may note that such a retardation often goes hand in hand with the close-up narratorial standpoint (see §3.4).

For the acceleration of speed we may turn to examples (48) and (49).

(48) E.M. Forster, *A Room with a View*, part 2, chapter 8:

> So it was that after the gropings and the misgivings of the afternoon they pulled themselves together and settled down to a very pleasant tea-party.

(49) Ovid, *Metamorphoses* 10.519–24:

> 'labitur occulte fallitque volatilis aetas,
> et nihil est annis velocius. Ille [. . .]
>   qui conditus arbore nuper,
> nuper erat genitus, modo formosissimus infans,
> iam iuvenis, iam vir, iam se formosior ipso est,
> iam placet et Veneri matrisque ulciscitur ignes.'

> 'Time glides by imperceptibly and in its flight escapes our attention, and nothing is swifter than years. That child [Adonis][. . .] who had only recently been hidden in the tree, who had only recently been born, one moment is a very beautiful child, the next already a youth, already a man, already more beautiful than his former self, already appeals even to Venus and avenges the passion of his mother.'

Example (48) follows at the end of a chapter devoted to a minute recording of the ('gropings and misgivings' of the) afternoon; the narrator speeds up as if to show that things now run smoothly. In (49) the secondary narrator Orpheus, after a detailed account of Adonis' birth, accelerates the rhythm of his narration when describing Adonis' life so as to fast-forward to Venus falling in love with the beautiful youth.

A narrator may even bring the flow of events to a complete standstill or *pause* (no FT corresponds to the ST), as in (50) and (51).

(50) Miguel de Cervantes, *Don Quixote*, book 1, chapter 16:

> Beyond the two came the carrier's bed, made, as we have said, of the saddles and all the trappings of the best two mules he had. He had twelve glossy, well-covered, splendid beasts, for he was one of the richest muleteers in Arevalo, as the author of this history tells [*follows a long digression on the author Cide Hamete Benengeli*]. But to return to the story. After the carrier had visited his mules [...]

(51) Herodotus, *Histories* 1.201–4:

> [...] ἐπεθύμησε Μασσαγέτας ὑπ' ἑωυτῷ ποιήσασθαι. τὸ δὲ ἔθνος τοῦτο
> καὶ μέγα λέγεται εἶναι καὶ ἄλκιμον, οἰκημένον δὲ πρὸς ἠῶ τε καὶ ἡλίου
> ἀνατολάς, πέρην τοῦ Ἀράξεω ποταμοῦ [...] ὁ δὲ Ἀράξης λέγεται [...]
> τοῦ ὦν δὴ πεδίου<τούτου>τοῦ μεγάλου οὐκ ἐλαχίστην μοῖραν μετέχουσι
> οἱ Μασσαγέται, ἐπ' οὕς ὁ Κῦρος ἔσχε προθυμίην στρατεύσασθαι.

> [...] he [Cyrus] desired to subdue the Massagetae. These are said to be a great and mighty people, dwelling towards the east and the sunrise, beyond the Araxes [...] The Araxes is said [...] [*there follow two chapters of geographical description*]. The greater part of this wide plain is the country of the Massagetae, against whom Cyrus desired to lead his army.

In passage (50) the external narrator himself qualifies the passage on his 'source', the historian Cide Hamete Benengeli, as a pause by emphatically marking his return to his story. In (51) the Herodotean narrator interrupts his story about the reign of the Persian King Cyrus in order to insert a geographical digression on the Massagetae. He picks up again the thread of his narrative, typically, with a verbal echo ('desired': ἔσχε προθυμίην ≈ ἐπεθύμησε).

Sometimes pauses are cleverly avoided (52–3).

(52) Alessandro Manzoni, *The Betrothed* (*I promessi sposi*), chapter 8:

> The boatmen made silently for the opposite shore [...] The silent passengers cast a melancholy look behind at the mountains and the landscape, illumined by the moon, and varied by multitudes of shadows. They discerned villages, houses, cottages; the palace of Don Roderick, raised above the huts that crowded the base of the promontory, like a savage prowling in the dark over his slumbering prey. Lucy beheld it, and shuddered; then cast a glance beyond the declivity, towards her own little home, and beheld the top of the fig-tree which towered in the court-yard; moved at the sight, she buried her face in her hands, and wept in silence. Farewell, mountains, source of waters! Farewell to your varied summits, familiar as the faces of friends! You torrents, whose voices have been heard from infancy. Of such a nature,

if not precisely the same, were the reflections of Lucy and her companions, as the bark carried them to the right bank of the Adda.

(53) Homer, *Odyssey* 13.95–113:

> τῆμος δὴ νήσῳ προσεπίλνατο ποντοπόρος νηῦς.
> Φόρκυνος δέ τίς ἐστι λιμήν, ἁλίοιο γέροντος,
> ἐν δήμῳ Ἰθάκης· δύο δὲ προβλῆτες ἐν αὐτῷ
> ἀκταὶ ἀπορρῶγες, λιμένος πότιπεπτηυῖαι [. . .]
> ἔνθ᾽ οἵ γ᾽ εἰσέλασαν [. . .]

At that time the sea-going ship started to approach the island. There is a
bay, called after Phorcys, the old man from the sea, on Ithaca: its two
headlands jut out sheer to sea and crouch over the bay [. . .] It was into
this bay that they [the Phaeacians] drove in [. . .]

In (52) the narrator fills the time the boat needs to cross the water
with the silent thoughts of his characters. In (53) he seems to interrupt his story to describe the bay of Phorcys, but when he picks up its
thread again, the Phaeacians turn out to have also progressed and
reached the end of the bay.

A final form of rhythm consists in passing over events or *ellipsis*
(gap; no ST corresponds to the FT). Instances may be casual and the
result of narrative efficiency (type: 'Some two weeks later . . . '), but
often they are meaningful or at least invite the narratees to fill in the
voids (54–5).

(54) F. Scott Fitzgerald, *The Great Gatsby*, chapter 2:

Then Mr. McKee turned and continued on out of the door. Taking my
hat from the chandelier I followed. 'Come to lunch some day,' he
suggested [. . .] 'All right,' I agreed, 'I'll be glad to.' . . . I was standing
behind his bed and he was sitting up between the sheets, clad in his
underwear, with a great portfolio in his hands. 'Beauty and the Beast
. . . Loneliness . . . Old Grocery Horse . . . Brook'n Bridge . . . ' Then I was
lying half asleep in the cold lower level of the Pennsylvania Station,
staring at the morning *Tribune*, and waiting for the four o'clock train.

(55) Virgil, *Aeneid* 12.725–7:

Iuppiter ipse duas aequato examine lances
sustinet et fata imponit diversa duorum,
quem damnet labor et quo vergat pondere letum.

Jupiter himself upholds two scales in evenly balance and places in them
the different fates of the two heroes [Aeneas and Turnus], to see whom
the strife dooms and through whose weight death sinks down.

In (54) the ellipses in the story, graphically marked by the dots, suggest the amnesia of the internal narrator, who is recording a party at which everyone got very drunk and at the end of which he came with one of the other guests, Mr McKee, a photographer, to his bedroom where he was shown some of his pictures. In (55) an element that is commonly found in 'weighing fates' scenes is lacking: the result of the weighing and the name of the man doomed to die. Some have explained the absence as due to the *Aeneid* being not finished. An attractive alternative is to see it as a deliberate ellipsis of the narrator, either to increase suspense (is Turnus really going to be killed?) or to make Aeneas' killing of Turnus do without Jupiter's sanctioning.

A special kind of ellipsis, which is highly relevant when discussing classical literature, is that occasioned by the fact that to a great degree this literature is traditional, that is, it deals with the same stock of mythical narratives over and over again. Counting on the narratees' prior knowledge, a narrator can thus tell a story in as elliptical a way he wants, presenting only parts of it or even merely alluding to them (56).

(56) Pindar, *Pythian* 11.17–22:

> τὸν δὴ φονευομένου πατρὸς Ἀρσινόα Κλυταιμήστρας
> χειρῶν ὕπο κρατερᾶν
>   ἐκ δόλου τροφὸς ἄνελε δυσπενθέος,
> ὁπότε Δαρδανίδα κόραν Πριάμου
>   Κασσάνδραν πολιῷ χαλκῷ σὺν Ἀγαμεμνονίᾳ
> ψυχᾷ πόρευ' Ἀχέροντος ἀκτὰν παρ' εὔσκιον
> νηλὴς γυνά.

[Orestes] whom, at the slaughter of his father, his nurse Arsinoa out from under the strong hands of Clytemnestra and away from her grievous treachery rescued, when with grey bronze she dispatched Cassandra, daughter of the Dardanian Priam, along with Agamemnon's soul to the shadowy shore of Acheron, pitiless woman.

The Pindaric narrator here relies heavily on his narratees' knowledge of the Oresteia myth, which they need in order to understand of what Clytemnestra's 'grievous treachery' consists, what Priam's daughter Cassandra is doing with Agamemnon, and why Clytemnestra kills Agamemnon.

4.6. FREQUENCY

A final temporal relationship between fabula and story is *frequency*: the number of times an event from the fabula is recounted in the story. The default form of frequency is *singulative* narration: each event is recounted once. But an event may be present more than once (*repetition*). An extreme example is Faulkner's novel *Absalom, Absalom!*, in which the story of its protagonist, Thomas Sutpen, is told four times by four different narrators. But small-scale repetitions (by the narrator, by characters, or by both) occur in virtually all narratives, and we have already come across many examples. Some more follow (57–8).

(57) John Galsworthy, *The Man of Property*, part 1, chapter 1:

> [James Forsyte:] 'Jolyon, he will have his own way. He's got no children'— and stopped, recollecting the continued existence of old Jolyon's son, young Jolyon, June's father, who had made such a mess of it, and done for himself by deserting his wife and children and running away with that foreign governess. [. . .] She [Aunt Ann] thought of June's father, young Jolyon, who had run away with a foreign girl! Ah, what a sad blow to his father and to them all. Such a promising young fellow! A sad blow, though there had been no public scandal, most fortunately, Jo's wife seeking for no divorce! [. . .] The two [old and young Jolyon] had not met for fourteen years. And not for the first time during those fourteen years old Jolyon wondered whether he had been a little to blame in the matter of his son.

(58) Virgil, *Aeneid* 4.281–2 and 360–1:

> ardet abire fuga dulcisque relinquere terras,
> attonitus tanto monitu imperioque deorum. [. . .]
> 'desine meque tuis incendere teque querelis;
> Italiam non sponte sequor.'
>
> He [Aeneas] is on fire to flee and leave the sweet country, awed by the forceful warning and divine command. [. . .] 'Stop putting me [Aeneas] and yourself [Dido] on fire with your complaints; not of free will do I search Italy.'

In (57) the repeated references to the *brouille* between father and son (old and young Jolyon) by different characters gradually fill in the narratees about its details. In (58) we first have the Virgilian narrator recounting Aeneas' reaction to Mercury's command to leave Carthage and Dido: although *dulcis*, 'sweet', reveals some regret in having to go and end his affair, he is eager to continue his mission. When Aeneas returns to the issue, facing Dido, he puts much more emphasis on his unwillingness to go, but that misfires dramatically: Dido does not forgive him, neither now nor when he repeats the argument in the Underworld (6.460).

The reverse of repetition is *iterative* narration, whereby several identical events are presented only once. Not surprisingly, this form is often used to convey characteristic habits or to accelerate speed (59–60).

(59) John Galsworthy, *The Man of Property*, part 1, chapter 1:

> They had all done so well for themselves, these Forsytes, that they were all what is called 'of a certain position'. They had shares in all sorts of things. They collected pictures, too, and were supporters of such charitable institutions as might be beneficial to their sick domestics [. . .] Like all Forsytes of a certain age they kept carriages of their own, and never took cabs if by any means they could avoid it.

(60) Homer, *Iliad* 1.488–92:

> αὐτὰρ ὁ μήνιε νηυσὶ παρήμενος ὠκυπόροισι
> διογενὴς Πηλῆος υἱός, πόδας ὠκὺς Ἀχιλλεύς·
> οὔτε ποτ' εἰς ἀγορὴν πωλέσκετο κυδιάνειραν
> οὔτε ποτ' ἐς πόλεμον, ἀλλὰ φθινύθεσκε φίλον κῆρ
> αὖθι μένων, ποθέεσκε δ' ἀϋτήν τε πτόλεμόν τε.

But he was sulking, sitting idle by his speedy ships, the royal son of Peleus, swift-footed Achilles. He never went to the assembly where men may win glory nor into the fighting, but he was wasting his heart out, staying where he was, and yearned for the clamour of battle.

In (59) the narrator is engaged in introducing the family that will form the centre of his story and in so doing employs the iterative mode: all members of the family share certain habits that are described collectively and only once. In (60) the iterative mode, marked by the use of the iterative infix in πωλέσκετο, φθινύθεσκε, and ποθέεσκε, conjures up the picture of Achilles doing (or not doing) the same things during the days of his wrath.

A variant of iterative narration is *omnitemporal* (gnomic, proverbial) narration, the situation when a narrator refers to things of all times, such as natural phenomena, human nature, and the habits of the immortal gods (61–2).

(61) George Eliot, *The Mill on the Floss*, book 1, chapter 5:

> 'O he is cruel!' Maggie sobbed aloud, finding a wretched pleasure in the hollow resonance that came through the long empty space of the attic. She never thought of beating or grinding her Fetish; she was too miserable to

be angry. These bitter sorrows of childhood!—when sorrow is all new and strange, when hope has not yet got wings to fly beyond the days and weeks, and the space from summer to summer seems measureless.

(62) Valerius Flaccus, *Argonautica* 6.613–16:

> tunc vero, stabulis qualis leo saevit opimis
> luxurians spargitque famem mutatque cruores,
> sic neque parte ferox nec caede moratur in una
> turbidus [. . .]

Then, indeed, like a lion that rages in the fertile stables and abundantly stills his appetite and passes from the one killing to the other, so fierce Jason, in his rage, does not tarry in one place or one killing [. . .]

In (61) the narrator reacts to the sorrow of her young protagonist with a comment on the 'bitter sorrows' of childhood in general. Passage (62) provides an example of one of the most frequent uses of omnitemporal narration in classical literature: a simile.

The manipulating of time in a narrative is one of the oldest tricks of the trade, and ancient narratives already display a varied and rich use of it. Ancient literary theory also paid much attention to it. The main contribution of narratology consists in systematizing and completing the many aspects of time as a formal characteristic of texts. Narratological 'time' does not help us to understand 'time' as a mental construct in antiquity. That is an entirely different topic. However, narratological time is a highly efficient means for identifying which accents a narrator wants to place, which events to foreground or downplay, and which relationships between events to make clear. It is thus helpful for confirming or questioning existing interpretations and for suggesting new ones.

FURTHER READING

Narratology

Bal, M., *Narratology: Introduction to the Theory of Narrative* (Toronto 1997; first published 1985).
Culler, J., 'Fabula and Sjuzhet in the Analysis of Narrative', *Poetics Today* 1, 1980, 27–37.
Dannenberg, H.P., *Coincidence and Counterfactuality: Plotting Time and Space in Narrative Fiction* (Lincoln, NE 2008).

Fleischman, S., *Tense and Narrativity: From Medieval Performance to Modern Fiction* (Austin 1990).

Fludernik, M., *An Introduction to Narratology* (London and New York 2009; first published in German 2006).

Forster, E.M., *Aspects of the Novel* (Harmondsworth 1979; first published 1927).

Genette, G., *Narrative Discourse: An Essay in Method* (Ithaca, NY 1980; first published in French 1972).

Genette, G., *Narrative Discourse Revisited* (Ithaca, NY 1988; first published in French 1983).

Hamon, P., 'Clausules', *Poétique* 6, 1975, 495–526.

Herman, D., *Basic Elements of Narrative* (Malden, Oxford, and Chichester 2009).

Lungo, A. del, *L'incipit romanesque* (Paris 2003; first published in Italian 1997).

Mendilow, A.A., *Time and the Novel* (London and New York 1952).

Miller, N. (ed.), *Romananfänge: Versuch zu einer Poetik des Romans* (Berlin 1965).

Morhange, J.L., 'Incipit narratifs: l'entrée du lecteur dans l'univers de la fiction', *Poétique* 104, 1995, 387–410.

Mortimer, A.K., *La clôture narrative* (Paris 1985).

Müller, G., *Die Bedeutung der Zeit in der Erzählkunst* (Bonn 1947).

Nuttall, A.D., *Openings: Narrative Beginnings from the Epic to the Novel* (Oxford 1992).

Prince, G., 'The Disnarrated', in *Narrative as Theme: Studies in French Fiction* (Lincoln, NE 1992), 28–38.

Richardson, B. (ed.), *Narrative Beginning: Theories and Practices* (Lincoln, NE 2008).

Ricoeur, P., *Time and Narrative*, vols I–II (Chicago and London 1984, 1985; first published in French 1983).

Schmid, W., *Narratologia: Elemente der Narratologie* (Berlin 2008; first published 2005).

Weinrich, H., *Tempus: Besprochene und erzählte Welt* (Stuttgart 1971; first published 1964).

Zeelander, S., *Closure in Biblical Narrative* (Leiden 2012).

Narratology and classics

Dunn, F.M., *Tragedy's End: Closure and Innovation in Euripidean Drama* (New York and Oxford 1996).

Dunn, F.M., and T. Cole (eds), *Beginnings in Classical Literature*, special issue of *Yale Classical Studies* 29 (Cambridge 1992).

Time   103

Fowler, D.P., 'First Thoughts on Closure: Problems and Prospects', in *Roman Constructions: Readings in Postmodern Latin* (Oxford 2000), 239–83 (first published 1989).

Fowler, D.P., 'Second Thoughts on Closure', in *Roman Constructions: Readings in Postmodern Latin* (Oxford 2000), 284–307 (first published 1997).

Fusillo, M., *Il tempo delle Argonautiche: un analisi del racconto in Apollonio Rodio* (Rome 1985).

Grethlein, J., *The Greeks and Their Past: Poetry, Oratory and History in the Fifth Century BCE* (Cambridge and New York 2010).

Griffith, D.R., 'In the Dark Backward: Time in Pindaric Narrative', *Poetics Today* 14, 1993, 607–23.

Hurst, A., 'Temps du récit chez Pindare (*Pyth.* 4) et Bacchylide (11)', *Museum Helveticum* 40, 1983, 154–68.

Jong, I.J.F. de, and R. Nünlist (eds), *Time in Ancient Greek Literature*, Studies in Ancient Greek Narrative 2 (Leiden 2007).

Kranz, W., '*Sphragis*: Ichform und Namensiegel als Eingangs-und Schluss-motive antiker Dichting', *Rheinisches Museum* 104, 1961, 3–46, 97–104.

Morrison, J.V., *Homeric Misdirection: False Predictions in the Iliad* (Ann Arbor 1992).

Pinheiro, M.P.F., 'Time and Narrative Technique in Heliodorus' *Aethiopica*', in W. Haase (ed.), *Aufstieg und Niedergang der römischen Welt*, vol. II (Berlin 1980), 3148–73.

Rengakos, A., 'Die *Argonautika* und das "kyklische Gedicht": Bemerkungen zur Erzähltechnik des griechischen Epos', in A. Bierl, A. Schmitt, and A. Willi (eds), *Antike Literatur in neuer Deutung (FS. J. Latacz)* (Munich 2004), 277–304.

Roberts, D.W., 'Afterword: Ending and Aftermath, Ancient and Modern', in D. Roberts, F. Dunn, and D. Fowler (eds), *Classical Closure: Reading the End in Greek and Latin Literature* (Princeton 1997), 251–73.

Roberts, D.W., F. Dunn, and D. Fowler (eds), *Classical Closure: Reading the End in Greek and Latin Literature* (Princeton 1997).

Rood, T., *Thucydides: Narrative and Explanation* (Oxford 1998).

Sistakou, E., '"Snapshots" of Myth: The Notion of Time in Hellenistic Epyllion', in J. Grethlein and A. Rengakos (eds), *Narratology and Interpretation: The Content of Narrative Form in Ancient Literature* (Berlin 2009), 293–319.

5

Space

The previous three chapters discussed heavily theorized aspects of narrative texts: the narrator, focalization, and time. The present chapter will deal with an aspect that has received far less theoretical attention until recently: space. Space is here understood in the broad sense of the setting of the action of a story, other localities that are referred to (e.g. as part of dreams or reports), and the objects that fill that space as 'props'. For a long time it was thought that space had no function other than supplying a background setting, a narratological category which was taken for granted by theorists rather than required attention. This theoretical neglect is belied by the practice of novelists, who for example often choose places for their titles: *Aethiopica, Wuthering Heights, Northanger Abbey, The Mill on the Floss, A Room with a View, Manhattan Transfer, Berlin-Alexanderplatz*, and so on. Indeed, as this chapter will show, space plays a vital role in the construction and interpretation of stories.

5.1. THE PLACE OF SPACE

There can be huge differences in the attention paid to space. Some narratives are full of detailed descriptions or semantically loaded settings, for example Charles Dickens's *Great Expectations*, and others, like Robert Musil's *Der Mann ohne Eigenschaften*, focus on plot or characters but leave their environments largely unspecified. Whether space is described in abundance or sparingly, narratologists agree it can never be presented in a narrative text in its totality: the narratees are offered a mere selection of details. The narrative evocation of space, therefore, always requires active cooperation on the part of the narratees. They are asked to summon the implications of 'Paris' or 'a dark wood' from their own memory, or to imagine a wonder-world like that in J.R.R. Tolkien's *Lord of the Rings*.

A narrative text may address not only the space of the events but also *the space of the narrator* (at the moment of narration), as in (1) and (2).

(1) F. Scott Fitzgerald, *The Great Gatsby*, chapter 9:

> Even when the East excited me most, even when I was most keenly aware of its superiority to the bored, sprawling, swollen towns beyond the Ohio, with their interminable inquisitions which spared only the children and the very old—even then it had always for me a quality of distortion. West Egg, especially, still figures in my more fantastic dreams. I see it as a night scene by El Greco: a hundred houses, at once conventional and grotesque, crouching under a sullen, overhanging sky and a lustreless moon [. . .]

(2) Thucydides, *Peleponnesian War* 5.26.5:

> καὶ ξυνέβη μοι φεύγειν τὴν ἐμαυτοῦ ἔτη εἴκοσι μετὰ τὴν ἐς Ἀμφίπολιν στρατηγίαν, καὶ γενομένῳ παρ' ἀμφοτέροις τοῖς πράγμασι, καὶ οὐχ ἧσσον τοῖς Πελοποννησίων διὰ τὴν φυγήν, καθ' ἡσυχίαν τι αὐτῶν μᾶλλον αἰσθέσθαι.

> It befell me also to be banished from my own city twenty years after my command of Amphipolis, and being conversant with affairs on both sides, especially with those of the Peloponnesians because of my banishment, to get to know more about them at leisure.

The narrator of (1) comes from and tells his story in the American Midwest ('the bored, sprawling, swollen towns beyond the Ohio'), a location that differs from that where he found himself when the events took place (West Egg and New York on the East Coast). In (2) Thucydides-narrator explains how being banished from Athens gave him the opportunity to get much information about the Peloponnesians.

There may also be continuity between the space of the events and that of the narrator (3–4).

(3) Sir Walter Scott, *Ivanhoe*, chapter 1:

> In that pleasant district of merry England which is watered by the river Don, there extended in ancient times a large forest, covering the greater part of the beautiful hills and valleys which lie between Sheffield and the

pleasant town of Doncaster. The remains of this extensive wood are still to be seen at the noble seat of Wentworth, of Wharncliffe Park, and around Rotherdam.

(4) Ovid, *Metamorphoses* 9.225–9:

> [...] in rigidos versum silices prior edidit aetas.
> nunc quoque in Euboico scopulus brevis eminet alto
> gurgite et humanae servat vestigia formae,
> quem, quasi sensurum, nautae calcare verentur
> appellantque Lichan.

[...] old tradition transmits that he [Lichas, hurled by Heracles into the sea] changed into hard stone. Even to this day in the Euboean sea a low rock rises from the deep and retains traces of a human figure, which sailors, as if it were sentient, fear to tread on, and call Lichas.

In (3) and (4) the narrator notes that a locale is still visible in his own times.

When analysing space we may further distinguish between the *setting*, that is, the location where the action takes place, which of course may change in the course of the narrative, and *frames*, locations that occur in thoughts, dreams, memories, or reports. Examples of a setting include (5) and (6).

(5) E.M. Forster, *A Room with a View*, chapter 2:

> It was pleasant to wake up in Florence, to open the eyes upon a bright bare room, with a floor of red tiles which look clean though they are not [...] It was pleasant, too, to fling wide the windows, pinching the fingers in unfamiliar fastenings, to lean out into sunshine with beautiful hills and trees and marble churches opposite, and close below, the Arno, gurgling against the embankment of the road.

(6) Longus, *Daphnis and Chloe* 1.1–2:

> πόλις ἐστὶ τῆς Λέσβου Μιτυλήνη, μεγάλη καὶ καλή· διείληπται γὰρ
> εὐρίποις ὑπεισρεούσης τῆς θαλάσσης καὶ κεκόσμηται γεφύραις ξεστοῦ
> καὶ λευκοῦ λίθου. νομίσεις οὐ πόλιν ὁρᾶν ἀλλὰ νῆσον. ταύτης τῆς πόλεως
> τῆς Μιτυλήνης ὅσον ἀπὸ σταδίων διακοσίων ἀγρὸς ἦν ἀνδρὸς
> εὐδαίμονος, κτῆμα κάλλιστον· ὄρη θηροτρόφα, πεδία πυροφόρα, γήλοφοι
> κλημάτων, νομαὶ ποιμνίων, καὶ ἡ θάλασσα προσέκλυζεν ἠιόνος
> ἐκτεταμένης ψάμμῳ μαλθακῇ.

There is a city on Lesbos called Mitylene, of great size and beauty; it is transected by channels that make the sea flow into the city, and ornamented with bridges of polished marble. You will think you see an island rather than a city. About two hundred stades from that city of Mitylene was a country estate of a wealthy man, a most beautiful possession: mountains feeding wild animals, plains where corn grew, slopes planted with vineyards, pastures with flocks, and the sea lapped on the soft sand of a large beach.

In (5) the setting of (the first part of) the novel, Florence is painted, fittingly, as the view from a hotel window. In (6) an anonymous external narrator panoramically introduces the stage where the ensuing events, the burgeoning love of Daphnis and Chloe, will take place: in the country estate, with the city Mitylene occasionally playing a role. By referring to a real place, Mitylene on Lesbos (described in the present tense), the narrator anchors the setting of his narrative in real geography with which his narratees would be familiar.

For frames we may think of (7) and (8).

(7) Gustave Flaubert, *Sentimental Education* (*L'education sentimentale*), chapter 13:

> The idea of being married no longer appeared to him preposterous. They might travel; they might go to Italy, to the East. And he saw her standing on a hillock, or gazing at a landscape, or else leaning on his arm in a Florentine gallery while she stood to look at the pictures. What a pleasure it would be to him merely to watch this good little creature expanding under the splendours of Art and Nature! When she had got free from the commonplace atmosphere in which she had lived, she would, in a little while, become a charming companion.

(8) Horace, *Ode* 2.19.1–4:

> Bacchum in remotis carmina rupibus
> vidi docentem, credite posteri,
> Nymphasque discentis et auris
> capripedum Satyrorum acutas.

> I saw Bacchus on remote rocks teaching songs—posterity, believe it—
> and Nymphs and the keen ears of goat-footed Satyrs learning.

In (7) the protagonist, young Fredric Moreau, dreams of travelling abroad with his beloved, the daughter of a rich landowner. In (8) the narrator 'Horace' describes his vision of the god of poetry, Bacchus, teaching his mythical pupils, Nymphs and Satyrs, 'on remote rocks'. His vision is revealed as a poetic construction by *credite posteri*, 'posterity, believe it'. Frames may bring in distant, inaccessible, hypothetical, or counterfactual locations, all of which expand the space of a story in significant ways.

Narratives embedded in ancient drama, in particular, make use of frames. First, there is the *extra-scenic* space, that which lies immediately offstage inside the *skēnē*-building (9).

(9) Euripides, *Alcestis* 162–76:

καὶ στᾶσα πρόσθεν Ἑστίας κατηύξατο· [...]
πάντας δὲ βωμούς, οἳ κατ᾽ Ἀδμήτου δόμους,
προσῆλθε κἀξέστεψε καὶ προσηύξατο,
πτόρθων ἀποσχίζουσα μυρσίνης φόβην [...]
κἄπειτα θάλαμον ἐσπεσοῦσα καὶ λέχος
ἐνταῦθα δὴ ᾽δάκρυσε καὶ λέγει τάδε·
'ὦ λέκτρον, ἔνθα παρθένει᾽ ἔλυσ᾽ ἐγὼ
κορεύματ᾽ ἐκ τοῦδ᾽ ἀνδρός, οὗ θνῄσκω πάρος,
χαῖρ᾽·'

And standing in front of Hestia's altar she [Alcestis] prayed. [...] She went to all the altars in Admetus' house and garlanded them and prayed, breaking off a spray of myrtle for each [...] Then she burst into the bedroom and on the bed; and there at last she wept and says: 'O marriage bed, where I yielded up my virginity to this man, for whom I die, farewell!'

A servant of Alcestis recounts the actions of her mistress, who has promised to die in the place of her husband Admetus, inside the house. The ancient tragedians could also introduce extra-scenic space by showing it literally on the *ekkyklēma* or 'roll-out machine', a wheeled platform rolled out through the door of the *skēnē*. This was used, for instance, in the case of the mad hero in Euripides' *Heracles*, who appears bound to a pillar of the home he has destroyed.

Second, there is *distanced* space, which lies much further offstage than the extra-scenic space (10).

(10) Seneca, *Heracles* 533–6:

intravit Scythiae multivagas domos
et gentes patriis sedibus hospitas,
calcavitque freti terga rigentia
et mutis tacitum litoribus mare.

He entered Scythia's nomad houses and tribes that are strangers to their fathers' dwellings, and he trod the frozen back of the sea, taciturn waters with silent shores.

The setting of the *Heracles* is Thebes, and its chorus here recounts Heracles' many labours that brought him to far-flung regions.

A last introductory question to be asked when analysing space is its distribution: are we dealing with longer, *synoptic* introductions or with *stray indications* sprinkled over the text, usually when the action requires them? An example of the latter is found in Virginia Woolf's *To the Lighthouse*, in which the idea of visiting the lighthouse is both suggested and postponed in the first sentence of the story ('"There'll be no landing at the Lighthouse tomorrow", said Charles Tansley'), the building is later seen from afar ('"Oh, how beautiful!" For the great plateful of blue water was before her; the hoary Lighthouse, distant, austere, in the midst'), and it is described in detail only at the end, when the visit finally takes place (11).

(11) Virginia Woolf, *To the Lighthouse*, part 3, chapter 8:

> James looked at the Lighthouse. He [...] could see that it was barred with black and white; he could see the windows in it; he could even see washing spread on the rocks to dry.

The same technique may be observed in Homer. References to Achilles' barrack are scattered throughout the *Iliad* (9.185; 16.221; 18–19; *passim*), but it is described in detail only when it becomes the focus of the story (that is, when Priam enters it on his dangerous mission to free the body of his son Hector from Achilles):

(12) Homer, *Iliad* 24.448–56:

> ἀλλ' ὅτε δὴ κλισίην Πηληϊάδεω ἀφίκοντο
> ὑψηλήν, τὴν Μυρμιδόνες ποίησαν ἄνακτι
> δοῦρ' ἐλάτης κέρσαντες· ἀτὰρ καθύπερθεν ἔρεψαν
> λαχνήεντ' ὄροφον λειμωνόθεν ἀμήσαντες·
> ἀμφὶ δέ οἱ μεγάλην αὐλὴν ποίησαν ἄνακτι
> σταυροῖσιν πυκινοῖσι· θύρην δ' ἔχε μοῦνος ἐπιβλὴς
> εἰλάτινος, τὸν τρεῖς μὲν ἐπιρρήσσεσκον Ἀχαιοί,
> τρεῖς δ' ἀναοίγεσκον μεγάλην κληῗδα θυράων,
> τῶν ἄλλων· Ἀχιλεὺς δ' ἄρ' ἐπιρρήσσεσκε καὶ οἶος·

> And when they came to the barrack of Peleus' son, a high building, which the Myrmidons had made for their king, having cut planks of pine. And above they had roofed it with shaggy thatch cut and taken from a meadow. And around it they had made a great yard for their king with close-set stakes. The gate was held by a single bar of pine-wood, which it needed three Greeks to push home, and three of the others could open the big door-bolt, but Achilles could push it open even by himself.

This long description, which brings about a retardation, marks the importance of the memorable moment when Priam and Achilles meet. It is also relevant to what follows: the detail that only Achilles could move the doorbolt by himself will soon figure in his dialogue with Priam, as the Greek hero guesses that a god must have helped the Trojan king enter the camp because 'no mortal man could easily push back the bar across our gates' (566–7).

For synoptic introductions of space we may turn to (13) and (14).

(13) E.M. Forster, *A Passage to India*, chapter 1:

> Except for the Marabar Caves—and they are twenty miles off—the city of Chandrapore presents nothing extraordinary. Edged rather than washed by the river Ganges, it trails for a couple of miles along the bank, scarcely distinguishable from the rubbish it deposits so freely [. . .] The streets are mean, the temples ineffective, and though a few fine houses exist they are hidden away in gardens or down alleys whose filth deters all but the invited guest.

(14) Ovid, *Metamorphoses* 1.168–76:

> est via sublimis, caelo manifesta sereno;
> lactea nomen habet, candore notabilis ipso.
> hac iter est superis ad magni tecta tonantis
> regalemque domum. dextra laevaque deorum
> atria nobilium valvis celebrantur apertis.
> plebs habitat diversa locis [. . .]
> hic locus est quem, si verbis audacia detur,
> haud timeam magni dixisse Palatia caeli.

> There is a road in the air, visible when the sky is clear. It has the name 'Milky [Way]', famed for its splendour. Here is the road for the gods to the halls and royal dwelling of the mighty Thunderer. On its right and left are the *atria* of the upper-class gods, frequently visited through open gates. The lesser gods dwell in a different area. [. . .] This is the place that, if boldness may be put into words, I would not hesitate to call the Palatine of high heaven.

In (13) the narrator introduces the main setting of his story, the fictional city of Chandrapore. In (14) the narrator introduces the habitat of the first secondary narrator of the *Metamorphoses*, Jupiter. By describing the heavenly palaces of the gods in unmistakably Roman terms and even explicitly comparing it to the real world ('I would not hesitate to call [it] the Palatine of high heaven'), he immediately alerts his narratees to important correspondences between their world and the world of the myths to be told.

The synoptic introduction of space and objects may take the form of a description, and this phenomenon merits a separate discussion.

5.2. DESCRIPTION

Description means that a narrator brings his story to a standstill and describes at length objects or scenery (or the outward appearance of persons, which is here left out). Consider, for example, (15–16).

(15) Ernest Hemingway, *Hills Like White Elephants*:

> The hills across the valley of the Ebro were long and white. On this side there was no shade and no trees and the station was between two lines of rails in the sun. Close against the side of the station there was the warm shadow of the building and a curtain, made of strings of bamboo beads, hung across the open door into the bar, to keep out the flies. The American and the girl with him sat at a table in the shade, outside the building.

(16) Homer, *Odyssey* 4.844–7:

> ἔστι δέ τις νῆσος μέσσῃ ἁλὶ πετρήεσσα,
> μεσσηγὺς Ἰθάκης τε Σάμοιό τε παιπαλοέσσης,
> Ἀστερίς, οὐ μεγάλη, λιμένες δ᾽ ἔνι ναύλοχοι αὐτῇ
> ἀμφίδυμοι· τῇ τόν γε μένον λοχόωντες Ἀχαιοί.

> There is a rocky island in mid-sea, halfway between Ithaca and rugged Samos, Asteris, not big, but there are two harbours in it with anchorage for ships. Here the Achaeans waited in hiding for him [Telemachus].

In (15) the narrator starts, as often, with a description of the setting. We may hesitate whether the description is focalized by the external narrator or by the characters, but features suggesting the latter include the use of past tenses and the definite article ('the hills', 'the station', 'the building'). In (16) the external narrator briefly interrupts the narrative to introduce the place where the suitors lay in ambush for Telemachus. The 'there is a place X' motif will become a staple of ancient storytelling (cf. example (14)).

A narrator can explicitly but paradoxically draw attention to the fact that he is giving a description by remarking that something *cannot* be described.

(17) William Shakespeare, *Antony and Cleopatra*, act 2, scene 2:

> I will tell you.
> The barge she [Cleopatra] sat in, like a burnished throne,
> burned on the water, the poop was beaten gold;
> purple the sails, and so perfumed that
> the winds were love-sick with them; the oars were silver [...]
> For her own person,
> it beggared all description: she did lie
> in her pavilion, cloth-of-gold of tissue,
> o'erpicturing that Venus where we see
> the fancy outwork nature. On each side [...]

(18) Josephus, *Jewish War* 5.176–7:

> κειμένοις δὲ πρὸς ἄρκτον αὐτοῖς ἔνδοθεν ἡ τοῦ βασιλέως αὐλὴ προσέζευκτο, παντὸς λόγου κρείσσων· οὔτε γὰρ πολυτελείας οὔτε κατασκευῆς τινος ἔλειπεν ὑπερβολήν, ἀλλὰ τετείχιστο μὲν ἅπασα τριάκοντα πήχεις τὸ ὕψος κύκλῳ, κατ᾽ ἴσον διάστημα κεκοσμημένοις δὲ πύργοις διείληπτο ἀνδρῶσί τε μεγίστοις καὶ εἰς ξενῶνας ἑκατοντακλίνους·

Adjoining and on the inner side of the towers was the king's palace, baffling all description; for in extravagance and equipment no building surpassed it, but it was completely enclosed within a wall thirty cubits high, broken at equal distances by ornamental towers, and contained immense banqueting halls and bedchambers for a hundred guests.

In both passages the narrator's comment that something 'beggared' or 'baffled' description actually does not stop him from describing it, and it serves to call attention to the description.

Narratees will in general have no trouble in recognizing a description when they read one. But in fact the boundaries between narration and description are permeable, since many descriptive passages also display some form of narrativity (19–20).

(19) Thomas Hardy, *Jude the Obscure*, part 1, chapter 1:

> It [the village of Marygreen, where the main character lives] was as old-fashioned as it was small, and it rested in the lap of an undulating upland adjoining the North Wessex downs. Old as it was, however, the well-shaft

was probably the only relic of the local history that remained absolutely unchanged. Many of the thatched and dormered dwelling-houses had been pulled down of late years, and many trees felled on the green.

(20) Virgil, *Aeneid* 7.789–92:

> at levem clipeum sublatis cornibus Io
> auro insignibat, iam saetis obsita, iam bos,
> (argumentum ingens), et custos virginis Argus,
> caelataque amnem fundens pater Inachus urna.

But the figure of Io with uplifted horns was emblazoned in gold on his polished shield, already covered with hair, already a cow (a huge emblem), and the maiden's warden Argus, and her father Inachus pouring his stream from an embossed urn.

In (19) the description of the village at first is static, focusing on its geographical location and outward appearance, but gradually it starts to acquire a narrative dimension by acknowledging its 'local history'. Passage (20) describes a static depiction on the shield of Turnus, but the repeated *iam*, 'already', evokes the story lying behind the picture, the girl Io turning into a cow.

And although a description often creates a pause in the story, this certainly is not always the case: it may transpire at the end of a description that time has ticked on, as in the description of the bay of Phorcys in the *Odyssey* (example (53) in Chapter 4), or the description may be made part of the action, as when an object is described while it is being made or a location while it is being traversed. This phenomenon of the narrativization of descriptions should be connected to the fact that, from early times onwards, narrators have invented all kinds of devices to integrate descriptions into the narrative flow of their stories as much as possible. More will be said about this in the next section.

When discussing descriptive passages, it may be relevant to pay attention to their organization: they can be organized as a refrain (he made X, he made Y, etc.), an enumeration (first, second, third, etc.), according to spatial principles (left, right, in front, behind, etc.), or other ideologically, culturally, or conventionally determined principles (21–2).

(21) Gustave Flaubert, *Madame Bovary*, chapter 1:

> [. . .] the 'new fellow', was still holding his cap on his knees even after prayers were over. It was one of those head-gears of composite order, in

which we can find traces of the bearskin, shako, billycock hat, sealskin cap, and cotton night-cap; one of those poor things, in fine, whose dumb ugliness has depths of expression, like an imbecile's face. Oval, stiffened with whalebone, it began with three round knobs; then came in succession lozenges of velvet and rabbit-skin separated by a red band; after that a sort of bag that ended in a cardboard polygon covered with complicated braiding, from which hung, at the end of a long thin cord, small twisted gold threads in the manner of a tassel.

(22) Apollonius of Rhodes, *Argonautica* 1.721–47:

> αὐτὰρ ὅγ᾽ ἀμφ᾽ ὤμοισι, θεᾶς Ἰτωνίδος ἔργον,
> δίπλακα πορφυρέην περονήσατο […]
> ἐν μὲν ἔσαν Κύκλωπες ἐπ᾽ ἀφθίτῳ ἥμενοι ἔργῳ,
> Ζηνὶ κεραυνὸν ἄνακτι πονεύμενοι· […]
> ἐν δ᾽ ἔσαν Ἀντιόπης Ἀσωπίδος υἱέε δοιώ […]
> ἐν δὲ βοῶν ἔσκεν λάσιος νομός. […]

And around his shoulder he [Jason] pinned a double cloak of purple, the work of the Itonian goddess […] Upon it were the Cyclopes seated at their ceaseless task, fashioning a thunderbolt for Zeus their king […] Upon it were the two sons of Antiope, daughter of Asopus […] Upon it was a thickly grassed pasture with cattle. […]

The organizing principle of the description in (21) is that of enumeration ('it began with', 'then came', 'after that'), while in (22) we are dealing with a refrain (of 'upon it').

Finally, of course, there may be no order at all, which is in itself significant (23).

(23) E.M. Forster, *A Room with a View*, chapter 2:

Now she [Lucy] entered the church depressed and humiliated, not even able to remember whether it was built by the Franciscans or the Dominicans. Of course, it must be a wonderful building. But how like a barn! And how very cold! Of course, it contained frescoes by Giotto, in the presence of whose tactile values she was capable of feeling what was proper. But who was to tell her which they were? She walked about disdainfully, unwilling to be enthusiastic over monuments of uncertain authorship or date. There was no one even to tell her which, of all the sepulchral slabs that paved the nave and transepts, was the one that was really beautiful […]

The young heroine of the novel has lost her guide and Baedeker and thus has to visit the Basilica of Santa Croce in Florence on her own, wandering aimlessly through the church; her focalization presents the narratees with a very random and incomplete description of its interior.

5.3. THE PRESENTATION AND INTEGRATION OF SPACE

Space, whether incidental details or synoptic descriptions, can be introduced to the narratees in various ways. One very common method is through the *focalization of the narrator* (24–5).

(24) Charles Dickens, *Little Dorrit*, book 1, chapter 6:

> Thirty years ago there stood, a few doors short of the church of Saint George, in the borough of Southwark, on the left-hand side of the way going southward, the Marshalsea Prison. It had stood there many years before, and it remained there some years afterwards; but it is gone now, and the world is none the worse without it. It was an oblong pile of barrack building, partitioned into squalid houses standing back to back, so that there were no back rooms; environed by a narrow paved yard, hemmed in by high walls duly spiked at top.

(25) Virgil, *Aeneid* 1.637–42:

> at domus interior regali splendida luxu
> instruitur, mediisque parant convivia tectis:
> arte laboratae vestes ostroque superbo,
> ingens argentum mensis, caelataque in auro
> fortia facta patrum, series longissima rerum
> per tot ducta viros antiqua ab origine gentis.

> But inside the palace is laid out with the glitter of royal pomp, and servants prepare for a banquet inside the halls: there are tapestries artfully embroidered and of proud purple, on the tables is heavy silver, and embossed in gold are the brave deeds of her forefathers, a very long line of history traced via many heroes from the beginning of her race.

In (24) the narrator sets the stage for the story to follow, the prison where little Dorrit lives with her father; his focalization transpires from a remark like 'it is gone now, and the world is none the worse without it'. In (25) the Virgilian narrator describes the richness of

Dido's palace and the dignity of her lineage, which will make her, in the eyes of the Roman narratees, a worthy partner of Aeneas.

Narrators are, however, often loath to interrupt the flow of their narrative and hence have looked for ways to introduce space to their stories more smoothly or naturally. A slightly more integrated method of description is therefore with an *anonymous focalizer* (see also §3.6), as in (26) and (27).

(26) George Eliot, *Adam Bede*, book 1, chapter 2:

> The Donnithorne Arms stood at the entrance of the village, and a small farmyard and stackyard which flanked it, indicating that there was a pretty take of land attached to the inn, gave the traveller a promise of good feed for himself and his horse, which might well console him for the ignorance in which the weather-beaten sign left him as to the heraldic bearings of that ancient family, the Donnithornes.

(27) Pausanias, *Description of Greece* 1.1:

> καὶ λιμήν τε παραπλεύσαντι τὴν ἄκραν ἐστὶ καὶ ναὸς Ἀθηνᾶς Σουνιάδος ἐπὶ κορυφῇ τῆς ἄκρας. πλέοντι δὲ ἐς τὸ πρόσω Λαύριόν τέ ἐστιν, ἔνθα ποτὲ Ἀθηναίοις ἦν ἀργύρου μέταλλα, καὶ νῆσος ἔρημος οὐ μεγάλη Πατρόκλου καλουμένη·

> When one has rounded the promontory [of Sunium] there is a harbour and a temple of Athena on the peak of the promontory. Sailing further there is Laurium, where once the Athenians had silver mines, and a small, uninhabited island, called the island of Patroclus.

In (26) the narrator introduces an anonymous traveller who looks at the inn and its surroundings (rather than describing them herself), while in (27) we are dealing with the widespread device of the anonymous focalizer in the guise of a dative participle (παραπλεύσαντι, πλέοντι), which goes back to the format of the *periplus*, a description of the ports and coastal landmarks that the captain of a vessel could expect to find along a shore.

By far the most widespread method of integrating space is by making *one of the characters focalize* a setting or object (28–9).

(28) E.M. Forster, *Howards End*, chapter 26:

> Next morning a fine mist covered the peninsula. The weather promised well, and the outline of the castle mound grew clearer each moment that Margaret watched it. Presently she saw the keep, and the sun painted the rubble gold, and charged the white sky with blue. The shadow of the

house gathered itself together and fell over the garden. A cat looked up at her window and mewed. Lastly the river appeared, still holding the mists between its banks and its overhanging alders, and only visible as far as a hill, which cut off its upper reaches.

(29) Apollonius of Rhodes, *Argonautica* 4.1245–9:

> οἱ δ᾽ ἀπὸ νηὸς ὄρουσαν, ἄχος δ᾽ ἕλεν εἰσορόωντας
> ἠέρα καὶ μεγάλης νῶτα χθονὸς ἠέρι ἶσα
> τηλοῦ ὑπερτείνοντα διηνεκές· οὐδέ τιν᾽ ἀρδμόν,
> οὐ πάτον, οὐκ ἀπάνευθε κατηυγάσσαντο βοτήρων
> αὖλιον, εὐκήλῳ δὲ κατείχετο πάντα γαλήνῃ.

They leapt from the ship, and grief seized them as they viewed the sky and the levels of vast land disappearing in the air and stretching far without break. They could see no source of fresh water, no path, no herdsmen's yard far off in the distance; everything was in the grip of perfect calm.

In (28) we look at the scenery around the house Oniton Grange through the eyes of Margaret ('watched it', 'she saw'), while in (29) the uninviting Syrtis, a shallow sandy gulf on the coast of Libya, is focalized by the Argonauts ('they viewed'), as is confirmed by the presentation through negation ('no source of fresh water') of what they had hoped to see. There are many variations on this pattern, for example a character looking through a window, entering a room, or travelling through a city or country.

A character may also *himself or herself describe* a place or object to another character (30–1).

(30) John Galsworthy, *The Man of Property*, part 1, chapter 8:

> I've tried to plan a house here with some self-respect of its own [. . .] This is for your pictures, divided from this court by curtains; draw them back and you'll have a space of fifty-one by twenty-three six. This double-faced stove in the centre, here, looks one way towards the court, one way towards the picture room; this end wall is all window; you've a south-east light from that, a north light from the court.

(31) Virgil, *Eclogue* 3.36–42:

> [. . .] pocula ponam
> fagina, caelatum divini opus Alcimedontis,
> lenta quibus torno facili superaddita vitis
> diffusos hedera vestit pallente corymbos.
> in medio duo signa, Conon et—quis fuit alter,

descripsit radio totum qui gentibus orbem,
tempora quae messor, quae curvus arator haberet?

[...] I will stake beechwood cups, the carved work of divine Alcimedon; on which a pliant vine, added by the skilful chisel, covers spreading clusters of light green ivy. In the centre are two figures, Conon and— who was the other, who described with his rod the whole circuit of the heavens for men, what seasons the reaper should keep in mind, what the bent ploughman?

In (30) the young architect Bosinney tries to enthuse his client, Soames Forsyte, by giving a lively description of the house he will build for him (note the gestures suggested by the deictic pronouns 'this' and 'here'). In (31) one of two herdsmen about to enter a singing contest describes his stakes to his opponent. The incompleteness of his description ('who was the other ... ?') characterizes him as a simple rustic but also incites the narratees to supply a name themselves (Hesiod or Aratus?) and thus ponder Virgil's literary models.

Finally, the most integrated or narrativized form of space-presentation is when *a character makes or handles an object* (32–3).

(32) Jules Verne, *Twenty Thousand Leagues under the Sea*, part 1, chapter 3:

At this order, which was relayed to the engine by means of a compressed-air device, the mechanics activated the start-up wheel. Steam rushed whistling into the gaping valves. Long horizontal pistons groaned and pushed the tie rods of the drive shaft. The blades of the propeller churned the waves with increasing speed, and the *Abraham Lincoln* moved out majestically amid a spectator-laden escort of some 100 ferries and tenders.

(33) Homer, *Iliad* 18.478–84:

ποίει δὲ πρώτιστα σάκος μέγα τε στιβαρόν τε
πάντοσε δαιδάλλων, περὶ δ' ἄντυγα βάλλε φαεινὴν
τρίπλακα μαρμαρέην, ἐκ δ' ἀργύρεον τελαμῶνα.
πέντε δ' ἄρ' αὐτοῦ ἔσαν σάκεος πτύχες· αὐτὰρ ἐν αὐτῷ
ποίει δαίδαλα πολλὰ ἰδυίῃσι πραπίδεσσιν.
ἐν μὲν γαῖαν ἔτευξ', ἐν δ' οὐρανόν, ἐν δὲ θάλασσαν,
ἠέλιόν τ' ἀκάμαντα σελήνην τε πλήθουσαν [...]

First he began to make a huge and massive shield, decorating it all over, and he put a triple rim around it, bright and gleaming, and hung a silver baldric from it. The shield was made of five layers. And on its surface he made many decorations with his cunning mind. On it he made the

earth, and sky, and sea, and the weariless sun and the moon waxing
full […]

What better way to describe a steamship than with it starting its
impressive engines (32), and what better way to describe Achilles'
new shield than by having it made before the narratees' eyes by the
divine artisan Hephaestus (33)? Example (33), like most of the
examples in Section 5.2, is an *ekphrasis*, and the presentation of this
type of description, ubiquitous in ancient literature and still found
regularly in modern literature, merits a fuller discussion.

5.4. THE PRESENTATION OF AN *EKPHRASIS* OF VISUAL ART

The term *ekphrasis* was used in antiquity to refer to a broad category
of descriptions: of settings, objects, works of art, and also of persons
and even of set pieces such as storms or battles. In modern times the
term became restricted to the description of works of art, and it is on
these that this section focuses. The presentation of such *ekphraseis* is
complex; no less than six parameters play a role. The first parameter,
of course, is the *narrator-focalizer*, who looking at the work of art and
putting his view into words, makes the narratees 'see' it in their
imagination. The *narratees*, who occasionally are explicitly invoked
in the form of 'you might have seen', are the second parameter. The
third parameter is *the artist* of the work of art, to whom the narrator
usually refers one way or another. The fourth parameter is the figure
of *the observer*: a narrator often makes one of the characters look at
the work of art, primarily to strengthen the integration of the description in the narrative. But the observer figure offers all kinds of extra
possibilities: he or she may react emotionally to the work of art and
interpret it, correctly or incorrectly. The fifth parameter is *the work
itself*, its material, colour, size, and so on. The last parameter is the
content of the work of art, *the images depicted on it*.

Let us start with taking a closer look at a modern example (34).

(34) W.H. Auden, *The Shield of Achilles*:

> She looked over his shoulder
> For vines and olive trees,

Marble well-governed cities
And ships upon untamed seas,
But there on the shining metal
His hands had put instead
An artificial wilderness
And a sky like lead.
[...]
The thin-lipped armouror,
Hephaestos, hobbled away,
Thetis of the shining breasts
Cried out in dismay
At what the god had wrought
To please her son, the strong
Iron-hearted man-slaying Achilles
Who would not live long.

In this poem we have the artist Hephaestus, who has just finished making a new shield for Achilles; an observer, Thetis, who looks at what he has made and does not see what she expected to see (the kind of images we find on the Homeric shield: vines, olive trees, cities); the work itself ('shining metal'); the images depicted ('an artificial wilderness and a sky like lead'); and a narrator-focalizer who sees it all (Thetis looking at the shield, Hephaestus hobbling away, and the shield itself). The narratees are not explicitly mentioned but are supposed to bring their knowledge of Homer's shield of Achilles (and therefore recognize what Thetis' expectations are based on) and of contemporary history (to recognize what Hephaestus does depict, most probably concentration camps or some other atrocity from a fascist regime). This beautiful poem nicely captures the intriguing ambiguities involved in all *ekphraseis*. Who is responsible for which detail of the description: the artist, the viewing character, or the narrator? Has Hephaestus made 'an artificial wilderness', is this Thetis' interpretation, or is it the focalization of the narrator?

For an ancient example, we may turn to the Shield of Aeneas (35).

(35) Virgil, *Aeneid* 8.617–56:

> ille, deae donis et tanto laetus honore
> expleri nequit atque oculos per singula volvit. [...]
> fecerat et viridi fetam Mavortis in antro
> procubuisse lupam [...]
> haud procul inde citae Mettum in diversa quadrigae
> distulerant (at tu dictis, Albane, maneres!) [...]

> illum indignanti similem similemque minanti
> aspiceres [...]
> atque hic auratis volitans argenteus anser
> porticibus Gallos in limine adesse canebat.

He [Aeneas], rejoicing in the gift of the goddess and such great honour, cannot be sated and turns his eyes from scene to scene. [...] He [Vulcan] had fashioned, too, the mother-wolf outstretched in the green cave of Mars [...] Not far thence speedy four-horse carts had torn Mettus apart (but you, Alban, should have stood by your words!) [...] Him [Porsenna] you might have seen resembling an angry one, resembling a threatening one [...] And here the silver goose, fluttering though gilded colonnades, cried that the Gauls were on the threshold.

In this *ekphrasis* we have Aeneas as observer figure, Vulcan as the artist, the Virgilian narrator-focalizer (whose presence is felt e.g. in the apostrophe *at tu dictis, Albane, maneres*), the narratees (who are involved in the description in *aspiceres*), the images depicted (e.g. the famous she-wolf, Porsenna attacking Rome and the sacred geese on the capitol warning the Romans for the Gauls), and the work of art itself (in *argenteus anser* and *auratis ... porticibus*). Once more the division of labour between the agents involved in the presentation of the *ekphrasis* is worth paying attention to: Aeneas is the observer but is revealed, after the *ekphrasis*, not to understand exactly what he sees; Vulcan, who is endowed with prophetic powers, made the images depicting the future of Rome; but it is arguably the narrator, 'Virgil', whose focalization mainly determines the interpretation of the narratees.

5.5. FUNCTIONS OF SPACE

Compared to plot, the most important characteristic of a narrative according to Aristotle and many narratologists after him, and characters, the main interest of a novel according to many modern writers, space has long seemed just a necessary ingredient and a mere ancillary to the story: the action and characters have to be situated somewhere, and the primary function of space is to set the scene. When taking the form of a long description, space would even seem to have merely an *ornamental* function, an idea which goes back to ancient rhetoric, which listed *descriptio* under the *ornatus* of a speech and considered it to be at home especially in digressions. A variant is the idea that detailed descriptions may serve to increase the reality effect of a story.

Few critics nowadays would like to leave it at that and ascribe space and description only a scene-setting, ornamental, or authenticating function. First, space may acquire a *thematic* function, when it is itself one of the main ingredients in a narrative. Modern examples that spring to mind are John Dos Passos's *Manhattan Transfer*, Alexander Döblin's *Berlin-Alexanderplatz*, and Jack Kerouac's *On the Road*. For classical literature we may think of Homer's *Odyssey*, as the interest in the exotic places visited by Odysseus reflects the expanding world of the Greeks in the eight and seventh centuries BC; Apollonius of Rhodes' *Argonautica*, in which the Greeks of Alexandria and else-where see their appropriation of large parts of the Mediterranean justified by heroic action of the past and the Argonauts visiting places and leaving their traces in the landscape; and Virgil's *Aeneid*, which offers a teleologically coloured view of early Italy, destined to become the Roman world.

A second function is involved when a place or object, fully described in the form of a synoptic description or *ekphrasis*, somehow mirrors the surrounding narrative. Such *mirror-descriptions*, as they might be called, are a subtype of the larger category of the *mise en abyme* (for which see §2.6). A poignant example is found in (36).

(36) William Shakespeare, *The Rape of Lucrece* 1366–70, 1453–9:

> At last she [Lucrece] called to mind where hangs a piece
> Of skilful painting, made for Priam's Troy:
> Before the which is drawn the power of Greece.
> For Helen's rape the city to destroy,
> Threat'ning cloud-kissing Ilion with annoy.
> [*There follows a description of this painting in no fewer than
> 200 lines, whereby the focalizing Lucrece explicitly looks for
> points of contact between the painting and her own situation*]
> To this well-painted piece is Lucrece come,
> To find a face where all distress is stell'd.
> Many she sees where cares have carved some,
> But none where all distress and dolour dwell'd,
> Till she despairing Hecuba beheld,
> Staring on Priam's wounds with her old eyes [. . .]

Lucrece has just been raped and is waiting anxiously for her husband to return as she scans a large painting of the Fall of Troy. It is also a story of a rape but above all a story full of female suffering. Mirror-descriptions often anticipate the plot (37).

(37) Homer, *Odyssey* 19.226–31:

> 'αὐτὰρ οἱ περόνη χρυσοῖο τέτυκτο
> αὐλοῖσιν διδύμοισι· πάροιθε δὲ δαίδαλον ἦεν·
> ἐν προτέροισι πόδεσσι κύων ἔχε ποικίλον ἐλλόν,
> ἀσπαίροντα λάων· τὸ δὲ θαυμάζεσκον ἅπαντες,
> ὡς οἱ χρύσεοι ἐόντες ὁ μὲν λάε νεβρὸν ἀπάγχων,
> αὐτὰρ ὁ ἐκφυγέειν μεμαὼς ἤσπαιρε πόδεσσι.'

'And on it [Odysseus' cloak] was a brooch of gold with double sheaths. On the face it was richly decorated: a dog held a dappled fawn in the grip of its front paws, keeping tight hold of it as it gasped. Everybody marvelled at it, how, though made of gold, the one holding the fawn in its grip throttled it, while the other, eager to escape, was jerking its feet, convulsed.'

'The Cretan'/Odysseus describes to Penelope a brooch he had seen Odysseus wearing in the past. Its image, a dog throttling a fawn, can be interpreted by the primary narratees as an anticipation of Odysseus (cast in the role of hunter or predator throughout the *Odyssey*) killing the suitors (typically portrayed as animals of prey).

A third function of space is the *symbolic* one. This means that places, often arranged in oppositions like 'inside' versus 'outside' and 'city' versus 'country', become semantically charged (38–9).

(38) William Thackeray, *Vanity Fair*, chapter 61:

> That second-floor arch in a London house, looking up and down the wall of the staircase, and commanding the main thoroughfare by which the inhabitants are passing [...]—that stair, up or down which babies are carried, old people are helped, guests are marshalled to the hall, the parson walks to the christening, the doctor to the sick-room, and the undertaker's men to the upper floor—what a memento of Life, Death, and Vanity it is—that arch and stair—if you choose to consider it, and sit on the landing, looking up and down the wall!

(39) Ovid, *Metamorphoses* 3.407–10:

> fons erat inlimis, nitidis argenteus undis,
> quem neque pastores neque pastae monte capellae
> contigerant aliudve pecus, quem nulla volucris
> nec fera turbaret nec lapsus ab arbore ramus;

There was a clear pool, silvery through its glittering water, which no shepherd or she-goat grazing in the mountains or any other cattle had ever come to, whose surface no bird or beast or falling bough from a tree ever ruffled [...]

In (38) the narrator helps us to see the arch and stair in symbolic terms, labelling them a 'memento of Life, Death, and Vanity'. In (39) the clear water of the pool and its untouched nature more implicitly symbolize the extreme virginity of Narcissus and, aptly, will become his death.

Some forms of space have acquired symbolic associations through literary convention (40–1).

(40) Lewis Carroll, *Alice in Wonderland*, chapter 1:

Alice started to her feet, for it flashed across her mind that she had never before seen a rabbit with either a waistcoat-pocket, or a watch to take out of it, and burning with curiosity, she ran across the field after it, and fortunately was just in time to see it pop down a large rabbit-hole under the hedge. In another moment down went Alice after it, never once considering how in the world she was to get out again. The rabbit-hole went straight on like a tunnel for some way, and then dipped suddenly down, so suddenly that Alice had not a moment to think about stopping herself before she found herself falling down a very deep well.

(41) Plato, *Phaedrus* 230b–c:

'νὴ τὴν Ἥραν, καλή γε ἡ καταγωγή. ἥ τε γὰρ πλάτανος αὕτη μάλ' ἀμφιλαφής τε καὶ ὑψηλή, τοῦ τε ἄγνου τὸ ὕψος καὶ τὸ σύσκιον πάγκαλον, καὶ ὡς ἀκμὴν ἔχει τῆς ἄνθης, ὡς ἂν εὐωδέστατον παρέχοι τὸν τόπον· ἥ τε αὖ πηγὴ χαριεστάτη ὑπὸ τῆς πλατάνου ῥεῖ μάλα ψυχροῦ ὕδατος, ὥστε γε τῷ ποδὶ τεκμήρασθαι. Νυμφῶν τέ τινων καὶ Ἀχελῴου ἱερὸν ἀπὸ τῶν κορῶν τε καὶ ἀγαλμάτων ἔοικεν εἶναι. εἰ δ' αὖ βούλει, τὸ εὔπνουν τοῦ τόπου ὡς ἀγαπητὸν καὶ σφόδρα ἡδύ· θερινόν τε καὶ λιγυρὸν ὑπηχεῖ τῷ τῶν τεττίγων χορῷ. πάντων δὲ κομψότατον τὸ τῆς πόας, ὅτι ἐν ἠρέμα προσάντει ἱκανὴ πέφυκε κατακλινέντι τὴν κεφαλὴν παγκάλως ἔχειν.'

'By Hera, what a beautiful resting place! This plane tree is very tall and spreading, and the height and shadiness of the chasteberry tree is absolutely fine. It's at the height of its flowering and so makes the place very sweet-smelling. And then the spring of cool water flows most delightfully under the plane tree—or at least that's the evidence of my feet! It appears from the images of maidens and other statues that it is sacred to Achelous and some of the nymphs. And again, if you please, see how lovely and extremely sweet is the airiness of the place. It resounds with a chorus of cicadas, the shrill sound of summer. But the most exquisite thing of all is the quality of the grass. It is sufficiently abundant for someone reclining slightly up the bank to keep his head in a comfortable position.'

In (40) we are dealing with the typical motif of a character overstepping a magical boundary (falling in a hole, stepping through a door, etc.) and entering a different world. In (41) Plato makes Socrates describe a typical *locus amoenus*: shade, cool water, a breeze, a pleasant smell, and grass. This setting has erotic associations and thus provides a fitting context for the first part of the dialogue, of which love will be a central theme.

Fourth, we may distinguish a *characterizing* function, when space reveals something about a person or his or her milieu, character, or situation (42–3).

(42) George Eliot, *Adam Bede*, book 1, chapter 6:

[. . .] the house-floor is perfectly clean again; as clean as everything else in that wonderful house-place, where the only chance of collecting a few grains of dust would be to climb on the salt-coffer, and put your finger on the high mantelshelf on which the glittering brass candlesticks are enjoying their summer sinecure [. . .]

(43) Plutarch, *Alcibiades* 16.1:

Ἐν δὲ τοῖς τοιούτοις πολιτεύμασι καὶ λόγοις καὶ φρονήματι καὶ δεινότητι πολλὴν αὖ πάλιν τὴν τρυφὴν τῆς διαίτης καὶ περὶ πότους καὶ ἔρωτας ὑβρίσματα, καὶ θηλύτητας ἐσθήτων ἁλουργῶν ἑλκομένων δι' ἀγορᾶς, καὶ πολυτέλειαν ὑπερήφανον, ἐκτομάς τε καταστρωμάτων ἐν ταῖς τριήρεσιν, ὅπως μαλακώτερον ἐγκαθεύδοι, κειρίαις, ἀλλὰ μὴ σανίσι, τῶν στρωμάτων ἐπιβαλλομένων, ἀσπίδος τε διαχρύσου ποίησιν οὐδὲν ἐπίσημον τῶν πατρίων ἔχουσαν, ἀλλ' Ἔρωτα κεραυνοφόρον [. . .]

But along with his statesmanship, eloquence, pride, and ingenuity went, by contrast, a luxurious lifestyle, overindulgence in drink and sex, effeminacy of dress—he would trail his purple-dyed clothing through the city square—and incredible extravagance. For instance, he had the decks of triremes altered so that he could lay his bedclothes on cords rather than on bare boards and so have a softer bed to sleep on, and he had a shield made, with golden tracery, which bore, instead of an ancestral device, an image of Eros holding a thunderbolt [. . .]

In (42) the description reveals the sober, hard-working, and industrious mentality of the inhabitants of the house, including the girl with whom the protagonist, Adam Bede, will fall in love. In (43) Alcibiades' clothing, bedding, and shield are explicitly mentioned by the biographical narrator to illustrate his extravagant and indulgent nature.

If space tells us something about a character's mood or feelings, we are dealing with the *psychologizing* function (44–5).

(44) Thomas Hardy, *Tess of the D'Urbervilles*, chapter 16:

> The bird's-eye perspective before her [Tess] was not so luxuriantly beautiful, perhaps, as that other one which she knew so well; yet it was more cheering. It lacked the intensely blue atmosphere of the rival vale, and its heavy soils and scants; the new air was clearer, more ethereal, buoyant, bracing [...] Either the change in the quality of the air from heavy to light, or the sense of being amid new scenes where there were no invidious eyes upon her, sent up her spirits wonderfully. Her hopes mingled with the sunshine in an ideal photosphere which surrounded her as she bounded along against the soft south wind.

(45) Plutarch, *Alexander* 20.13:

> ὡς δ' εἶδε μὲν ὄλκια καὶ κρωσσοὺς καὶ πυέλους καὶ ἀλαβάστρους, πάντα χρυσοῦ, διησκημένα περιττῶς, ὠδώδει δὲ θεσπέσιον οἷον ὑπ' ἀρωμάτων καὶ μύρων ὁ οἶκος, ἐκ δὲ τούτου παρῆλθεν εἰς σκηνὴν ὕψει τε καὶ μεγέθει καὶ τῷ περὶ τὴν στρωμνὴν καὶ τὰς τραπέζας καὶ τὸ δεῖπνον αὐτὸ κόσμῳ θαύματος ἀξίαν, διαβλέψας πρὸς τοὺς ἑταίρους, 'τοῦτ' ἦν, ὡς ἔοικεν' ἔφη 'τὸ βασιλεύειν.'

> And when Alexander saw the bowls, pitchers, wash-basins, and perfume-jars, all of gold and elaborately wrought, when he smelt how marvellously the forechamber was scented with aromatic herbs and spices, and when he passed from there into the tent which was amazing for its height and size, its gorgeous couch and tables, and the actual food served upon them, he looked at his companions and said: 'This, I suppose, is what it was to be king.'

After an earlier debacle, young Tess in (44) is ready to make a new start and leave her home a second time, now to become a milkmaid in a neighbouring vale. Her hopeful mood is reflected in the way she looks at the scenery. Example (45) clearly reveals Alexander's emotions at the sight of the belongings and residence of his defeated Persian opponent, King Darius, but what are they? Do we see the first inklings of Alexander's later attraction to Eastern luxury and habits, or is he still the hardened soldier who looks with contempt and pity upon a king who bases his royal status merely on wealth?

The symbolic, characterizing, and psychologizing functions are not always easy to distinguish, and the terms are often used indiscriminately. Moreover, they may come into play at the same time. As a rule of thumb we may consider symbolic functions to be cultural and collective whereas the characterizing and psychologizing functions concern individuals. The characterizing function refers to a character's permanent traits, the psychological to his or her mood of the moment.

A particular form of semantic loading of space is *personification* (or *pathetic fallacy*), the projection of qualities normally associated with human beings upon inanimate objects or nature, and animals (46).

(46) John Steinbeck, *The Grapes of Wrath*, chapter 1:

> The wind grew stronger, whisked under stones, carried up straws and old leaves, and even little clods, marking its course as it sailed across the fields. The air and the sky darkened and through them the sun shone redly, and there was a raw sting in the air. During a night the wind raced faster over the land, dug cunningly among the rootlets of the corn, and the corn fought the wind with its weakened leaves until the roots were freed by the prying wind and then each stalk settled wearily sideways toward the earth and pointed the direction of the wind.

In this example it is the narrator who turns to personification, endowing the wind or stalks with all kind of human traits ('whisked under', 'raced', 'cunningly', 'wearily'). When focalizing characters do so, the device also acquires a psychologizing function. Personification is found throughout classical literature, from as early as Homer. However, it may be difficult to determine whether we are already dealing with a literary device or still with a mode of thought, that is, a manifestation of the ease with which the Greeks anthropomorphize nature, in the earliest instances. But a genuine literary instance of personification is seen in example (47).

(47) Virgil, *Eclogue* 5.24–8:

> non ulli pastos illis egere diebus
> frigida, Daphni, boves ad flumina; nulla neque amnem
> libavit quadripes nec graminis attigit herbam.
> Daphni, tuum Poenos etiam ingemuisse leones
> interitum montesque feri silvaeque loquuntur.

On those days, Daphnis, no herdsman drove his cattle to the cool streams; no four-footer tasted the brook or touched the leaves of grass. The desolate mountains and woods tell, Daphnis, that even Punic lions moaned over your death.

Virgil makes his secondary narrator, the herdsman Mopsus, sing a song about Daphnis, the archetypal herdsman, in which nature weeps over his death. We are in fact dealing with a double pathetic fallacy in that nature, mountains, and woods, are supposed to *tell* (through the rustle of leaves) the story of Daphnis being *mourned* by nature.

Space has long been underestimated in narratological theory. Closer inspection of its many forms and functions, however, has revealed it to be an effective category of signification in narrative. Classical literature has always shown greater affinity with space, in particular in the form of the ubiquitous *ekphrasis*. When reading ancient texts it always pays to be on the lookout for the symbolic, characterizing, or psychologizing function of space.

FURTHER READING

Narratology

Bachelard, G., *La poétique de l'espace* (Paris 1957).

Dannenberg, H.P., *Coincidence and Counterfactuality: Plotting Time and Space in Narrative Fiction* (Lincoln, NE 2008).

Dennerlein, K., *Narratologie des Raumes* (Berlin 2009).

Hallet, W., and B. Neumann (eds), *Raum und Bewegung in der Literatur: Die Literaturwissenschaften und der Spatial Turn* (Bielefeld 2009).

Hamon, P., *Du descriptif* (Paris 1993; first published 1981).

Heffernan, J.A.W., *Museum of Words: The Poetics of Ekphrasis from Homer to Ashbery* (Chicago 1993).

Hoffmann, G., *Raum, Situation, erzählte Wirklichkeit: Poetologische und historische Studien zum englischen und amerikanischen Roman* (Stuttgart 1978).

Lopes, J.M., *Foregrounded Description in Prose Fiction: Five Cross-Literary Studies* (Toronto 1995).

Lukács, G., 'Narrate or Describe?', in *Writer and Critic and Other Essays* (London 1970; first published 1936), 110–48.

Meyer, H., 'Raumgestaltung und Raumsymbolik in der Erzählkunst', in A. Ritter (ed.), *Landschaft und Raum in der Erzählkunst* (Darmstadt 1975; first published 1957), 208–31.

Petsch, R., 'Raum in der Erzählung', in A. Ritter (ed.), *Landschaft und Raum in der Erzählkunst* (Darmstadt 1975; first published 1934), 36–44.

Ronen, R., 'Space in Fiction', *Poetics Today* 7, 1986, 421–38.

Warf, B., and S. Arias (eds), *The Spatial Turn: Interdisciplinary Perspectives* (New York 2009).

Zoran, G., 'Towards a Theory of Space in Narrative', *Poetics Today* 5, 1984, 309–35.

Narratology and classics

Barchiesi, A., 'Virgilian Narrative (b)-Ecphrasis', in C. Martindale (ed.), *The Cambridge Companion to Virgil* (Cambridge 1997), 271–81.

Bartsch, S., *Decoding the Ancient Novel: The Reader and the Role of Description in Heliodorus and Achilles Tatius* (Princeton 1989).

Bartsch, S., and J. Elsner (eds), Special Issue on Ekphrasis, *Classical Philology* 102, 2007.

Becker, A.S., *The Shield of Achilles and the Poetics of Ekphrasis* (London 1995).

Bonnafé, A., J.C. Decourt, and B. Helly (eds), *L'espace et ses représentations* (Lyons 2000).

Clay, J.S., *Homer's Trojan Theater: Space, Vision, and Memory in the Iliad* (Cambridge 2011).

Elliger, W., *Die Darstellung der Landschaft in der griechischen Dichtung* (Berlin 1975).

Elsner, J. (ed.), Special Issue on Ekphrasis, *Ramus* 31, 2002.

Fowler, D., 'Narrate and Describe: The Problem of Ekphrasis', in *Roman Constructions: Readings in Postmodern Latin* (Oxford 2000; first published 1991), 64–85.

Harrison, S.J., 'Picturing the Future: The Proleptic Ekphrasis from Homer to Vergil', in S.J. Harrison (ed.), *Texts, Ideas, and the Classics: Scholarship, Theory and Classical Literature* (Oxford 2001), 70–92.

Harrison, S.J., 'Picturing the Future Again: Proleptic Ekphrasis in Silius' *Punica*', in A. Augoustakis (ed.), *Brill's Companion to Silius Italicus* (Leiden 2010), 279–92.

Hass, P., *Der locus amoenus in der antiken Literatur: Zu Theorie und Geschichte eines literarischen Motivs* (Bamberg 1998).

Hinds, S., 'Landscape with Figures: Aesthetics of Place in the *Metamophoses* and Its Traditions', in P. Hardie (ed.), *The Cambridge Companion to Ovid* (Cambridge 2002), 122–49.

Jong, I.J.F. de, 'The Shield of Achilles: From Metalepsis to *Mise en Abyme*', *Ramus* 40, 2011, 1–14.

Jong, I.J.F. de (ed.), *Space in Ancient Greek Literature*, Studies in Ancient Greek Narrative 3 (Leiden 2012).

Laird, A., 'Sounding Out Ecphrasis: Art and Text in *Catullus* 64', *Journal of Roman Studies* 83, 1993, 18–30.

Paschalis, M., and S. Frangoulidis (eds), *Space in the Ancient Novel* (Groningen 2002).

Purves, A.C., *Space and Time in Ancient Greek Narrative* (New York 2010).

Putnam, M.C.J., *Virgil's Epic Designs: Ekphrasis in the Aeneid* (New Haven and London 1998).

Rehm, R., *The Play of Space: Spatial Transformation in Greek Tragedy* (Princeton 2002).

Segal, C.P., *Landscape in Ovid's Metamorphoses: A Study in the Transformations of a Literary Symbol* (Wiesbaden 1969).

Thalmann, W.G., *Apollonius of Rhodes and the Spaces of Hellenism* (Oxford and New York 2011).

Vetta, M., C. Catenacci, and M. di Marzio (eds), *I luoghi e la poesia nella Grecia Antica* (Alessandria 2006).

Webb, R., *Ekphrasis, Imagination, and Persuasion in Ancient Rhetorical Theory and Practice* (Farnham and Burlington 2009).

Part II

Narratological Close Readings

6

Narratology and Epic

Homeric Hymn to Aphrodite *45-291* *(Aphrodite and Anchises)*

6.1. INTRODUCTION

The step to apply narratology to epic is logical and easy. Epic is the narrative genre par excellence in antiquity and, via the ancient novel, the direct model and precursor of our modern novel. Epic introduced many of the stock-in-trade storytelling devices: the Muses, beginning *in medias res*, prolepsis and analepsis, retardation, *ekphrasis*, and embedded focalization. We are now more aware than we used to be that the word 'introduced' is perhaps not entirely apt: precedents for quite a few of these narrative devices can be found in Near Eastern literature, for example the Gilgamesh epic. But the Greek texts are usually much more sophisticated and complex, and later European literatures used them, not the Near Eastern texts, as models.

In view of this formative nature of early Greek epic, it is not surprising that its most famous exponent, Homer, features regularly in narratological classics. Erich Auerbach devotes the first chapter of his celebrated *Mimesis: The Representation of Reality in Western Literature* to a comparison between the narrative styles of Homer and the Old Testament. While in the Old Testament time and space are undefined and thoughts and feelings remain unexpressed, in Homer all events are given equal attention and take place in a spatial and temporal present that is absolute. Nothing is left unexpressed and everything is externalized; in Auerbach's words, 'a continuous rhythmic procession of phenomena passes by, and never is there a form left fragmentary or half-illuminated, never a lacuna, never a gap, never a glimpse of unplumbed depths'.[1] His ideas about Homer have not remained unchallenged; there is much more suspense, gaps, perspective, and psychological complexity in that text than he suggested.[2]

In the first chapter of *The Rhetoric of Fiction*, Wayne Booth refers to Homer and the Old Testament as examples of authoritative narration:

> Homer writes scarcely a page [*sic!*] without some kind of direct clarification of motives, of expectations, and of the relative importance of events. [...] In the opening lines of the *Iliad*, for example, we are told, under the half-pretense of an invocation, precisely what the tale is to be about: 'the anger of Peleus' son Achilles and its devastation'. We are directly told that we are to care more about the Greeks than the Trojans. We are told that they were 'heroes' with 'strong souls'. We are told that it was the will of Zeus that they should be 'the delicate feasting of dogs'. And we learn that the particular conflict between Agamemnon, 'the lord of men', and 'brilliant' Achilles was set on by Apollo. We could never be sure of any of this information in real life, yet we are sure as we move through the *Iliad* with Homer constantly at our elbow, controlling rigorously our beliefs, our interests, and our sympathies.[3]

When writing this assessment of Homer as a paragon of authoritative narration, Booth was unaware that actually Homer had been seen from Aristotle onwards as the master of 'showing' (as opposed to 'telling'). The truth may lie somewhere in-between.[4]

Finally, Gérard Genette illustrates the working of anachrony (the changing of the chronological order of events of the fabula into the effective order of the story) on the basis of the opening of the *Iliad* in his *Narrative Discourse*. Starting from the wrath of Achilles, the very first word of the poem, the Homeric narrator first works his way back in time: the wrath was the result of Achilles' quarrel with Agamemnon, which had been caused by the plague, which had been sent by Apollo to punish the Greeks and above all Agamemnon for their harsh treatment of the priest Chryses. At this point the narrator starts the full narration of his story and devotes the rest of his first book to a leisured presentation, in chronological order, of Agamemnon's abuse of the priest, the plague, the quarrel, and Achilles' wrath:

[1] Auerbach [1946] 1953: 6–7.
[2] See Köhnken [1976] 2009: 44–61 and de Jong 1999.
[3] Booth [1961] 1983: 4–5.   [4] See de Jong [1987] 2004; 2005.

We know that this beginning *in medias res*, followed by an expository
return to an earlier point of time, will become one of the formal topoi of
epic, and we also know how faithfully the style of novelistic narration
follows in this respect the style of its remote ancestor, even in the heart
of the 'realistic' nineteenth century. To be convinced of this one need
only think of certain of Balzac's openings, such as those in *César
Birotteau* or *La Duchesse de Langeais*. [...] We will thus not be so
foolish as to claim that anachrony is either a rarity or a modern
invention. On the contrary, it is one of the traditional resources of
literary narration.[5]

In view of this place of honour in narratological history, it is not
surprising to see that many Greek and Latin epic texts (and their main
successor, the ancient novel) have already benefited from narratological analysis, as can be seen from the bibliography at the end of
Chapter 1. In this chapter we will take a closer look at a specimen of
epic narrative from one of the *Homeric Hymns*.

6.2. *HOMERIC HYMNS*

The *Homeric Hymns* are a collection of thirty-three poems, of which
at least one had been ascribed in antiquity to Homer and therefore
became known as the *Homeric Hymns*. They resemble the Homeric
epics in style and language, but probably none actually is the work of
that poet. For one thing, the collection contains some examples that
are clearly from a much later period.

   The poems are called hymns because they deal with the life and
deeds of gods and as such resemble the cultic hymns that played a
major role in Greek society: a chorus would sing a song while walking
in a procession or standing around an altar. The song is a gift to the
god, comparable to sacrifices or libations, and intended to win his or
her goodwill. The *Homeric Hymns* differ from these cultic hymns in
that they were recited by one person only and are composed in
dactylic hexameters rather than lyric metres. Their exact status and
function is the subject of much debate: were they sung by way of

[5] Genette [1972] 1980: 36.

proem to epic recitations that took place during festivals, were they perhaps specifically sung at festivals for the gods hymned, or were they autonomous, non-cultic poems sung at the symposium?

For the purpose of this book such questions must be left unanswered.[6] What is relevant is that most hymns, in particular the four longer ones (to Demeter, to Apollo, to Hermes, and to Aphrodite), contain narratives. Thus, a Homeric hymn typically consists of an opening in which the god to be hymned is mentioned, a descriptive section in which the typical attributes of the hymned god are listed, a narrative section in which a characteristic event in the life of the god is recounted, and a conclusion in which the hymnic speaker says farewell to the god (usually with the verb *chairein* which is also found in cultic hymns). When embarking on his narrative, the hymnic speaker, who usually refers to himself in the 'I' form at the opening or end of his poem, changes into a primary external narrator. The modest scale of hymnic narrative makes it an excellent exercise for the narratological analysis of epic narration.

The *Homeric Hymn to Aphrodite* in particular offers an intriguing narrative (45–291). Its *fabula* can be summed up in a few words: Zeus, whom Aphrodite has often caused to fall in love with mortal women, turns the tables on that goddess by inflaming her desire for a mortal man, the Trojan prince Anchises; Aphrodite, presenting herself to Anchises in the shape of a Phrygian princess, makes love to him on Mount Ida; afterwards, she reveals her true identity and announces the birth of their son Aeneas. This fabula is an expansion of the traditional *material,* such as we know it from for example *Iliad* 2.820–1 (Αἰνείας, τὸν ὑπ᾽ Ἀγχίσῃ τέκε δῖ᾽ Ἀφροδίτη | Ἴδης ἐν κνημοῖσι θεὰ βροτῷ εὐνηθεῖσα, 'Aeneas, whom Aphrodite bore to Anchises, after having slept with him on the glades of the Ida, goddess with mortal') or Hesiod *Theogony* 1008–10. When we turn to the level of the *story,* however, the picture is less clear. Does Anchises know that he is facing a goddess? Does Aphrodite know that it was Zeus who made her fall in love with Anchises? And how do the narratees understand what happens and why? When answering these (and other) interpretative questions, the many verbal echoes in the *text* will prove to be of great importance.

---

[6] For a recent overview, see Richardson 2010: 1–32 and Faulkner 2011.

6.3. NARRATOLOGICAL CLOSE READING OF HOMERIC *HYMN TO APHRODITE* 45–291[7]

45–52

τῇ δὲ καὶ αὐτῇ Ζεὺς γλυκὺν ἵμερον ἔμβαλε θυμῷ   (45)
ἀνδρὶ καταθνητῷ μιχθήμεναι, ὄφρα τάχιστα
μηδ' αὐτὴ βροτέης εὐνῆς ἀποεργμένη εἴη
καί ποτ' ἐπευξαμένη εἴπῃ μετὰ πᾶσι θεοῖσιν
ἡδὺ γελοιήσασα φιλομμειδὴς Ἀφροδίτη
ὥς ῥα θεοὺς συνέμειξε καταθνητῇσι γυναιξί   (50)
καί τε καταθνητοὺς υἷας τέκον ἀθανάτοισιν,
ὥς τε θεὰς ἀνέμειξε καταθνητοῖς ἀνθρώποις.

But for herself, too, Zeus cast sweet desire in her heart   (45)
to join in love with a mortal man, so that as quickly as possible
she would not herself be separated from a mortal bed
and would not boast anymore among all the gods,
laughing sweetly smile-loving Aphrodite,
how she joins in love gods with mortal women,   (50)
—and they bear mortal sons to immortals—
and how she joins in love goddesses to mortal men.

The narrative of the *Hymn to Aphrodite* follows quite naturally and smoothly from the opening (1–2a) and attributive section of the hymn (2b–44): the hymnic speaker announces as his subject the ἔργα Ἀφροδίτης, 'works of Aphrodite', and then describes the goddess' power: Aphrodite makes all creatures (mortals, animals, and gods—except Athena, Artemis, and Hestia) fall in love. She even makes the most powerful god of all, Zeus, fall in love and couples him with mortal women.[8] With the detail of a god sleeping with a

---

[7] There is quite a bibliography on the *H. Aphr.*, which is excellently summarized and discussed in Faulkner 2008. I will therefore mainly refer to him, or, for narratologically important points, to Smith 1981 and Clay 1989. This chapter is a thoroughly revised and expanded version of de Jong 1989. The text is that of Faulkner 2008; the translations are my own.

[8] I interpret the aorists ἤγαγε (36) and συνέμειξε (39), with e.g. Smith 1981: 17 and Faulkner 2008: ad 36, as omnitemporal, on account of the presence of epic τε. Van der Ben 1986: 4–5 and Clay 1989: 163 take them as past tenses, since they assume that as a result of the events to be told Aphrodite *no longer* couples gods and mortals; see n. 51.

mortal the hymnic speaker starts to zoom in and prepare for the narrative to follow.

The narrative begins when we turn to singulative narration, the moment when Zeus decides to turn the tables on Aphrodite and make her fall in love herself with a mortal man. The verbal echo γλυκὺν ἵμερον ἔμβαλε θυμῷ (45) ≈ ἐπὶ γλυκὺν ἵμερον ὦρσεν (2) underscores his intention to beat Aphrodite with her own weapons.[9] There is no indication why Zeus wants to teach Aphrodite a lesson at this specific point, but that it would be this god who takes the initiative is not surprising; as the narratees would know, for example from his famous catalogue of loves at *Iliad* 14.315–28, he is one of her most frequent divine 'victims'. He is also the only god who is powerful enough to assume the power of another god: although he cannot resist Aphrodite when she beguiles his strong mind, he can take her place and himself engender love. There is also a marked tendency in the longer *Homeric Hymns* to portray Zeus as a kind of judge or referee between gods (cf. in *H. Dem.*: Demeter vs Hades; *H. Herm.*: Hermes vs Apollo); in the *Hymn to Aphrodite*. Zeus, acting on behalf of all gods, puts Aphrodite in her place.

Zeus' intentions to take revenge on Aphrodite are presented in the form of embedded focalization: the long clause which begins with ὄφρα τάχιστα + optative and subjunctive (46–52). He wants Aphrodite to join in love with a mortal herself to know how this feels (as we will see, this is not a pure pleasure for a god, and it may entail negative consequences) and, as a consequence, to stop boasting about her capacity to couple gods and mortals and have children born out of such encounters.[10] The narratees know well about such children, for example from Homer *Odyssey* 11.235–327; Hesiod *Catalogue of Women* or *Theogony* 943–1020. The observation that Zeus' motifs are presented in embedded focalization is highly relevant in that it means that not only Anchises will be unaware of the divine machinery underlying what happens to him (as mortals usually are) but also Aphrodite. Only the narratees have been privy to Zeus' hidden thoughts.

---

[9] Scholars are divided as to where the narrative starts: according to Smith 1981: 39, Faulkner 2008: 1 and ad 45–52, it begins at 53; according to Van der Ben 1986: 4–5, at 36. I follow Clay 1989: 164 in putting its beginning at 45, since Zeus' plan and Aphrodite's evaluation at 247–55 clearly form a ring (see 239–55).

[10] The aorists συνέμειξε (50) and ἀνέμειξε (52) are omnitemporal.

53–7

Ἀγχίσεω δ' ἄρα οἱ γλυκὺν ἵμερον ἔμβαλε θυμῷ,
ὃς τότ' ἐν ἀκροπόλοις ὄρεσιν πολυπιδάκου Ἴδης
βουκολέεσκεν βοῦς δέμας ἀθανάτοισιν ἐοικώς.   (55)
τὸν δὴπειτα ἰδοῦσα φιλομμειδὴς Ἀφροδίτη
ἠράσατ', ἐκπάγλως δὲ κατὰ φρένας ἵμερος εἷλεν.

It was for Anchises that he cast a sweet desire in her heart,
who at that time on the heights of Ida with many springs
was tending cattle, in build resembling the gods.   (55)
As a result, seeing him smile-loving Aphrodite
fell in love, and desire took hold of her heart forcefully.

Zeus starts executing his plan (γλυκὺν ἵμερον ἔμβαλε θυμῷ at 53 resumes the action of 45: γλυκὺν ἵμερον ἔμβαλε θυμῷ, after the exposition of the god's motives), and it is now revealed that Anchises is the mortal man with whom Aphrodite is to fall in love.

The way in which Zeus inflames Aphrodite's passion is by making her see Anchises. It is not indicated where Aphrodite finds herself, but wherever she is she is able to perceive the youth on Mount Ida. Greek gods are able to see (and hear) from a great distance; thus Poseidon spots Odysseus sailing home on a raft while looking 'from afar from the mountains of Solymi' (*Od.* 5.282–3) and Thetis hears her son Achilles praying to her on the beach of Troy while she is sitting in the depths of the sea (*Il.* 1.357–8).

Who is focalizing the introduction of Anchises at 54–5? Is it Zeus, who chooses Anchises because of his divine beauty, or is it Aphrodite, who falls in love with him because of that beauty? Perhaps it is most attractive to understand it as being focalized by both of them, with Zeus aptly choosing a man whom Aphrodite will like. The way in which Anchises' beauty is described is conventional: he resembles the gods in build (cf. e.g. δέμας ἀθανάτοισιν ὁμοῖος at *Od.* 3.468, of Telemachus, or γυνὴ ἐϊκθῖα θεῇσι at *Il.* 19.286, of Briseis). But at the same time it is significant in that there are so many role-reversals between god and mortal in this hymnic narrative: Anchises resembles the gods, and the goddess Aphrodite will soon do her utmost to resemble a mortal.

Anchises' introduction also presents us with a first indication of the setting of the upcoming narrative: the mountainside of Ida. This setting belongs to the material of the erotic encounter of Aphrodite and Anchises (cf. *Il.* 2.821; Hes. *Th.* 1010) but also recalls that of Zeus' seduction by Hera in *Iliad* 14.166–15.77, a passage which very likely served as an intertext for the hymnic poet of the *Hymn to Aphrodite*. Anchises is tending cattle, as youngsters of royal lineage do in epic (cf. e.g. *Il.* 20.91, 188–90, where we hear about Aeneas doing the same). With τότ' (54) the narrator also indicates something of a temporal setting: 'at that time', that is, at the moment Aphrodite first sets eyes on him. Later on we will get more particulars about the time of day (78–9).

Aphrodite falls in love with Anchises the moment she spots him, the coincident aorist participle ἰδοῦσα creating a 'love at first sight' effect. The connection between sight and eros is typical (cf. e.g. Anchises at 84–91 and Zeus at *Il.* 14.294). The verbal echo in line 57 confirms that Zeus' plan of planting desire in Aphrodite's heart has been successful (κατὰ φρένας ἵμερος εἷλεν ≈ ἵμερον ἔμβαλε θυμῷ: 45, 53), indeed, as the addition of ἐκπάγλως suggests, has been very successful.

58–65

ἐς Κύπρον δ' ἐλθοῦσα θυώδεα νηὸν ἔδυνεν
ἐς Πάφον· ἔνθα δέ οἱ τέμενος βωμός τε θυώδης·
ἔνθ' ἥ γ' εἰσελθοῦσα θύρας ἐπέθηκε φαεινάς.   (60)
ἔνθα δέ μιν Χάριτες λοῦσαν καὶ χρῖσαν ἐλαίῳ
ἀμβρότῳ, οἷα θεοὺς ἐπενήνοθεν αἰὲν ἐόντας,
ἀμβροσίῳ ἑδανῷ, τό ῥά οἱ τεθυωμένον ἦεν.
ἑσσαμένη δ' εὖ πάντα περὶ χροῒ εἵματα καλά
χρυσῷ κοσμηθεῖσα φιλομμειδὴς Ἀφροδίτη [. . .]   (65)

She went to Cyprus and entered her fragrant temple
at Paphos; there she has a precinct and fragrant altar.
There she entered and closed the shining doors.   (60)
There the Charites bathed her and anointed her with olive oil,
immortal, such as covers the eternally living gods,
immortal and sweet, which was ready perfumed for her.
Having dressed herself well with all beautiful clothes about her body
and adorned herself with gold, smile-loving Aphrodite [. . .]   (65)

After having been inflamed with desire for Anchises, Aphrodite prepares to seduce him. From now on the action evolves according to the 'seduction' type-scene, which we also find, for example, in Hera's seduction of Zeus in *Iliad* 14: (1) toilette (58–67); (2) approach (68–80); (3) reaction of seduced (81–106); (4) seducer's false tale

(107–42); (5) reaction of seduced (143–54); (6) intercourse and sleep (155–79); and (7) awakening (180–291). Aphrodite's toilette differs from that of Hera. The latter washes and adorns herself in her private bedroom, while Aphrodite goes to her temple at Paphos and has herself taken care of by her attendants, the Charites. In other words, she prepares for her seduction very much in her capacity of goddess of love, with unforeseen consequences (see 92–106). A second difference is that Hera's clothes and jewellery are described in detail while she adorns herself but not mentioned at the moment Zeus sees her. Aphrodite's clothes and jewellery are only mentioned briefly during her toilette but described in full when Anchises first sets eyes on her (an instance of narrative delay or paralipsis).

66–75

[...] σεύατ' ἐπὶ Τροίης προλιποῦσ' εὐώδεα Κύπρον
ὕψι μετὰ νέφεσιν ῥίμφα πρήσσουσα κέλευθον.
Ἴδην δ' ἵκανεν πολυπίδακα, μητέρα θηρῶν,
βῆ δ' ἰθὺς σταθμοῖο δι' οὔρεος· οἱ δὲ μετ' αὐτήν
σαίνοντες πολιοί τε λύκοι χαροποί τε λέοντες   (70)
ἄρκτοι παρδάλιές τε θοαὶ προκάδων ἀκόρητοι
ᾖσαν· ἡ δ' ὁρόωσα μετὰ φρεσὶ τέρπετο θυμόν
καὶ τοῖς ἐν στήθεσσι βάλ' ἵμερον, οἱ δ' ἅμα πάντες
σύνδυο κοιμήσαντο κατὰ σκιόεντας ἐναύλους.
αὐτὴ δ' ἐς κλισίας εὐποιήτους ἀφίκανε·   (75)

[...] sped towards Troy leaving fragrant Cyprus
high among the clouds quickly making her way.
She reached Ida with many springs, mother of wild animals,
and went straight for his steading across the mountain. And after her
went fawning grey wolves and fierce-eyed lions,   (70)
bears, and swift leopards, insatiable for deer.
And seeing them she rejoiced in her heart
and she cast desire in their hearts, and they all
lay down in pairs in their shadowy lairs.
But she herself reached his well-built hut.   (75)

In epic, gods travel in various ways and narrators choose what best suits their narrative: they can walk on foot, ride in a chariot, fly through the air, or simply reach their destination without an indication of how exactly they transported themselves.[11] The last method was used in 58–9, where Aphrodite simply arrives on Cyprus and in Paphos, the narrator fast-forwarding to the goddess adorning herself. Now the narrator first makes Aphrodite fly from Cyprus to Mount Ida, as the reference to clouds suggests, and then walk for the last part of her trip. There is a good reason for this choice: making Aphrodite walk across the mountain allows the narrator to show her exercising her power as goddess of love on wild animals (cf. 4).

Mount Ida is typically called 'mother of wild animals', and this spatial detail is here given a characterizing function: a set of wild animals, including wolves, lions, and leopards, fawn at Aphrodite. This behaviour already suggests that they recognize Aphrodite's authority (cf. *Il.* 13.27–9, where the power of the sea-god Poseidon, riding the waves on his chariot, is recognized by sea beasts who 'gather from their lairs and gambol at his coming'). She next tests her power on the wild animals, as it were, by arousing desire in them before using it with Anchises (βάλ' ἵμερον: 73 ≈ γλυκὺν ἵμερον ἔμβαλε θυμῷ: 143). The animals respond as desired and immediately all start mating. It remains to be seen whether Aphrodite will overpower Anchises just as easily.

> *76–80*
> τὸν δ' εὗρε σταθμοῖσι λελειμμένον οἷον ἀπ' ἄλλων
> Ἀγχίσην ἥρωα θεῶν ἄπο κάλλος ἔχοντα.
> οἱ δ' ἅμα βουσὶν ἕποντο νομοὺς κάτα ποιήεντας
> πάντες, ὁ δὲ σταθμοῖσι λελειμμένος οἷος ἀπ' ἄλλων
> πωλεῖτ' ἔνθα καὶ ἔνθα διαπρύσιον κιθαρίζων.   (80)
>
> Him she found alone left behind by the others in the steading,
> the hero Anchises, having his beauty from the gods.
> The others were all following cattle over the grassy pastures,
> but, alone left behind by the others in the steading,
> he was walking up and down, playing loudly on his lyre.   (80)

When epic characters arrive at their destination, they typically focalize the situation they find (cf. the marker εὗρε). The bucolic setting, briefly indicated at 54–5, now comes into full view. Aphrodite notes that Anchises is conveniently alone, and she has occasion to admire his divine beauty again. The information about the other herdsmen in

---

[11] See de Jong 2012: 43–8.

the grassy pastures (78) is best included in Aphrodite's focalization, since later it appears that she is aware of their existence when she starts bringing her meeting with Anchises to a close 'at the time when herdsmen drive their cattle and sheep back to the shed' (168–71). Her focalization can be again explained in reference to her divine sight (cf. 54–5). The alternative is to take 78 as an intrusion of the primary narrator upon her focalization (paralepsis). Anchises is not actually herding cows but playing on a lyre. This activity conveys a double message: it shows him to be a hero[12] rather than a simple shepherd (who would play the panpipe) and also a man who potentially is in the mood for love (the lyre is mentioned in one breath with the ἔργα Ἀφροδίτης e.g. at *Il.* 3.54, and Anchises might be supposed to be singing of love, as later literary shepherds tend to do).[13]

81–91

στῆ δ᾽ αὐτοῦ προπάροιθε Διὸς θυγάτηρ Ἀφροδίτη
παρθένῳ ἀδμήτῃ μέγεθος καὶ εἶδος ὁμοίη,
μή μιν ταρβήσειεν ἐν ὀφθαλμοῖσι νοήσας.
Ἀγχίσης δ᾽ ὁρόων ἐφράζετο θάμβαινέν τε
εἶδός τε μέγεθός τε καὶ εἵματα σιγαλόεντα.   (85)
πέπλον μὲν γὰρ ἔεστο φαεινότερον πυρὸς αὐγῆς,
εἶχε δ᾽ ἐπιγναμπτὰς ἕλικας κάλυκάς τε φαεινάς,
ὅρμοι δ᾽ ἀμφ᾽ ἁπαλῇ δειρῇ περικαλλέες ἦσαν
καλοὶ χρύσειοι παμποίκιλοι· ὡς δὲ σελήνη
στήθεσιν ἀμφ᾽ ἁπαλοῖσιν ἐλάμπετο, θαῦμα ἰδέσθαι.   (90)
Ἀγχίσην δ᾽ ἔρος εἷλεν, ἔπος δέ μιν ἀντίον ηὔδα·

She placed herself before him, daughter of Zeus, Aphrodite,
resembling in height and build an unwedded virgin,
so that, when he saw her with his eyes, he would not be frightened.
Anchises, seeing her took stock and was amazed
at her build, height, and shining clothes.   (85)
For the dress which she wore was brighter than fire,
and she wore twisted bracelets and shining ear-rings,
and around her tender neck there were very beautiful necklaces,
fair, of gold, and elaborately wrought. Like the moon
it shone around her tender breasts, a wonder to behold.   (90)
And desire gripped Anchises, and he addressed her:

---

[12] As Clay 1989: 172 notes, the word *heros* appears only here in the hymns.
[13] See Faulkner 2008: ad 80.

From this point onwards Aphrodite's seduction of Anchises starts diverging from its Iliadic counterpart, Hera's seduction of Zeus, because it involves a god and a mortal and hence merges with a 'god meets mortal' type-scene: this means that a god assumes a mortal disguise in order to converse with a mortal, usually revealing his or her divine identity at the end of the meeting (sometimes as an epiphany, with the god appearing to the mortal in divine shape).[14]

The mortal shape adopted by gods is always carefully chosen: they want their mortal addressees to do something (here, exceptionally, go to bed with them), and hence either look for authority or try to win their confidence. Aphrodite here assumes the identity of an unmarried mortal virgin: innocent, sexually inexperienced, and vulnerable, that is, the opposite of her true identity in every way. The narrator adds Aphrodite's motive for choosing this disguise in the form of embedded focalization (marker: μή + optative): she wants to prevent Anchises from fearing her. Fear is a common reaction of mortals to encountering gods[15] and mortals run special risks if they make love to a god (see *180–90*). Will Aphrodite succeed?

For the first time in the story we turn to Anchises' focalization.[16] The shift is reflected on the level of the text in the chiastic order μή . . . ταρβήσειεν ἐν ὀφθαλμοῖσι νοήσας . . . ὁρόων ἐφράζετο θάμβαινέν τε. What does Anchises see? A young virgin or a goddess? Both positions have been defended. Thus Bergren compares the description of Aphrodite's outfit with that of Pandora, the first human female, in Hesiod *Theogony* 571–84 and *Works and Days* 70–82, and concludes that what Anchises sees is a typical bride.[17] Most scholars assume, however, that Aphrodite's true divine status is still somehow discernible despite her adoption of the identity of a virgin mortal. What strikes Anchises most is the glitter of her appearance; a full description of her spectacular clothes and jewellery was omitted earlier by the narrator, but it is now very effectively given through the hero's eyes (see *58–65*). This is the first indication that he takes her for a goddess,[18] since gods are radiant.[19] Anchises' amazement

[14] See de Jong 2001: ad 1.96–324.
[15] Cf. e.g. *Il.* 24.170; *Od.* 16.179; *H. Dem.* 281–3, 293; *H. Ap.* 47–8.
[16] Cf. Smith 1981: 44: 'we share some of Anchises' reaction to the radiantly impressive young woman who suddenly stands before him'.
[17] Bergren 1989: 11.
[18] Thus e.g. Smith 1981: 44–5 and Faulkner 2008: ad 83–90.
[19] Cf. e.g. Demeter in *H. Dem.* 189, 278–9; Apollo in *H. Ap.* 202–3, 440–2.

(θάμβαινέν) points in the same direction,[20] as does the expression θαῦμα ἰδέσθαι, which typically refers to the admiration of a mortal for immortal things or persons in epic.[21]

But the definite answer to the question of what exactly Anchises sees comes from the way he addresses the girl in front of him, when he turns from (secondary) focalizer into (secondary) narrator-focalizer.

92–106

'χαῖρε ἄνασσ', ἥ τις μακάρων τάδε δώμαθ' ἱκάνεις,
Ἄρτεμις ἢ Λητὼ ἠὲ χρυσῆ Ἀφροδίτη
ἢ Θέμις ἠϋγενὴς ἠὲ γλαυκῶπις Ἀθήνη
ἤ πού τις Χαρίτων δεῦρ' ἤλυθες, αἵ τε θεοῖσι   (95)
πᾶσιν ἑταιρίζουσι καὶ ἀθάνατοι καλέονται,
ἤ τις νυμφάων αἵ τ' ἄλσεα καλὰ νέμονται,
ἢ νυμφῶν αἳ καλὸν ὄρος τόδε ναιετάουσι
καὶ πηγὰς ποταμῶν καὶ πίσεα ποιήεντα.
σοὶ δ' ἐγὼ ἐν σκοπιῇ, περιφαινομένῳ ἐνὶ χώρῳ,   (100)
βωμὸν ποιήσω, ῥέξω δέ τοι ἱερὰ καλὰ
ὥρῃσιν πάσῃσι· σὺ δ' εὔφρονα θυμὸν ἔχουσα
δός με μετὰ Τρώεσσιν ἀριπρεπέ' ἔμμεναι ἄνδρα,
ποίει δ' εἰσοπίσω θαλερὸν γόνον, αὐτὰρ ἔμ' αὐτόν
δηρὸν ἔϋ ζώειν καὶ ὁρᾶν φάος ἠελίοιο   (105)
ὄλβιον ἐν λαοῖς καὶ γήραος οὐδὸν ἱκέσθαι.'

'Hail, Lady, whoever you are of the blessed ones that arrive at
    this dwelling,
Artemis, or Leto or golden Aphrodite
or fair-born Themis or owl-eyed Athena
or perhaps you came here one of the Charites, who   (95)
accompany all the gods and are called immortal,
or one of the nymphs who live in the lovely forest groves
or one of the nymphs who inhabit this beautiful mountain,
and the springs of rivers and grassy meadows.
For you I will build on a hilltop, in a conspicuous place   (100)
an altar and I will perform fair sacrifices for you
in all seasons. But you in return with kind spirit
give that I will be an outstanding man among the Trojans
and make my offspring thriving in time to come, and that
    I myself
live long and well and see the light of the sun   (105)
prosperous among my people and reach old age.'

---

[20] Cf. e.g. *Il.* 3.398; *Od.* 1.323; 3.372.   [21] See de Jong [1987] 2004: 48–9.

Incited by what he has just seen, Anchises takes the initiative and addresses the girl before him. This is in accordance with the epic convention of a 'host' welcoming a stranger to his house (cf. τάδε δώμαθ': 92) speaking first.[22] Also, embedded focalization in epic regularly leads to speech, the so-called 'action–perception–reaction' motif.[23]

Anchises' speech has the typical shape of a prayer, here with a hymnic flavour (but of course hymn and prayer are closely connected): (1) invocation (featuring the hymnic 'Χαῖρε' and the kind of relative expansions typical of hymnic attributive sections); (2) promise; and (3) request. This suggests once more that Anchises is taking the woman before him for a goddess, although he does not know which goddess (he mentions Aphrodite only as one among many). It has been suggested that Anchises might not be sincere in addressing the young woman as a goddess and that he might be merely adopting the same diplomatic attitude that Odysseus used to address Nausikaa in *Odyssey* 6.149–85.[24] The nature of the favours that Anchises prays for makes this improbable, however. Whereas Odysseus asks to be shown the way to the city and to be provided with clothes to hide his nakedness (*Od.* 6.178–9), requests with which a human being like Nausikaa can easily comply, Anchises asks for status, offspring, and old age, requests which only a god can fulfil. There can be no other conclusion than that at this stage Anchises is convinced that he is facing a goddess.

Anchises' speech in the first place serves to portray him as a pious man: although we heard that *eros* gripped him upon seeing the female before him, he controls his desire and reacts in a way appropriate in the presence of a goddess. At the same time, his speech is a masterful stroke on the part of the primary narrator. It confirms that Aphrodite has only been partly successful in her disguise. She has managed to allay his fear and instil *eros* by assuming the guise of a young mortal virgin, yet she has 'pimped' herself too professionally in her temple at Paphos. As a result the suspense mounts: will Aphrodite 'get' her Trojan prince? Will her desire be fulfilled? Will Zeus' plan be fulfilled? Of course, the answer can only be 'yes', but it remains to be seen how Aphrodite convinces Anchises that she is not a god. She

---

[22] Smith 1981: 46.   [23] de Jong 2001: ad 5.279–90.
[24] See the discussion in Faulkner 2008: ad 92–106.

must seduce him not only with her outward appearance, but also with words. As Clay noted, whereas the wild beasts of Mount Ida had easily succumbed to her power and their desire had led to immediate consummation, 'humans are subject to certain scruples and constraints, whether social or religious, that restrict sexual license. Human beings, like animals, copulate, but the art of seduction, used to overcome inhibitions and restrictions, distinguishes them from beasts.'[25]

Although Aphrodite's plan seems to misfire for the time being and Anchises does not talk about sex, his speech does touch on some issues which will become relevant later on in the narrative: offspring and a long life, including old age.

107-16

τὸν δ' ἠμείβετ' ἔπειτα Διὸς θυγάτηρ Ἀφροδίτη·
'Ἀγχίση, κύδιστε χαμαιγενέων ἀνθρώπων,
οὔ τίς τοι θεός εἰμι· τί μ' ἀθανάτῃσιν ἐΐσκεις;
ἀλλὰ καταθνητή τε, γυνὴ δέ με γείνατο μήτηρ.   (110)
'Οτρεὺς δ' ἐστὶ πατὴρ ὀνομάκλυτος, εἴ που ἀκούεις,
ὃς πάσης Φρυγίης εὐτειχήτοιο ἀνάσσει.
γλῶσσαν δ' ὑμετέρην τε καὶ ἡμετέρην σάφα οἶδα·
Τρωὰς γὰρ μεγάρῳ με τροφὸς τρέφεν, ἡ δὲ διάπρο
σμικρὴν παῖδ' ἀτίταλλε φίλης παρὰ μητρὸς ἑλοῦσα.   (115)
ὣς δή τοι γλῶσσάν γε καὶ ὑμετέρην εὖ οἶδα.'

Him answered next Zeus' daughter Aphrodite:
'Anchises, most glorious of earth-born men,
be sure I am no goddess—why liken me to the gods?—
but a mortal, and a mortal woman bore me as my mother.   (110)
Otreus is my father, with famous name, if perhaps you have
      heard it,
who rules over the whole of well-walled Phrygia.
Your language I know well, as well as my own.
For a Trojan nurse reared me in the palace, and she raised
      me throughout,
having taken me over from my dear mother when I was
      very young.   (115)
Thus I happen to know your language well, too.'

[25] Clay 1989: 175.

In order to make her seduction of Anchises a success, Aphrodite has to flesh out her assumed identity of a young woman with a fictitious biography. This takes the form of a lying tale (107–42), such as we know from other epic gods and mortals (mainly Odysseus) in disguise.[26] That the goddess of love uses deception in order to win over Anchises, of course, also suits her nature: as the attributive section of the hymn made clear, the working of Aphrodite involves deceit (7, 33, 38). Aphrodite will do an excellent job: she poses as a modest maiden who would not think of premarital sex, yet actually offers Anchises her social status, her virginity, and divinely ordained marriage with him as bait to lure him into having sex with her.

She begins by making herself daughter of a real person, the Phrygian King Otreus (cf. *Il.* 3.184–9, where we hear of Priam fighting with this king against the Amazons), of whom Anchises will have heard but who lives far enough away to preclude an all too intimate knowledge of his family. Posing as the daughter of a king means that she is a good match. Eager to convince Anchises, Aphrodite even uses a unique circumstantial detail that is not before found in epic narrative. Epic characters conventionally are able to talk with each other, whether Greek, Trojan, Phrygian, or Laystrygonian; but Aphrodite explains how she can talk to Anchises in his own, Trojan, language in a brief external analepsis on her nurse.[27] For all the profusion of details, Aphrodite does leave out one thing: her own name.[28] Indeed, gods in disguise never give themselves names (while lying mortals do). Perhaps epic narrators felt a religious constraint from making their immortal characters do so. In order to explain how she arrived in a remote mountainscape in full, glamorous regalia, Aphrodite resorts to another, longer external analepsis.

117–30
ʻνῦν δέ μ' ἀνήρπαξε χρυσόρραπις Ἀργειφόντης
ἐκ χοροῦ Ἀρτέμιδος χρυσηλακάτου κελαδεινῆς.
πολλαὶ δὲ νύμφαι καὶ παρθένοι ἀλφεσίβοιαι
παίζομεν, ἀμφὶ δ' ὅμιλος ἀπείριτος ἐστεφάνωτο·   (120)

---

[26] See de Jong 2001: ad 13.253–86.
[27] Faulkner 2008: ad 113–16 suggests that this detail may be due to the hymn originating in the Troad, an area with a long tradition of Greek and Phrygian interaction.
[28] Cf. Smith 1981: 51.

ἔνθεν μ' ἥρπαξε χρυσόρραπις Ἀργειφόντης,
πολλὰ δ' ἔπ' ἤγαγεν ἔργα καταθνητῶν ἀνθρώπων,
πολλὴν δ' ἄκληρόν τε καὶ ἄκτιτον, ἣν διὰ θῆρες
ὠμοφάγοι φοιτῶσι κατὰ σκιόεντας ἐναύλους,
οὐδὲ ποσὶ ψαύειν ἐδόκουν φυσιζόου αἴης·   (125)
Ἀγχίσεω δέ με φάσκε παραὶ λέχεσιν καλέεσθαι
κουριδίην ἄλοχον, σοὶ δ' ἀγλαὰ τέκνα τεκεῖσθαι.
αὐτὰρ ἐπεὶ δὴ δεῖξε καὶ ἔφρασεν, ἤτοι ὅ γ' αὖτις
ἀθανάτων μετὰ φῦλ' ἀπέβη κρατὺς Ἀργειφόντης·
αὐτὰρ ἐγώ σ' ἱκόμην, κρατερὴ δέ μοι ἔπλετ' ἀνάγκη.'   (130)

'But now the gold-wanded Argus-slayer has carried me off
    from the dance for Artemis of the gold shafts and hailed with
    shouting.
Many of us, young married women and maidens who bring a
    great bride price,
were dancing, and a vast crowd stood around us.   (120)
From there he carried me off, the gold-wanded Argus-slayer,
and over many worked fields of mortal men he transported me
and much ownerless and unworked land too, where
raw flesh-eating beasts roam about their shadowy lairs,
and it seemed my feet were not touching the life-giving
    earth.   (125)
And of Anchises he said that I sharing his bed would be called
the lawful wife, and would bear you splendid children.
And after he had shown the way and indicated (my future),
    he went
back to rejoin the families of the gods, the mighty Argus-slayer.
But I came to you, for a strong compulsion forced me.'   (130)

By describing herself participating in a dance for Artemis, Aphrodite
underscores her virginity and nuptibility[29] and explains her splendid
outfit; by referring to a vast admiring crowd and great bride price, she
increases her desirability (cf. Nausikaa at *Od.* 6.279). Introducing
Hermes explains how she could travel so quickly from Phrygia to
the top of Mount Ida and how she knows who Anchises is, conveys

---

[29] Young women dance in honour of Artemis at all kind of cultic occasions, but
Clay 1989: 176 suggests that 'the dance in honor of Artemis by girls approaching the
age of marriage performed the function of a debut or showcase for the display of
marriageable maidens, who are generally kept in seclusion'.

the message that it is the will of the gods that she becomes Anchises' wife, and also hints at sex, since gods normally abduct women for that purpose.[30]

Lying tales typically are a blend of the true and the invented, and the narratees may note that Aphrodite's reference to the wild beasts and their shadowy lairs recalls her real voyage (cf. the verbatim repetition κατὰ σκιόεντας ἐναύλους 124b = 74b). Whereas in reality she walked across the mountain (see 66–75), here scholars are divided over the question of how Hermes transported her: were they flying high up through the air or were they skimming over the land?[31] Whichever option we choose, and the second seems more likely, we are dealing with an early example of the panoramic standpoint (cf. the repeated πολλά and πολλήν).

Although playing the role of a mortal maiden, Aphrodite shrewdly manages to grant one of Anchises' requests when she recounts how Hermes announced that she would bear Anchises' offspring. At this important point she actually intrudes upon the (indirect) quotation of Hermes' words and turns from third person ('Hermes said that I would be called the lawful wife of *Anchises*') to second person ('and would bear *you* children'). At the same time, the narratees may note the dramatic irony of her lie that the gods arranged her marriage with Anchises: Aphrodite does not know Zeus' plan to make her fall in love, as set out at 45–52, but unwittingly speaks the truth.

To speak about her marriage to Anchises in terms of a 'strong compulsion' suits her assumed persona of a young and innocent girl: it is inconceivable that she initiated this erotic adventure herself; it was forced upon her by others. Likewise, Persephone stressed her unwillingness when she was carried off by Hades (*H. Dem.* 19, 30, 72, 344, 413, 432).[32] But again dramatic irony is involved; the narratees know that there is indeed an external force at work, Zeus, and soon will be reminded of it by the narrator at 166–7. Finally, Aphrodite's remark makes clear that what we are witnessing is how love 'overcoming' people, a feature mentioned emphatically in the attributive section (ἐδάμασσατο: 3, δάμναται: 17), works in practice.

---

[30] Clay 1989: 176–7.   [31] For discussions, see Faulkner 2008: ad 122–5.
[32] Faulkner 2008: ad 129.

131–42

ἀλλά σε πρὸς Ζηνὸς γουνάζομαι ἠδὲ τοκήων
ἐσθλῶν· οὐ μὲν γάρ κε κακοὶ τοιόνδε τέκοιεν·
ἀδμήτην μ᾽ ἀγαγὼν καὶ ἀπειρήτην φιλότητος
πατρί τε σῷ δεῖξον καὶ μητέρι κεδνὰ εἰδυίῃ
σοῖς τε κασιγνήτοις οἵ τοι ὁμόθεν γεγάασιν·   (135)
οὔ σφιν ἀεικελίη νυὸς ἔσσομαι, ἀλλ᾽ εἰκυῖα.
πέμψαι δ᾽ ἄγγελον ὦκα μετὰ Φρύγας αἰολοπώλους
εἰπεῖν πατρί τ᾽ ἐμῷ καὶ μητέρι κηδομένῃ περ·
οἱ δέ κέ τοι χρυσόν τε ἅλις ἐσθῆτά θ᾽ ὑφαντήν
πέμψουσιν, σὺ δὲ πολλὰ καὶ ἀγλαὰ δέχθαι ἄποινα.   (140)
ταῦτα δὲ ποιήσας δαίνυ γάμον ἱμερόεντα
τίμιον ἀνθρώποισι καὶ ἀθανάτοισι θεοῖσιν.᾽

'But now I beseech you, by Zeus and your parents,
who must be noble, for no humble people would have produced
    such a child as you:
take me unwedded and without experience of sex with you
and show me to your father and your dutiful mother
and your brothers who are born from the same stock.   (135)
I will not be an unfitting daughter-in-law for them, but a fitting one.
And quickly send a messenger to the Phrygians of the darting steeds,
to tell my father and my anxious mother.
They will send you gold in plenty and woven clothing, too,
and you must accept the many splendid gifts.   (140)
Once you have done all that, hold a delightful marriage party,
one to be held in honour by both men and immortal gods.'

Aphrodite continues playing the role of decent and attractive maiden, referring to an official marriage and a bride-gift[33] and coyly bringing in her family. At the same time, by urging Anchises to take her with him '*un*wedded and without experience of sex', she actually hints at the opposite, the possibility of having premarital sex.[34] Her begging 'by Zeus' and her reference to a 'marriage party [...] held in honour by both men and immortal gods' are additional instances of dramatic irony: the narratees are reminded of Zeus' plan to punish Aphrodite on behalf of the other gods. Soon Aphrodite herself will come to realize that her

[33] For the remarkable ἄποινα at 140, normally meaning 'ransom', see Faulkner 2008: ad 140.
[34] Smith 1981: 53.

union with Anchises will only bring her the reproach of her fellow gods
(247–8).

143–54

ὣς εἰποῦσα θεὰ γλυκὺν ἵμερον ἔμβαλε θυμῷ.
Ἀγχίσην δ' ἔρος εἷλεν, ἔπος τ' ἔφατ' ἔκ τ' ὀνόμαζεν·
'εἰ μὲν θνητή τ' ἐσσί, γυνὴ δέ σε γείνατο μήτηρ,   (145)
Ὀτρεὺς δ' ἐστὶ πατὴρ ὀνομάκλυτος, ὡς ἀγορεύεις,
ἀθανάτου δὲ ἕκητι διακτόρου ἐνθάδ' ἱκάνεις
Ἑρμέω, ἐμὴ δ' ἄλοχος κεκλήσεαι ἤματα πάντα,
οὔ τις ἔπειτα θεῶν οὔτε θνητῶν ἀνθρώπων
ἐνθάδε με σχήσει πρὶν σῇ φιλότητι μιγῆναι   (150)
αὐτίκα νῦν, οὐδ' εἴ κεν ἐκηβόλος αὐτὸς Ἀπόλλων
τόξου ἀπ' ἀργυρέου προΐῃ βέλεα στονόεντα.
βουλοίμην κεν ἔπειτα, γύναι εἰκυῖα θεῇσι,
σῆς εὐνῆς ἐπιβὰς δῦναι δόμον Ἄϊδος εἴσω.'

By thus speaking Aphrodite cast sweet desire in his heart.
And eros seized Anchises, and he spoke and addressed her:
'If truly you are mortal and a mortal woman bore you as your
    mother,   (145)
and Otreus is your father, with famous name, as you say,
and you have come here by the will of the immortal go-between
Hermes, and you will be called my wife forever,
then no one of the gods or mortal men
is going to hold me back here from making love to you   (150)
right away, not even if far-shooting Apollo himself
should discharge baleful arrows from his silver bow.
I would be prepared in that case, woman who resembles the
    goddesses,
having once mounted your bed to go down to Hades' house.'

The narrator, capping Aphrodite's speech, shows her exercising
her power as goddess of love, casting desire into Anchises via her
words. Does Anchises believe her story? According to Smith, 'he does
not wholly believe what he has heard but is prepared nonetheless
to act as though he did'.[35] It seems most likely that Anchises remains
rationally sceptical about the alleged human nature of the woman
facing him, yet emotionally (and under the influence of the desire
which Aphrodite has just cast into him) lets himself be swayed by
her words. His caution in the first place appears from the combination

---

[35] Smith 1981: 55.

εἰ + indicative in 145–8, which, according to Rijksbaron, 'often suggests a certain scepticism on the part of the speaker'.³⁶ Anchises also repeats Aphrodite's assertions with juridical precision (145–6 ≈ 110–11, 148 ≈ 127), thereby passing the responsibility on to her.³⁷ Next, there is his substitution of ὡς ἀγορεύεις (146) for Aphrodite's εἴ που ἀκούεις (111): instead of acknowledging that he has heard of Otreus, as Aphrodite invited him to do, he stresses that *she claims* to be his daughter. His vocative address γύναι εἰκυῖα θεῇσι, finally, can be taken as laudatory but may also reflect his uncertainty.³⁸

Despite all his caution, however, his passion mounts in the course of the speech, and he ends with the forceful declaration that he would be prepared to die as long as he can make love to her now. This passionate declaration recalls that of Hermes, who expresses himself willing to be, like Ares, enchained and laughed at by the other gods if only he can sleep with Aphrodite (*Od.* 8.340–2; Demodocus' song of Ares and Aphrodite is another probable intertext of our hymnic poet).³⁹ Anchises' desire for a long life (104–5) is temporarily forgotten! The detail that he thinks of death by the hands of *a god* perhaps is another hint that he is still considering the possibility that he is facing a goddess: gods do not tend to intervene in mortal love affairs, but there are precedents for gods killing the mortal lovers of goddesses (cf. *Od.* 5.121–8).

155–67

ὣς εἰπὼν λάβε χεῖρα· φιλομμειδὴς δ' Ἀφροδίτη   (155)
ἕρπε μεταστρεφθεῖσα κατ' ὄμματα καλὰ βαλοῦσα
ἐς λέχος εὔστρωτον, ὅθι περ πάρος ἔσκεν ἄνακτι
χλαίνῃσιν μαλακῆς ἐστρωμένον· αὐτὰρ ὕπερθεν
ἄρκτων δέρματ' ἔκειτο βαρυφθόγγων τε λεόντων,
τοὺς αὐτὸς κατέπεφνεν ἐν οὔρεσιν ὑψηλοῖσιν.   (160)
οἱ δ' ἐπεὶ οὖν λεχέων εὐποιήτων ἐπέβησαν,
κόσμον μέν οἱ πρῶτον ἀπὸ χροὸς εἷλε φαεινόν,
πόρπας τε γναμπτάς θ' ἕλικας κάλυκάς τε καὶ ὅρμους.
λῦσε δέ οἱ ζώνην ἰδὲ εἵματα σιγαλόεντα
ἔκδυε καὶ κατέθηκεν ἐπὶ θρόνου ἀργυροήλου   (165)
Ἀγχίσης· ὁ δ' ἔπειτα θεῶν ἰότητι καὶ αἴσῃ
ἀθανάτῃ παρέλεκτο θεᾷ βροτός, οὐ σάφα εἰδώς.

³⁶ Rijksbaron 1984: 69, n. 1.
³⁷ Cf. Priam at *Il.* 24.406–7, who does the same with the words of 'the Myrmidon'/ Hermes.
³⁸ Smith 1981: 57.   ³⁹ See Walcot 1991.

Having thus spoken he took her hand. And smile-loving Aphrodite (155)
went turning away her face and casting down her beautiful eyes
to the well-laid bed, where, as always, it was ready for its owner
spread with soft blankets. On top of them
lay skins of bears and deep-roaring lions,
which he himself had slain in the high mountains.   (160)
And after they had mounted the well-wrought bed,
he first took off from her body the shining adornment,
the brooches, twisting bracelets, necklaces and ear-rings.
He loosed her girdle and removed her gleaming clothes
and laid them on a silver-studded chair,   (165)
Anchises. He then by the will of the gods and destiny
lay with the immortal goddess, himself mortal, not knowing for sure.

Aphrodite continues to play the role of bashful maiden, casting down
her eyes, while Anchises is shown in command, leading her to the bed
and undressing her. His bed-covers have a characterizing and symbolic function: they mark Anchises as strong (a hunter of wild beasts)
and, as Faulkner noted, underline Aphrodite's 'loss of power in the
face of Anchises' momentary strength; she is now conquered on top
of the very beasts she earlier controlled'.[40] Likewise, the detailed
description of the removal of the jewellery and clothes which she
had so painstakingly put on in her temple on Paphos—a retardation
with zooming effect—signals that the goddess is now naked and
devoid of her divine power, just a woman in love. Soon she will put
on her clothes again and regain her divine power, and then it will be
Aeneas' turn to avert his eyes (see *180–90*).

The actual consummation is described very briefly (166–7), in
comparison to the long preparation for it and even longer evaluation
of it afterwards. This temporal rhythm suggests that this event, after
all, is not the main point of the story. Indeed, rather than scenically
giving details of the love-making, the narrator, having reached the
middle of his narrative, presents a summary of what it is about: a
mortal lies with an immortal through the will of the gods. A similar
kind of summary is found in the middle of the *Odyssey*, where it is
said that the ship of the Phaeacians carried home 'a man, having
godlike plans, who before had suffered many sorrows, experiencing
wars against men and sorrowful waves' (13.89–92). The final οὐ σάφα

---

[40] Faulkner 2008: ad 158–60; cf. also Smith 1981: 59.

εἰδώς confirms that Anchises is not certain about the status of the woman with whom he is sleeping (see *143–54*).[41]

168–79

ἦμος δ᾽ ἂψ εἰς αὖλιν ἀποκλίνουσι νομῆες
βοῦς τε καὶ ἴφια μῆλα νομῶν ἐξ ἀνθεμοέντων,
τῆμος ἄρ᾽ Ἀγχίσῃ μὲν ἐπὶ γλυκὺν ὕπνον ἔχευε   (170)
νήδυμον, αὐτὴ δὲ χροῒ ἕννυτο εἵματα καλά.
ἑσσαμένη δ᾽ εὖ πάντα περὶ χροῒ δῖα θεάων
ἔστη ἄρα κλισίῃ, εὐποιήτοιο μελάθρου
κῦρε κάρη, κάλλος δὲ παρειάων ἀπέλαμπεν
ἄμβροτον, οἷόν τ᾽ ἐστὶν ἐϋστεφάνου Κυθερείης.   (175)
ἐξ ὕπνου τ᾽ ἀνέγειρεν, ἔπος τ᾽ ἔφατ᾽ ἔκ τ᾽ ὀνόμαζεν·
'ὄρσεο, Δαρδανίδη· τί νυ νήγρετον ὕπνον ἰαύεις;
καὶ φράσαι εἴ τοι ὁμοίη ἐγὼν ἰνδάλλομαι εἶναι
οἵην δή με τὸ πρῶτον ἐν ὀφθαλμοῖσι νόησας.'

At the time when herdsmen drive back to the steading
their cattle and fat sheep from the flowery pastures,
then she shed sweet sleep over Anchises,   (170)
pleasant, and herself put on her fine garments.
Having dressed herself well all around her body, bright goddess,
she stood in the steading, and her head touched
the well-fashioned roof, and from her cheeks shone beauty,
divine, such as belongs to fair-crowned Cytherea.   (175)
She roused him from his sleep and spoke and addressed him:
'Get up, descendant of Dardanus—Why do you slumber in
     unbroken sleep?—
and observe whether I seem to you to be the same
as when you first set eyes on me.'

The temporal marker 'at the time when herdsmen . . . ', though phrased omnitemporally (in the present tense), suggests the return of Anchises' fellow herdsmen and hence signals to Aphrodite that the time for her to disappear has come.[42] Aphrodite sheds sleep over Anchises, an action which only gods can perform (cf. e.g. *Od.* 5.491–2), and puts on her clothes again, and both actions show her resuming her divine identity. Her radiance and supernatural stature indicate an epiphany,[43] such as is common at the end of a 'god meets mortal' scene. But it is

[41] For discussion of σάφα εἰδώς, see Faulkner 2008: ad 167.
[42] Smith 1981: 61.
[43] For radiance, see n. 19; for supernatural stature, see e.g. *H. Dem.* 188–9.

focalized by the external primary narrator, not by Anchises, who is asleep.[44] His moment of recognition is postponed. When she has finished dressing, Aphrodite wakes up Anchises with a speech.

Her speech resembles a 'dream' speech, and this again betrays Aphrodite's resumed divine status, since dreams in epic typically take the form of gods talking to mortals in their sleep. Her chiding question 'Why do you sleep?' is typical of dreams (cf. *Il.* 2.23; 23.69; 24.683–4; *Od.* 4.804), but is all the more unfair since she herself put Anchises to sleep. Rather than revealing her true identity herself, she is set on Anchises recognizing her.

> *180–90*
> ὣς φάθ'· ὁ δ' ἐξ ὕπνοιο μάλ' ἐμμαπέως ὑπάκουσεν.   (180)
> ὡς δὲ ἴδεν δειρήν τε καὶ ὄμματα κάλ' Ἀφροδίτης
> τάρβησέν τε καὶ ὄσσε παρακλιδὸν ἔτραπεν ἄλλῃ.
> ἂψ δ' αὖτις χλαίνῃ τε καλύψατο καλὰ πρόσωπα,
> καί μιν λισσόμενος ἔπεα πτερόεντα προσηύδα·
> 'αὐτίκα σ' ὡς τὰ πρῶτα, θεά, ἴδον ὀφθαλμοῖσιν   (185)
> ἔγνων ὡς θεὸς ἦσθα· σὺ δ' οὐ νημερτὲς ἔειπες.
> ἀλλά σε πρὸς Ζηνὸς γουνάζομαι αἰγιόχοιο,
> μή με ζῶντ' ἀμενηνὸν ἐν ἀνθρώποισιν ἐάσῃς
> ναίειν, ἀλλ' ἐλέαιρ'· ἐπεὶ οὐ βιοθάλμιος ἀνὴρ
> γίγνεται ὅς τε θεαῖς εὐνάζεται ἀθανάτῃσιν.'   (190)

So she spoke, and woken from his sleep he heard her at once.   (180)
And when he saw the neck and beautiful eyes of Aphrodite,
he was afraid and averted his eyes.
And he covered his handsome face back again in his blanket,
and begging her spoke winged words:
'At once when I first saw you, goddess, with my eyes,   (185)
I knew you were a god; but you did not speak the truth.
But now I beseech you by Zeus holding the aegis:
do not leave me to dwell among men as an enfeebled
creature, but have pity. For a man loses his procreative forces,
who goes to bed with immortal goddesses.'   (190)

Anchises' reaction to Aphrodite's epiphany takes the form of embedded focalization (181), followed by speech (185–90). He seems to recognize the goddess before him mainly on account of her eyes, just as Achilles recognizes Athena because of her δεινὼ ... ὄσσε, 'fearful

---

[44] Faulkner 2008: ad 168–83.

eyes' (*Il.* 1.199–200), and Helen Aphrodite on account of her ὄμματα μαρμαίροντα, 'sparkling eyes' (*Il.* 3.396–7). His reaction, typically, is fear.[45] It is not certain that even now Anchises knows which goddess he is facing. The name 'Aphrodite' in 181 may very well derive from the primary narrator-focalizer, intruding upon Anchises' focalization (an instance of paralepsis);[46] in his ensuing speech Anchises will refer to her as θεά and θεός, and Aphrodite will mention her name only at 287.

In his speech he gives expression to his fear and puts the respon-sibility for what has just happened, a mortal sleeping with a goddess, with the goddess. His internal analepsis is correct (he *had* recognized the goddess at first and she *had* countered this by a lying tale), but he seems to have a selective memory (he leaves out his bravado acceptance of death if only he can go to bed with her). He ends with a supplication to save him, which, matching the earlier supplica-tion of 'the girl'/Aphrodite (131–42), shows how the roles have been reversed. He repeats his own earlier prayer: his plea not to be left an enfeebled creature and to keep his procreative powers equates with his earlier request for a long life and offspring (104–6). Now that he knows that he has certainly slept with a goddess, which is a dangerous activity for mortals (cf. Odysseus asking Circe to swear that having sex with her will not harm him: *Od.* 10.299–301, 341), his request has a more urgent undertone.[47] This is the last time Anchises speaks in the story.

The goddess Aphrodite, of course, has the last word (191–290). She starts by reassuring Anchises: he will not suffer any harm from her or any of the other gods, since he is dear to the gods, and he will get the offspring he had hoped for. The name of the child and accompanying etymology, however, give a first indication that, in contrast to Anchises, who gets everything he asked for, the outcome of their affair is less positive for her: 'his name shall be Aeneas, because a terrible (αἰνόν) sorrow took me, since I fell into a mortal man's bed' (198–9).

She backs up her claim that Anchises and the family he belongs to are 'dear to the gods' (195, 200–1) by telling two embedded narratives which recount erotic encounters between gods and members of his family: Ganymedes, who was carried off by Zeus to Olympus (202–17), and Tithonus, who was carried off by Eos to her palace at the end of the

---

[45] See n. 15.   [46] Cf. e.g. *Il.* 3.191–2, and see de Jong [1987] 2004: 104–5.
[47] See Faulkner 2008: ad 184–90 and 188–90.

earth (*218–38*). The first narrative ends on a positive note (Ganymedes is made 'immortal and ageless', and his father is glad when he is informed about his son's well-being and compensated in the form of speedy horses), but the second strikes a different chord.[48]

218–38

῾ὣς δ᾽ αὖ Τιθωνὸν χρυσόθρονος ἥρπασεν Ἠώς
ὑμετέρης γενεῆς ἐπιείκελον ἀθανάτοισι.
βῆ δ᾽ ἴμεν αἰτήσουσα κελαινεφέα Κρονίωνα   (220)
ἀθάνατόν τ᾽ εἶναι καὶ ζώειν ἤματα πάντα·
τῇ δὲ Ζεὺς ἐπένευσε καὶ ἐκρήηνεν ἐέλδωρ.
νηπίη, οὐδ᾽ ἐνόησε μετὰ φρεσὶ πότνια Ἠώς
ἥβην αἰτῆσαι, ξῦσαί τ᾽ ἄπο γῆρας ὀλοιόν.
τὸν δ᾽ ἤτοι εἵως μὲν ἔχεν πολυήρατος ἥβη,   (225)
Ἠοῖ τερπόμενος χρυσοθρόνῳ ἠριγενείῃ
ναῖε παρ᾽ Ὠκεανοῖο ῥοῆς ἐπὶ πείρασι γαίης·
αὐτὰρ ἐπεὶ πρῶται πολιαὶ κατέχυντο ἔθειραι
καλῆς ἐκ κεφαλῆς εὐηγενέος τε γενείου,
τοῦ δ᾽ ἤτοι εὐνῆς μὲν ἀπείχετο πότνια Ἠώς,   (230)
αὐτὸν δ᾽ αὖτ᾽ ἀτίταλλεν ἐνὶ μεγάροισιν ἔχουσα
σίτῳ τ᾽ ἀμβροσίῃ τε καὶ εἵματα καλὰ διδοῦσα.
ἀλλ᾽ ὅτε δὴ πάμπαν στυγερὸν κατὰ γῆρας ἔπειγεν
οὐδέ τι κινῆσαι μελέων δύνατ᾽ οὐδ᾽ ἀναεῖραι,
ἥδε δέ οἱ κατὰ θυμὸν ἀρίστη φαίνετο βουλή·   (235)
ἐν θαλάμῳ κατέθηκε, θύρας δ᾽ ἐπέθηκε φαεινάς.
τοῦ δ᾽ ἤτοι φωνὴ ῥεῖ ἄσπετος, οὐδέ τι κῖκυς
ἔσθ᾽ οἵη πάρος ἔσκεν ἐνὶ γναμπτοῖσι μέλεσσιν.᾽

'In the same way Tithonus was seized by golden-throned Eos,
a man of your family and like the immortals.
She went to ask the dark-clouded son of Cronus   (220)
that he be immortal and live forever.
And Zeus nodded his assent and fulfilled her wish.
Foolish woman, for mighty Eos did not think of asking
youth for him, and the stripping away of baneful old age.
So long as lovely youth possessed him,   (225)
taking his delight in golden-throned and early born Eos,
he lived by Ocean's streams at the end of the earth.
But when the first grey hairs came to show down
from his handsome head and noble chin,

---

[48] Smith 1981: 73–4 already detects negative notes in the first story. Walcot 1991: 48–50 sees the second story as a corrective of the first.

mighty Eos stopped going to bed with him, (230)
but she kept him in her palace and tended
him with bread and ambrosia and gave him fine clothing.
But, once hateful old age pressed fully upon him,
and he could not move or lift any of his limbs,
this seemed to her the best thing to do: (235)
she put him away in a bedroom and closed its shining doors.
His voice flows unendlessly, but there is none of the strength
that there used to be in his pliant limbs.'

Aphrodite, an external secondary narrator, uses an effective rhythm: she starts her narrative scenically (the moment of Tithonus' abduction and Eos' requesting Zeus for his immortality), turns to a summary (the period of their happy relationship), uses a scene again (to recount in full detail the appearance of the first grey hairs), turns to a summary (for Eos' reaction), uses another scene (for the arrival of old age), and ends with a summary (which makes clear the perpetual status of poor Tithonus). Her focalization appears from a comment like 'foolish woman' and the repeated qualification of old age as 'baneful' and 'hateful'. Her narrative strategies serve to make clear the crucial difference between Ganymedes and Tithonus: the first is immortal and ageless, and his father was glad about his son's status; the second is immortal but not ageless, and he becomes a burden to his lover Eos. The change in tone leads up to Aphrodite's conclusion.

239-55

'οὐκ ἂν ἐγώ γε σὲ τοῖον ἐν ἀθανάτοισιν ἑλοίμην
ἀθάνατόν τ' εἶναι καὶ ζώειν ἤματα πάντα. (240)
ἀλλ' εἰ μὲν τοιοῦτος ἐὼν εἶδός τε δέμας τε
ζώοις, ἡμέτερός τε πόσις κεκλημένος εἴης,
οὐκ ἂν ἔπειτά μ' ἄχος πυκινὰς φρένας ἀμφικαλύπτοι.
νῦν δέ σε μὲν τάχα γῆρας ὁμοίιον ἀμφικαλύψει
νηλειές, τό τ' ἔπειτα παρίσταται ἀνθρώποισιν, (245)
οὐλόμενον καματηρόν, ὅ τε στυγέουσι θεοί περ.
αὐτὰρ ἐμοὶ μέγ' ὄνειδος ἐν ἀθανάτοισι θεοῖσιν
ἔσσεται ἤματα πάντα διαμπερὲς εἵνεκα σεῖο,
οἳ πρὶν ἐμοὺς ὀάρους καὶ μήτιας, αἷς ποτε πάντας
ἀθανάτους συνέμιξα καταθνητῇσι γυναιξί, (250)
τάρβεσκον· πάντας γὰρ ἐμὸν δάμνασκε νόημα.
νῦν δὲ δὴ οὐκέτι μοι στόμα χείσεται ἐξονομῆναι
τοῦτο μετ' ἀθανάτοισιν, ἐπεὶ μάλα πολλὸν ἀάσθην
σχέτλιον οὐκ ὀνομαστόν, ἀπεπλάγχθην δὲ νόοιο,
παῖδα δ' ὑπὸ ζώνῃ ἐθέμην βροτῷ εὐνηθεῖσα.' (255)

'I would not choose you to be immortal and live forever
in such a condition among the gods.   (240)
If you could go on living being such in appearance and build
   (as you are now)
and be called my husband,
in that case sorrow would not enfold my mind.
But as it is, hostile old age will soon enfold you,
grim, which attends men in times to come,   (245)
destructive and wearying, which the gods abhor.
But for me there will be reproach among the immortal gods
all days for ever on your account,
who in the past were afraid of my whisperings and wiles, by which
I used to couple all the immortals with mortal women.   (250)
For my mind overcame them all.
But now my mouth will no longer open wide to mention
this among the immortals, since I have been so thoroughly foolish,
terribly, unspeakably, and was driven out of my senses,
and have conceived a child under my girdle through going to
   bed with a mortal.'   (255)

It now turns out that Aphrodite has told the story of Eos and Tithonus
to explain her take on the events that have just occured. Her lover
Anchises is bound to become old like Tithonus, and while this is
for him a goal to pray for (cf. 106), it is a horror for Aphrodite and
all other immortals (244–6). She could have avoided Eos' mistake and
asked Zeus to make Anchises 'ageless', but she instinctively feels that
Zeus is not likely to be of service to her and she moreover seems loath
to have Anchises around her 'forever' because his presence would
'forever' remind the other gods of her misalliance.[49] (For the same
reason, she will soon give instructions to have her son raised by others.)
We see that with the resumption of her divine shape (and having
fulfilled her erotic desire!) Aphrodite also regained her divine perspective, and she now regrets her romance with a mortal, calling it a grave
mistake (253–4). And while the argument function of the embedded
narratives (see §2.6) at first consisted in reassuring Anchises and
showing him the goodwill of the gods towards his family, it gradually
changes into preparing him for the goddess' announcement that she

---

[49] Cf. Faulkner 2008: ad 239–55. According to Smith 1981: 87–8, Aphrodite not
asking Zeus for Anchises' immortality is simply illogical; Clay 1989: 190 contends that
Aphrodite knows about Zeus' plan and that she therefore *knows* she has no chance.

is *not* going to follow the pattern set out in them and will *not* take Anchises with her.⁵⁰

The affair will not only bring Aphrodite ἄχος, 'sorrow' but also ὄνειδος, 'reproach' (247). Because she made the mistake that she so often caused other gods to make (ἀπεπλάγχθην . . . νόοιο: 254 ≈ παρὲκ Ζηνὸς νόον ἤγαγε: 36), namely of falling in love with a mortal (and begetting a mortal child), she has lost face considerably. The consequence she lays out is crucial and confirms, to the narratees, that Zeus' plan (45–52) has succeeded: she will no longer (οὐκέτι: 252 ≈ μηδ᾽ . . . ποτ᾽: 47–8) pride herself (ἐξονομῆναι τοῦτο: 252–3 ≈ ἐπευξαμένη εἴπῃ: 48) amidst her fellow gods (μετ᾽ ἀθανάτοισιν: 253 ≈ μετὰ πᾶσι θεοῖσιν: 48) on her power to couple them with mortals (τοῦτο = πάντας ἀθανάτους συνέμιξα καταθνητῇσι γυναιξί: 253, 249–50 ≈ θεοὺς συνέμιξε καταθνητῇσι γυναιξί . . . θεὰς ἀνέμιξε καταθνητοῖς ἀνθρώποις: 50, 52).⁵¹

The final part of Aphrodite's speech is filled with instructions concerning their child Aeneas (256–90) and is a variant of the instructions by gods concerning their cult, which are commonly found at the end of hymnic narratives (cf. *H. Ap.* 475–85, 532–44 and *H. Dem.* 256–74, 473–82). Aeneas is the visible sign of her mistake, so he must be concealed, that is, passed off as the child of a nymph from Mount Ida. A threatening tone is typical in the context of such instructions, and that Aphrodite adopts such a tone towards the man who was her lover only some hours before shows her to have completely regained her divine status: 'But if you speak out and foolishly boast of having united in love with fair-garlanded Cytherea, Zeus will be angry and will strike you with a smoking bolt' (286–8). Her instruction to Anchises mirrors her own resolve never to boast about her power to couple mortals and gods again, which, as we saw, was Zeus' intention. Her reference to Zeus' punishment of Anchises is one last instance of dramatic irony; she *herself* has been 'punished' by Zeus.

The narrative ends at 291 with an element which in itself is typical (the return of a god after his or her meeting with a mortal: cf. Hermes

⁵⁰ Anchises had not asked for this (see Faulkner 2008: ad 188–9 and 239–55), but Aphrodite naturally is thinking about the future of her lover as she will hereafter think of that of their child.
⁵¹ Van der Ben 1986: 33 and Clay 1989: 165–6, 183, 192–3 take a further step: they assume that from now on Aphrodite will stop coupling gods and mortals altogether and that this means the end of the heroic age. For arguments contra, see Faulkner 2008: 10–18.

at 129),[52] but which in the present context underscores Aphrodite's words: she goes back to her own world and leaves her mortal lover in his. After this, the hymn itself closes with a typical concluding formula (the hymnic speaker greeting the goddess and saying farewell), which once again confirms that Aphrodite has regained her divine status.

6.4. CONCLUSION: A TRAGICOMEDY OF ERRORS

What are the narratees to make of this story? Are we dealing with a comedy (Podbielski), an 'encomium' on the Aeneads (Reinhardt),[53] an answer to the question of how Aphrodite lost her power to unite gods and mortals in love and hence how the generation of semi-divine heroes came to an end (Van der Ben and Clay),[54] or a paradigmatic tale on mortality (Smith)?

The story of the encounter between Aphrodite and Anchises can also be read as a comedy of errors, or rather, since for Aphrodite not 'all ends well', a 'tragicomedy of errors'. There are a striking number of reversals of roles. Zeus plays the role of Aphrodite. Aphrodite pretends not to be Aphrodite (τί μ' ἀθανάτῃσιν ἐΐσκεις: 109), assumes the role of a mortal maiden (παρθένῳ... ὁμοίη: 82), and is addressed by Anchises first as a goddess (ἄνασσ', ἥ τις: 92), then as a 'woman who resembles the goddesses' (γύναι εἰκυῖα θεῇσι, 153), and finally as goddess again (θεά: 185). Anchises is a mortal, yet looks like an immortal (δέμας ἀθανάτοισιν ἐοικώς: 55, θεῶν ἄπο κάλλος ἔχοντα: 77), just like other members of his family (ἀγχίθεοι... εἶδός τε φυήν τε: 200–1; ἐπιείκελον ἀθανάτοισι: 220). These similarities and dissimulations have perplexing results: Aphrodite manages to deceive Anchises, but her triumph entails her own defeat, and Zeus, her former victim, is the one who sits pretty in the end.[55]

---

[52] See de Jong 2001: ad 6.41–7. Clay 1989: 200, not realizing the typical nature of such statements, attaches too much weight to it here: 'Aphrodite's brusk departure to Olympus signals the end of an epoch in which gods and mortals shared a now vanished intimacy.'

[53] Reinhardt 1956; for arguments contra, see Faulkner 2008: 3–7.

[54] See n. 51.

[55] This is the position of de Jong 1989 and Walcot 1991.

However we label it, this hymn does what all Homeric hymns do: it illustrates the nature of the individual god hymned (as in the *H. Herm.*, the illustration taking the form of a *leçon par l'exemple*: Hermes, patron of thieves, steals Apollo's cattle; Aphrodite, goddess of love, falls in love herself), it shows the superior power of Zeus,[56] and it defines the relationship between gods and mortals.

FURTHER READING

Auerbach, E., *Mimesis: The Representation of Reality in Western Literature* (Princeton 1953; first published in German 1946).
Bergren, A.L.T., 'The Homeric Hymn to Aphrodite: Tradition and Rhetoric, Praise and Blame', *Classical Antiquity* 8, 1989, 1–41.
Booth, W.C., *The Rhetoric of Fiction* (Chicago 1983; first published 1961).
Clay, J.S., *The Politics of Olympus: Form and Meaning in the Major Homeric Hymns* (Princeton 1989).
Faulkner, A., *The Homeric Hymn to Aphrodite* (Oxford 2008).
Faulkner, A., 'Introduction: Modern Scholarship on the Homeric Hymns: Foundational Issues', in A. Faulkner (ed.), *The Homeric Hymns: Interpretative Essays* (Oxford 2011), 1–25.
Genette, G., *Narrative Discourse: An Essay in Method* (Ithaca, NY 1980; first published in French 1972).
Janko, R., *The Iliad: A Commentary: Books 13–16* (Cambridge 1992).
Jong, I.J.F. de, 'Auerbach and Homer', in J.N. Kazazis and A. Rengakos (eds), *Euphrosyne: Studies in Ancient Epic and Its Legacy in Honor of Dimitris N. Maronitis* (Stuttgart 1999), 154–64.
Jong, I.J.F. de, *Narrators and Focalizers: The Presentation of the Story in the Iliad* (London 2004; first published 1987).
Jong, I.J.F. de, 'Aristotle on the Homeric Narrator', *Classical Quarterly* 55, 2005, 616–21.
Jong, I.J.F. de, 'The Biter Bit: A Narratological Analysis of *H. Aphr.* 45–291', *Wiener Studien* 23, 1989, 13–26.
Jong, I.J.F. de, *A Narratological Commentary on the Odyssey* (Cambridge 2001).
Jong, I.J.F. de, *Narrators and Focalizers: The Presentation of the Story in the Iliad* (London 2004; first published Amsterdam 1987).
Jong, I.J.F. de, 'The Homeric Hymns', in I.J.F. de. Jong (ed.), *Space in Ancient Greek Literature*, Studies in Ancient Greek Narrative 3 (Leiden 2012), 39–53.
Köhnken, A., 'Odysseus' Scar: An Essay on Homeric Epic Narrative Technique', in L.E. Doherty (ed.), *Oxford Readings in Classical Studies: Homer's Odyssey* (Oxford 2009), 44–61 (first published in German 1976).

[56] See Clay 1989: 15, 268.

Podbielski, H., *La structure de l'Hymne homérique à Aphrodite* (Wrocław 1971).

Reinhardt, K., 'Zum homerischen Aphroditehymnus', in *Festschrift Bruno Snell zum 60: Geburtstag* (Munich 1956), 1–14.

Richardson, N., *Three Homeric Hymns: To Apollo, Hermes, and Aphrodite* (Cambridge 2010).

Rijksbaron, A., *The Syntax and Semantics of the Verb in Classical Greek: An Introduction* (Amsterdam 1984).

Segal, C., 'Tithonus and The Homeric Hymn to Aphrodite: A Comment', *Arethusa* 19, 1986, 37–47.

Smith, P.M., *Nursling of Mortality: A Study of the Homeric Hymn to Aphrodite* (Frankfurt 1981).

Van der Ben, N., '*Hymn to Aphrodite* 36–292: Notes on the Pars Epica of the Homeric Hymn to Aphrodite', *Mnemosyne* 39, 1986, 1–41.

Walcot, P., 'The Homeric Hymn to Aphrodite: A Literary Appraisal', *Greece & Rome* 38, 1991, 137–55.

7

Narratology and Historiography

Herodotus, Histories *1.34–45 (Atys and Adrastus)*

7.1. INTRODUCTION

Can narratology be applied to historiographical texts? In 1966, one of the founding fathers of narratology, Roland Barthes, wholeheartedly said 'yes': 'There are countless forms of narrative in the world [. . .] Narrative is present in myth, legend, fables, tales, short stories, epics, history, tragedy, comedy, pantomime, paintings, stained-glass windows, local news, conversation.'[1] However, he spoke briefly and only once about the theoretical side of narratology and historiography (in the paper 'The Discourse of History')[2] and never undertook a sustained narratological analysis of a historical text.

About a decade later a forceful plea for historiography as a form of fiction, that is to say as a form of discourse which uses the same literary techniques as novels, was made by Hayden White, an American philosopher of history, in a number of publications. Here is a typical example:

> What all this points to is the need to revise the distinction conventionally drawn between poetic and prose discourse in discussion of such narrative forms as historiography and to recognize that the distinction, as old as Aristotle, between history and poetry obscures as much as it illuminates about both. If there is an element of poetry in all poetry, there is an element of poetry in every historical account. This is because in our account of the historical world we are dependent [. . .] on the techniques of figurative language both for our characterization of the

<hr>

[1] Barthes 1966: 1.   [2] Barthes [1967] 1981.

objects of our narrative representations and for the strategies by which to constitute narrative accounts of the transformations of those objects in time.[3]

In his analyses of historiographical texts, he concentrates on their emplotment: historians usually present their facts in narrative form, and for this they need to decide what the beginning and end of their narrative is and above all whether it is a story of decline or progress, a moralistic or a tragic tale, and so on.

In 1991 the narratologist Gérard Genette explicitly and elaborately put the narratological approach to factual texts on the agenda.[4] He noted that, despite Barthes's claim, hardly any narratological analyses of historiographical texts had been produced. Reviewing a number of narratological categories, such as analepses and prolepses, rhythm, focalization, and the status of the narrator, he concluded that most of these narrative devices can be and indeed are used by historians too. The only differences that he could detect concern scenic rhythm, whose inclusion of speeches is taken as a sign of fictionalization in historiography, and the embedded focalization of historical figures, in which a historian must use modifiers like 'I think' or motivate his knowledge by referring to ego-documents such as letters or diaries. But in general narrative devices can cross over from factual to fictional genres and back again. Sometimes the factual or fictional status of a text can be determined only on the basis of paratextual information, such as its title.

When he claimed that there existed no detailed narratological studies of historiographical texts, Genette could not know that a study that used narratology for the analysis of three histories of the French revolution had just been published by Ann Rigney in 1990. Narratology helped her to show the different accents that the three historians placed when recounting what is, after all, the same material.

Another detailed theoretical discussion is that of narratologist Dorrit Cohn in her study *The Distinction of Fiction* of 1999. In the book, she argues that fictional texts do have certain distinctive characteristics in comparison to non-fictional texts, and she sketches out how narratology can help to identify them. In a chapter on 'The

---

[3] White 1978: 60.   [4] Genette 1991: 65–93.

Signposts of Fictionality', she notes that narratologists had been making general claims too easily until that point:

> most narratological studies, including such classics of the discipline as Roland Barthes' 'Introduction to the Structural Analysis of Narrative' and Gérard Genette's *Narrative Discourse*, don't explicitly restrict their field, and some even quite expressly announce that they intend to encompass non-fiction as well. In the absence of counter-indications of any sort, a narrative poetics of this overarching kind leads one to believe that the entire panoply of conventions, 'figures', structural types, and discursive modes that it identifies applies equally within and without fiction, even though its textual exemplifications are drawn exclusively from the novelistic canon.[5]

She next sets out to identify signposts of fictionality through a comparison of fictional and historiographical narrative and proposes 'some rudiments for a historiographic narratology'.

The first signpost concerns the well-known fabula–story–text distinction. In the case of historiography, Cohn suggests, we must add a fourth level: that of 'the more or less reliably documented evidence of past events out of which the historian fashions his story'. The existence of this level, which in principle lies outside the domain of the text, can nevertheless sometimes be gleaned in the text from what she calls the 'testimonial stratum', or places where a historian indicates the sources of his or her story. This book works with such a fourth level, the *material*, not only for historiographical texts, but for all narrative texts (see §2.7).

The second signpost concerns the category of time. Cohn agrees with Genette that the same kind of analepses and prolepses are found in historiographical texts as in fictional ones, but she nevertheless sees a difference in the ways in which they are used:

> This is not to say that historians 'play' with time in the same sense as novelists: their departures from chronology and isochrony tend to be functional, dictated by the nature of their source materials, their subject matter, and their interpretative arguments rather than by aesthetic concerns or formal experimentation.[6]

She also remarks that summary is the default rhythm in historiography, but that the scenic rhythm is dominant in most novels.

---

[5] Cohn 1999: 109.   [6] Cohn 1999: 116.

The third signpost Cohn considers is focalization. Here she is more radical than Genette: whereas the former said that embedded focalization in historiographical narrative has to be modified or at least motivated, she contends that this narrative device is simply impossible: a historian can never know what a historical character thought or felt and can only work with (other characters' or his own) inferences. She also draws attention to the fact that historiography is often concerned with collective mentalities, rather than individual minds; this would call for a new category of focalization.

The final signpost of fictionality that Cohn points out is the distinction between narrator and author: in fictional texts we must always make that distinction, even if the narrator does not refer to himself, whereas the narrator is identical to the author as mentioned on the title page in the case of a historiographical text.

We may conclude that after an initial claim of universality for narratology, some narratologists have started to argue for a distinction between fictional narratology and historiographic narratology. It remains to be seen whether this is necessary for ancient historiography too. What the Roman professor of rhetoric Quintilian has to say on this topic seems pretty much the *communis opinio* of antiquity:

> est enim [historia] proxima poetis, et quodam modo carmen solutum est, et scribitur ad narrandum, non ad probandum, totumque opus non ad actum rei pugnamque praesentem, sed ad memoriam posteritatis et ingenii famam componitur.

> For it [historiography] is very close to poetry, and it is some kind of prose poem, and it is written in order to narrate, not to prove, something, and the entire work is designed not for immediate effect or the instant necessities of battles in court, but to record events for posterity and to win glory for the author.

> (Quintilian, *Institutio oratoria* X.1.31)

Indeed, when we look at, for example, Herodotus and Thucydides, they use embedded focalization amply. Sometimes they add a modifier, but mostly they simply represent the thoughts and emotions of their historical characters. Ancient historians also freely embed the focalization of the masses, a famous example being Thucydides' description of the feelings of the Athenians when embarking on the expedition to Sicily:

καὶ ἔρως ἐνέπεσε τοῖς πᾶσιν ὁμοίως ἐκπλεῦσαι· τοῖς μὲν γὰρ πρεσβυτέροις ὡς ἢ καταστρεψομένοις ἐφ᾽ ἃ ἔπλεον ἢ οὐδὲν ἂν σφαλεῖσαν μεγάλην δύναμιν, τοῖς δ᾽ ἐν τῇ ἡλικίᾳ τῆς τε ἀπούσης πόθῳ ὄψεως καὶ θεωρίας, καὶ εὐέλπιδες ὄντες σωθήσεσθαι· ὁ δὲ πολὺς ὅμιλος καὶ στρατιώτης ἔν τε τῷ παρόντι ἀργύριον οἴσειν καὶ προσκτήσεσθαι δύναμιν ὅθεν ἀίδιον μισθοφορὰν ὑπάρξειν.

And upon all alike there fell an eager desire to sail, upon the elders, from a belief that they would either subdue the places they were sailing against, or that at any rate a great force would suffer no disaster; upon those in the flower of their age, through a longing for far-off sights and scenes, in good hopes that they would return safely. And the great multitude, the soldiers, hoped not only to get money for the present but also to enlarge the empire, which would always be an inexhaustible source of pay.

(Thucydides, *Peloponnesian War* 6.24.3)

As for scenic rhythm, which includes the quotation of speech (one of Cohn's signposts of fictionality), it is often found in ancient histories. *Amplificatio*, the elaboration of the bare facts with all kinds of circumstantial detail, was a standard technique of ancient historians.[7] Although it was clear that historians wrote the speeches themselves, as Thucydides openly said, their substance was considered to be close to the original and hence historically reliable. Regarding speeches spoken in the more distant past, as in Herodotus, it would seem that the example of Homer, amply quoting his heroic heroes, had made the presence of speeches an acceptable tool for historians.

Cohn's suggestion that the narrator is the author in historiography (as opposed to fiction) seems naïve in the case of ancient historiography: the narrators of historiographical texts, even when they give their name, as do Herodotus and Thucydides and this name happens to be the same as that of the author, nevertheless create personae. We may assume that Herodotus the author travelled, although this point is contested, but not every conversation with local inhabitants that he records needs to be historically true. Ancient historians, in fact, had a rich arsenal of devices for authoritative self-presentation at their disposal.[8]

All in all, for ancient historiography our position can be more that of Barthes, White, and Genette: ancient historians make use of the same narrative devices as their literary counterparts. The reason is not

---

[7] See Fornara 1983: 134–7.   [8] See Marincola 1997.

difficult to imagine: the first historians were heavily indebted to the Homeric epics, in terms of both content (the focus on individuals) and form (the speeches and prolepses/analepses).[9] Where the narrator of the Homeric epics could rely on the Muses, later historians had to use their own eyes, ears, and reasoning but still adopted much from the traditional epic format. Therefore, there is no need to develop a separate historiographic narratology, and narratology can help to detect how historians adapt traditional narrative devices or invent new ones to convey their view of the past.

7.2. HERODOTUS' *HISTORIES*

The *Histories* are presented by an external narrator who effortlessly recounts events taking place at very different locations, from the intimacy of the bedchamber to the expanse of the battlefield, from Sardis to Sparta, and who not only knows and reveals the outcome of events but can also read his characters' minds. To modern minds it may seem odd that a historian acts like an omniscient and omnipresent narrator, but here the Herodotean narrator is clearly indebted to the Homeric narrator. But unlike that narrator, the Herodotean narrator has no Muses to help him, and at times he admits that he does *not* know something, gives more than one motive for a character's actions, and reaches the 'borders' of his story and is unable to tell what lies outside them. This narrator is also overt and dramatized: he is present in his own text as a person who travels and talks with informants and, as a *histor*, compares and weighs stories.

The main story of the *Histories* comprises some eighty years (*c.*560–478 BC), but a much longer period (*c.*3000–431 BC) is incorporated by means of external analepses and prolepses. The principal framework of the *Histories* is furnished by Eastern history, namely the successive reigns of the kings Croesus, Cyrus, Cambyses, Darius, and Xerxes. Why an Eastern framework in the work of a Greek historian? Scholars have suggested that no adequate Greek chronology was available, whereas lists of Eastern kings were. Also, the Greek history of this period is very fragmentary. But an ideological reason may be at

---

[9] See Strasburger 1972 and Rengakos 2006.

play too. The *Histories* tell the story of the Persian wars, starting from the first contact between East and West. An important issue in ancient as in modern warfare is the question of who started the hostilities: the initiator is morally to blame. The Herodotean narrator devotes the first five chapters of his work to the debate about who was responsible for the enmity between East and West, putting forward the Lydian Croesus as his own candidate. When he then goes on to spend four books on the expansion of Eastern imperialism, his procedure arguably has an ideological significance: it marks the Persians as the aggressors. The Persians say that it was the Greeks who began the war between East and West (cf. 7.8, 9, 11), and the *Histories* may be considered one long discussion of this issue.

The narrative chosen for analysis in this chapter, the death of Croesus' son Atys at the hands of Adrastus (1.34–45), forms part of the Lydian *logos* (1.7–94), which starts with Gyges and ends with Croesus. Gyges is a servant of the Lydian King Candaules, who manages to usurp his power. When Gyges asks the Oracle of Delphi whether his kingship is rightful, the Pythia says it is but adds 'that the Heraclidae will take their revenge on Gyges' descendants in the fifth generation, an utterance of which the Lydians and their kings took no notice until it was fulfilled' (1.13.2). The fifth generation includes Croesus and the narratees thus know from the beginning that he is doomed.[10] At first he is highly successful and manages to conquer many nations and acquire a great deal of wealth. At this point he is visited by the Athenian Solon (1.29–33). Croesus asks him who is 'the most fortunate' (ὀλβιώτατος) of men, expecting Solon to point at him, since he 'was convinced that he himself was the most fortunate of men'. Solon, however, comes up with other people, and when Croesus asks him why he does not choose him, a powerful and wealthy king, Solon answers that human fortune (συμφορή) is never stable and warns him that his luck can change into disaster anytime. Croesus dismisses the Athenian and considers his advice worthless.

At this point we find the Atys and Adrastus story, which recounts the tragic death of Croesus' son Atys. After he has recovered from this blow, Croesus will attack the Persians, be defeated, and lose his wealth

---

[10] Cf. Stahl 1975: 4: 'we see his success against the background of his expected doom, and all his smart reasoning appears to us as the cleverness of the ignorant, if not worse: of the forgetful, who could know better but belong to those who do not pay attention.'

and power (but not his life). Thus, the story of the death of Atys is the first moment when this ruler's luck starts to topple and the first proof of the validity of Solon's warning. The *material* on which Herodotus bases himself is historical; it is known that the Lydian King Croesus had two sons and a daughter and that one of his sons met a violent death.[11] But, as so often, he turns a historical event into a quintessentially Greek narrative with a beginning, middle, and end, replete with dreams, speeches, and instances of dramatic irony.[12]

7.3. NARRATOLOGICAL CLOSE READING OF *HISTORIES* 1.34–45

34.1

(1) μετὰ δὲ Σόλωνα οἰχόμενον ἔλαβε ἐκ θεοῦ νέμεσις μεγάλη Κροῖσον, ὡς εἰκάσαι, ὅτι ἐνόμισε ἑωυτὸν εἶναι ἀνθρώπων ἁπάντων ὀλβιώτατον.

(1) After Solon's departure, a great vengeance from the god visited Croesus, most likely because he considered himself to be the most fortunate of all men.

The narrative begins with a summary announcement of what is to come. This is the header technique that we find throughout the history of Greek narrative[13] and that can be considered the oral counterpart of our modern-age chapter heading. After all, Herodotus' *Histories* most likely started life as a series of public lectures, and verbal signs must structure the text for its hearers (or, even after the text had been written down, function as the paratextual apparatus which was as yet largely lacking).[14] Such headers may be unobtrusive (type: 'This is how Sardes was taken'), but they can also serve to create tension and direct the interpretation of the narratees. Thus here the events to come are qualified by the narrator as 'vengeance from the god' triggered by Croesus considering himself 'the most fortunate of all men'. The

---

[11] See Asheri, Lloyd, and Corcella 2007: ad 1.34–45.

[12] For discussions of the Atys and Adrastus story, see Hellmann 1934: 58–68; Stahl 1975; Rieks 1975; Szabó 1978; Long 1987: 74–105; and Arieti 1995: 54–66. This chapter is a thoroughly revised version of de Jong 2005. The texts are that of Hude (OCT), and translations are my own.

[13] See de Jong and Nünlist 2007: index s.v. 'header' device and 'initial summary with subsequent elaboration'; for Herodotus see also Munson 2001: 24–32.

[14] See de Jong 2004.

narrator employs the word νέμεσις only here, but the concept of the divine being 'jealous' of successful mortals and having the habit of 'cutting down what is surpassing in bigness' is widespread in the *Histories*.[15] Indeed, he follows up on what Solon had said only just before to Croesus: 'the god offers prosperity to men, but then destroys them utterly and completely' (1.32.1).[16] As often where the gods are concerned, the Herodotean narrator is modest and does not simply read their minds but adds a modifier ('most likely').[17]

34.2

(2) αὐτίκα δέ οἱ εὕδοντι ἐπέστη ὄνειρος, ὅς οἱ τὴν ἀληθείην ἔφαινε τῶν μελλόντων γενέσθαι κακῶν κατὰ **τὸν παῖδα**. ἦσαν δὲ τῷ Κροίσῳ δύο παῖδες, τῶν οὕτερος μὲν διέφθαρτο, ἦν γὰρ δὴ κωφός, ὁ δὲ ἕτερος τῶν ἡλίκων μακρῷ τὰ πάντα πρῶτος· οὔνομα δέ οἱ ἦν Ἄτυς. τοῦτον δὴ ὦν τὸν Ἄτυν **σημαίνει** τῷ Κροίσῳ ὁ ὄνειρος, ὡς ἀπολέει μιν αἰχμῇ σιδηρέῃ βληθέντα.

(2) Immediately he was visited in his sleep by a dream-figure, who revealed the truth of the mishap that was to befall him regarding **his son**. For Croesus had two sons, of whom the one was handicapped, for he was deaf and dumb, but the other was by far the most outstanding of his peers in all respects. His name was Atys. Concerning that Atys, the dream **indicates** to Croesus that he will lose him after being hit by an iron spear.

The action proper begins with a dream. The detail 'immediately' looks innocent enough, but it actually serves to endorse the narrator's hypothesis that the events to follow are a case of divine vengeance: dreams in Herodotus are sent by gods, and the occurrence of a dream right after Croesus' conversation with Solon in which his prosperity had been the main topic (the aorist ἐνόμισε refers to this particular moment) reveals the hand of the gods.[18]

Dreams are a recurrent and characteristic element in Herodotus' *Histories*. In the sixteen accounts of a person having a dream, the

---

[15] See Amasis in 3.40.2 and Artabanus in 7.10.2, and Harrison 2000: 39–40.

[16] For the close relationship between the Herodotean narrator and Solon, see Stahl 1975: 7 and Shapiro 1996. As Szabó 1978: 10 notes, in the Atys and Adrastus story the Herodotean narrator makes clear for the first time 'die in der Solon-Episode formulierten Ansichten mit einem konkreten Beispiel'.

[17] Cf. Harrison 2000: 182–91. Differently Frisch 1968: 20 (through this modifier Herodotus shrinks back from definitely connecting the dream with Croesus' dangerous claim to be most fortunate).

[18] Cf. Stein 1901: ad 34 ('Αὐτίκα δέ schliesst sich an den Nebengedanken ὅτι ἐνόμισε ὀλβ. um Vergehen und Strafe in nahen Bezug zu bringen').

event can be merely mentioned (6.118) but usually is developed in a 'dream' scene, which has three stages: the dream, its interpretation by the dreamer, and its fulfilment. Herodotus may have taken the motif of the dream from Homer (who was his model in so many other respects) or from Near Eastern sources, or it may simply be considered a universal of storytelling.[19] The dream can take the form of a 'symbolic scene' (the dreamer *sees* something with a symbolic meaning) or involve a 'messenger' (the dreamer is visited by a dream-figure who *tells* him something), or be a combination of the two.[20] Like oracles, dreams are ambiguous to their recipient within the story (who more often than not interprets them wrongly) but usually also to the narratees (who are only rarely informed right away by the narrator about their true meaning).

Croesus' dream is of the 'messenger' type: he is *told* that his son will die by the spear but does not *see* how this event will take place. As a result he will misinterpret the dream and take the wrong precautionary measures. That Croesus fails to understand the true meaning of the dream is signalled by the narrator through his use of the *de conatu* imperfect ἔφαινε ('the dream tried to make clear').[21] The narratees thus know that Croesus is going to misunderstand the dream, but apart from this hint, they too are for the time being left in the dark as to what is going to happen. They can only be sure that what the dream announces will happen, since the narrator calls its message 'the truth' and uses the verb μέλλω, which indicates that Atys' death is fated.[22] Usually μέλλω is followed by either present or future infinitive. The aorist infinitive, which we find here, is rare and leaves open *when* the fated event will happen; it can take place immediately or at some point in the distant future. This adds to the suspense for the narratees, who have no indication about when the announced death will take place.

The introduction of Atys makes clear that he is Croesus' most treasured son and that his loss will affect him greatly (and hence truly be 'a great vengeance' from the god). The formulation, 'by far

[19] For dreams in antiquity, see Harris 2009; in Herodotus Frisch 1968; Lévy 1995; de Jong 2006.
[20] 'Messenger' dreams: 1.34; 2.139, 141; 5.55–6; 7.12, 14, 17–18; 'symbolic scene' dreams: 1.107, 108, 209; 3.124; 6.107, 131; 7.19; combination: 3.30.
[21] Stein 1901: *ad loc.*: 'freilich umsonst, daher das Imperfekt'; Szabó 1978: 11. Cf. προέφαινε at 1.210.1; 3.65.4, also in the context of misunderstood dreams.
[22] For fatalistic μέλλω, see Rijksbaron 2002: 103–4, n. 2.

the most outstanding in all respects of his peers', also prepares for his acts later on in the narrative: since he does not want to be seen lagging behind his peers, he adopts a course of action that will lead to his death (see *37.1–3*). Later, the narratees, knowing the fates of both Atys and the mute son, who speaks once and thereby saves his father's life (1.85.4), may see the ironic contrast between the son who can speak but whose speaking will prove fatal and the mute son who only speaks once but in a beneficiary way.[23]

34.3

(3) ὁ δὲ ἐπείτε ἐξηγέρθη καὶ ἑωυτῷ λόγον ἔδωκε, καταρρωδήσας τὸν ὄνειρον ἄγεται μὲν τῷ παιδὶ γυναῖκα, ἐωθότα δὲ στρατηγέειν μιν τῶν Λυδῶν οὐδαμῇ ἔτι ἐπὶ τοιοῦτο πρῆγμα ἐξέπεμπε, ἀκόντια δὲ καὶ δοράτια καὶ τὰ τοιαῦτα πάντα τοῖσι χρέωνται ἐς πόλεμον ἄνθρωποι, ἐκ τῶν ἀνδρεώνων ἐκκομίσας ἐς τοὺς θαλάμους συνένησε, μή τί οἱ κρεμάμενον τῷ παιδὶ ἐμπέσῃ.

(3) When he awoke and reflected, Croesus, fearing the dream, **finds** a wife for his son and, although **his son** had regularly commanded the Lydians, he no longer sent him anywhere on that kind of business, and he removed all javelins, spears, and all similar things that people use for war from the men's quarters and piled them in storerooms to prevent any of them from falling **on his son** from where it hung.

Croesus does not discuss his dream with dream experts (*oneiropoloi*), as other Eastern monarchs do (e.g. 1.107), but instead interprets it himself. The reason is that that he wants to keep the dream a secret as part of his strategy to wriggle out of the fate it predicts. His secretiveness puts the responsibility of the dream's exegesis solely with him (the man to be punished by the gods) and also allows for a renewed, fatal interpretation by the son later on in the story (see *39.1–2*).

The measures that Croesus takes to avoid the death of his son reveal that he primarily associates the spear of the dream with war: he has his son marry, forbids him to lead military expeditions, and removes all weapons 'that people use for war' from the men's quarters. However, one of the conventions of early Greek literature is that fate is inescapable once it is announced. Throughout his *Histories* Herodotus shows human beings grappling with fate as announced in dreams, oracles, prophecies, and warnings from mortal advisers.[24] They try to avoid it either by simply rejecting the warnings or by

[23] Sebeok and Brady 1979.   [24] For an overview, see Harrison 2000: 122–57.

178   *Narratology and Classics*

taking precautions. In all cases the final result is the same (the announced fate takes place all the same), but often the persons involved actively bring it about themselves through their own precautions. Thus, Croesus' precaution of his son's marriage will backfire and actually induce the fulfilment of fate (see *37.1–3*).[25]

35.1–4

(1) ἔχοντος δέ οἱ ἐν χερσὶ **τοῦ παιδὸς** τὸν γάμον **ἀπικνέεται** ἐς τὰς Σάρδις ἀνὴρ **συμφορῇ** ἐχόμενος καὶ οὐ καθαρὸς χεῖρας, ἐὼν Φρὺξ μὲν γενεῇ, γένεος δὲ τοῦ βασιληίου. παρελθὼν δὲ οὗτος ἐς τὰ Κροίσου οἰκία κατὰ νόμους τοὺς ἐπιχωρίους καθαρσίου ἐδέετο ἐπικυρῆσαι, Κροῖσος δέ μιν ἐκάθηρε. (2) ἔστι δὲ παραπλησίη ἡ κάθαρσις τοῖσι Λυδοῖσι καὶ τοῖσι Ἕλλησι. Ἐπείτε δὲ τὰ νομιζόμενα ἐποίησε ὁ Κροῖσος, ἐπυνθάνετο ὁκόθεν τε καὶ τίς εἴη, λέγων τάδε· (3) 'ὤνθρωπε, τίς τε ἐὼν καὶ κόθεν τῆς Φρυγίης ἥκων ἐπίστιός μοι ἐγένεο; τίνα τε ἀνδρῶν ἢ γυναικῶν ἐφόνευσας;' ὁ δὲ ἀμείβετο· 'ὦ βασιλεῦ, Γορδίεω μὲν τοῦ Μίδεω εἰμὶ παῖς, ὀνομάζομαι δὲ Ἄδρηστος, φονεύσας δὲ ἀδελφεὸν ἐμεωυτοῦ ἀέκων πάρειμι ἐξεληλαμένος τε ὑπὸ τοῦ πατρὸς καὶ ἐστερημένος πάντων.' (4) Κροῖσος δέ μιν ἀμείβετο τοισίδε· 'ἀνδρῶν τε φίλων τυγχάνεις ἔκγονος ἐὼν καὶ ἐλήλυθας ἐς φίλους, ἔνθα ἀμηχανήσεις χρήματος οὐδενὸς μένων ἐν ἡμετέρου. συμφορήν τε ταύτην ὡς κουφότατα φέρων κερδανέεις πλεῖστον.'

(1) While he was busy with **his** son's marriage, a man **arrives** in Sardis in the grip of **misfortune** and not clean as regards his hand, a Phrygian by birth and of royal blood. That man, having come to Croesus' home, asked if he could obtain a purification in accordance with local customs, and Croesus purified him. (2) The rite of purification is nearly the same for Lydians as it is for Greeks. After he had performed the customary rites, Croesus asked him where he came from and who he was: (3) 'O man, who are you and from where in Phrygia have you come to my hearth? Which man or woman did you kill?' And he answered: 'King, I am the son of Midas, son of Gordias, and Adrastus is my name. Having involuntarily killed my own brother I am here, after I was expelled from my house by my father and stripped of everything.' (4) Croesus answered with the following words: 'You happen to be the offspring of friends and have come to friends, where you will be lacking in nothing staying in my house and you will gain most by taking your **misfortune** as lightly as possible.'

---

[25] Arieti 1995: 57 has missed the point: he argues that Croesus marries off his son to assure himself that an heir will be born as quickly as possible.

The story continues with an event that at first does not seem connected with it: the arrival of a stranger. The narrator gives a subtle signal, however, that the event is relevant after all: the historic present ἀπικνέεται. Historic presents are an important device that narrators use to highlight decisive moments. These moments need not belong to the climax of the story only, but may also, as here, concern earlier steps leading up to that climax.[26] When we look at the Atys and Adrastus story as a whole, we see a string of historic presents that form, as it were, the backbone of the story and mark its decisive steps (34.2, 3; 35.1; 37.1; 41.1; 43.2 [bis]; 45.2; 45.3;[27] the instances are highlighted in bold).

The narrator postpones mentioning the name of the stranger, first, ominously, introducing him as 'a man in the grip of misfortune' (35.1), then announcing the question for his name in indirect speech, and finally asking for it once more in direct speech. This repetitious rhythm maximizes the emphasis on the stranger's name when it is finally disclosed. Although the narrator does not spell it out (as the Homeric narrator usually does), the name is a speaking one: Adrastus means 'No-escape' (*alpha privans* and *didrasko*). His misfortune and status as 'Mr No-escape' consist in his involuntarily killing his own brother; soon we will see him falling prey to the same mishap a second time. His is therefore a paradigmatic case of the impossibility of human beings escaping their fate, a rule that will also apply to a rich and mighty man like Croesus in the end. His exemplary status is perhaps reflected in Croesus addressing him with the generic 'man', Ὤνθρωπε.[28]

Croesus' kind advice to Adrastus to take his 'misfortune' as lightly as possible has the ring of a cliché,[29] but in the present context it has a special significance because it contains the leitmotif of this story: συμφορή.[30] The Herodotean narrator often uses the repetition of a word to indicate a central theme. In the story of Atys and Adrastus the word συμφορή occurs no less than six times (35.1, 4; 41.1; 42.1;

---

[26] See Sicking and Stork 1997; Allan 2011.
[27] Verbs of speaking are often in the present tense in Herodotus and are left out of the account here.
[28] Differently Long 1987: 81, who connects Ὤνθρωπε with the ἄνθρωποι of 1.34.3 and suggests that this form of address marks Adrastus as the possible agent of Atys' death.
[29] Cf. e.g. E. *Med.* 1018: κούφως φέρειν . . . συμφοράς.
[30] See Hellmann 1934: 58–9; Rieks 1975: 40–1; Long 1987: 79–80.

44.2; 45.1; the instances are highlighted in bold). The word is used most of the time in connection with Adrastus but once with Croesus himself, which suggests a crucial link between their fates (see §7.4). It seems characteristic of Croesus, who measures well-being in terms of material goods, that he uses a metaphor derived from financial profit: κερδανέεις, 'you will profit'.[31]

36.1–3

(1) ὁ μὲν δὴ δίαιταν εἶχε ἐν Κροίσου, ἐν δὲ τῷ αὐτῷ χρόνῳ τούτῳ ἐν τῷ Μυσίῳ Ὀλύμπῳ ὑὸς χρῆμα **γίνεται** μέγα· ὁρμώμενος δὲ οὗτος ἐκ τοῦ ὄρεος τούτου τὰ τῶν Μυσῶν ἔργα διαφθείρεσκε, πολλάκις δὲ οἱ Μυσοὶ ἐπ᾽ αὐτὸν ἐξελθόντες ποιέεσκον μὲν κακὸν οὐδέν, ἔπασχον δὲ πρὸς αὐτοῦ. (2) τέλος δὲ ἀπικόμενοι παρὰ τὸν Κροῖσον τῶν Μυσῶν ἄγγελοι ἔλεγον τάδε· 'ὦ βασιλεῦ, ὑὸς χρῆμα μέγιστον ἀνεφάνη ἡμῖν ἐν τῇ χώρῃ, ὃς τὰ ἔργα διαφθείρει.τοῦτον προθυμεόμενοι ἑλεῖν οὐ δυνάμεθα. νῦν ὦν προσδεόμεθά σεο τὸν παῖδα καὶ λογάδας νεηνίας καὶ κύνας συμπέμψαι ἡμῖν, ὡς ἄν μιν ἐξέλωμεν ἐκ τῆς χώρης.' (3) οἱ μὲν δὴ τούτων ἐδέοντο, Κροῖσος δὲ μνημονεύων τοῦ ὀνείρου τὰ ἔπεα ἔλεγέ σφι τάδε· 'παιδὸς μὲν περὶ τοῦ ἐμοῦ μὴ μνησθῆτε ἔτι· οὐ γὰρ ἂν ὑμῖν συμπέμψαιμι· **νεόγαμός** τε γάρ ἐστι καὶ ταῦτά οἱ νῦν μέλει. Λυδῶν μέντοι λογάδας καὶ τὸ κυνηγέσιον πᾶν συμπέμψω καὶ διακελεύσομαι τοῖσι ἰοῦσι εἶναι ὡς προθυμοτάτοισι συνεξελεῖν ὑμῖν τὸ θηρίον ἐκ τῆς χώρης.'

(1) So he spent his life in Croesus' house, but in that same time a huge monster of a boar **appears** on Mount Olympus in Mysia. Coming down from that mountain, he repeatedly ruined the fields of the Mysians, and the Mysians often went out after him but failed to do him any harm, but themselves were hurt. (2) At last a delegation of Mysians arrived with Croesus and said: 'King, an enormous monster of a boar has appeared in our land, which ruins our fields. Although we try hard we are not able to catch him. Now we implore you to send your son and chosen young men and dogs with us so that we can drive him away from our land.' (3) They asked for those men, but Croesus, remembering his dream, spoke the following words to them: 'Don't mention my son anymore, for I will not send him with you. For he is a **just-married** man and that is what is on his mind now. Of the Lydians, however, I will send chosen men and my whole pack of hunting dogs, and I will order those who go that they will do their utmost to drive the beast out of your land together with you.'

[31] Arieti 1995: 59.

Once again a new storyline is introduced that does at first sight not seem related to the first, the dream about Atys, or the second, the arrival of Adrastus: a boar wreaks havoc in Mysia. The narrator gives two signals, however, that the events around the Mysian boar are relevant to the story: in the first place, there is the historic present γίνεται. In the second place, the narrator leaves the Adrastus storyline with an imperfect, δίαιταν εἶχε, which indicates that it has not ended yet but will be taken up again.[32] So the narratees are given to understand that Adrastus will return and again play a role in the story.

The narrator recounts the Mysians' unsuccessful dealings with the boar, information that is repeated in a brief internal analepsis by the Mysians asking Croesus for help. Their frightened focalization becomes clear in the substitution of μέγιστον for the narrator's μέγα. Croesus' reaction brings the dream storyline and the Mysian boar storyline together: he remembers the dream (and hence makes the narratees recall it) and thus refuses to send his son to their rescue. As motive for his refusal, he refers to his son's marriage rather than the dream in an attempt to keep the dream secret.

37.1–3

(1) ταῦτα ἀμείψατο. ἀποχρεωμένων δὲ τούτοισι τῶν Μυσῶν **ἐπεσέρχεται** ὁ τοῦ Κροίσου **παῖς** ἀκηκοὼς τῶν ἐδέοντο οἱ Μυσοί. οὐ φαμένου δὲ τοῦ Κροίσου **τόν γε παῖδά** σφι συμπέμψειν λέγει πρὸς αὐτὸν ὁ **νεηνίης** τάδε· (2) 'ὦ πάτερ, τὰ κάλλιστα πρότερόν κοτε καὶ γενναιότατα ἡμῖν ἦν ἔς τε πολέμους καὶ ἐς ἄγρας φοιτέοντας εὐδοκιμέειν. νῦν δὲ ἀμφοτέρων με τούτων ἀποκληίσας ἔχεις, οὔτε τινὰ δειλίην μοι παριδὼν οὔτε ἀθυμίην. νῦν τε τέοισί με χρὴ ὄμμασι ἔς τε ἀγορὴν καὶ ἐξ ἀγορῆς φοιτέοντα φαίνεσθαι; (3) κοῖος μέν τις τοῖσι πολιήτῃσι δόξω εἶναι, κοῖος δέ τις τῇ **νεογάμῳ** γυναικί; κοίῳ δὲ ἐκείνη δόξει ἀνδρὶ συνοικέειν; ἐμὲ ὧν σὺ ἢ μέθες ἰέναι ἐπὶ τὴν θήρην, ἢ λόγῳ ἀνάπεισον ὅκως μοι ἀμείνω ἐστὶ ταῦτα οὕτω ποιεόμενα.'

(1) That was his answer. And while the Mysians accepted that, **the son** of Croesus, having heard what the Mysians asked, **steps in**. When Croesus kept on saying that he would not send **his son** with them, the **youth** says to him: (2) 'Father, in the past the most admirable and noble things for me to do were to go to war and hunt and win distinction. Now you keep me debarred from both these activities, although you can discern neither cowardice nor faint-heartedness in me. Now what impression do you think I must give when I come and go to the

---

[32] See Rijksbaron 1988.

marketplace? (3) What kind of man will I appear to be to my fellow citizens, what man to my **just-married** wife? With what kind of man will she think she is living? Therefore please let me go to the hunt, or convince me with words that it is better for me to do the things you say.'

For a brief moment everything seems to go well for Croesus, since the Mysians accept his offer of other young men. But then the son himself enters the stage, and this crucial moment is of course marked by a historic present: ἐπεσέρχεται.

When about to speak, the son is referred to as ὁ νεηνίης. So far, he has consistently been referred to as ὁ παῖς, 'the son', but here he is suddenly 'the youth'. Why? The Herodotean narrator is making effective use of the technique of 'periphrastic denomination', in which a character is referred to not by his proper name but by a circumlocution.[33] Atys so far has been referred to as 'the son' because that is his role in the story: he is the son of Croesus who is going to die young (see 34.2, 3; 35.1; 37.1; the instances are highlighted in bold). When he is now referred to as ὁ νεηνίης, this signals that he will speak as a young man: he feels he is one of 'the chosen young men' (λογάδας νεηνίας) the Mysians asked for at 36.3. At 39.1 he will once more speak as a νεηνίης, but after this scene he will be again called παῖς, which marks his role of fated son (see 43.2, 3; 45.3).[34]

One of the arguments Atys uses to persuade his father is that he does not want to disappoint his new wife. This is the moment when we see Croesus' first measure backfire: he had hoped that having his son married would make him *less* interested in fighting, but instead it makes him *more* eager. The backfiring is underlined by the narrator through the repetition of νεόγαμος, which occurs first in Croesus' answer to the Mysians (36.3), then in his son's speech (37.3).

38.1–2

(1) ἀμείβεται Κροῖσος τοῖσδε· 'ὦ παῖ, οὔτε δειλίην οὔτε ἄλλο οὐδὲν ἄχαρι παριδών τοι ποιέω ταῦτα, ἀλλά μοι ὄψις ὀνείρου ἐν τῷ ὕπνῳ ἐπιστᾶσα ἔφη σε ὀλιγοχρόνιον ἔσεσθαι, ὑπὸ γὰρ αἰχμῆς σιδηρέης ἀπολέεσθαι. (2) πρὸς ὦν τὴν ὄψιν ταύτην τόν τε γάμον τοι τοῦτον ἔσπευσα

---

[33] See de Jong 1993 for examples from Homer.

[34] Long 1987: 88–9 has noticed the same pattern in the periphrastic denomination but gives it a different interpretation: Croesus speaks of Λυδῶν . . . λογάδας instead of the λογάδας νεηνίας of the Mysians (and thus tries to exclude his son), but the use of νεηνίης 'shows the inevitability of Atys's being included in the promised hunting party'.

καὶ ἐπὶ τὰ παραλαμβανόμενα οὐκ ἀποπέμπω, φυλακὴν ἔχων, εἴ κως
δυναίμην ἐπὶ τῆς ἐμῆς σε ζόης διακλέψαι. εἰς γάρ μοι μοῦνος τυγχάνεις
ἐὼν παῖς· τὸν γὰρ δὴ ἕτερον, διεφθαρμένον τὴν ἀκοήν, οὐκ εἶναί μοι
λογίζομαι.'

(1) Croesus answers with the following words: 'Son, I do not do these
things because I notice cowardice or any other defect in you, but a
dream visiting me in my sleep said that you are to be short-lived, since
you are to die by an iron spear. (2) With an eye on that dream therefore
I was anxious to affect your marriage and I do not send you out on
the expedition undertaken, taking precautions in the hope that I will
somehow steal you (from fate) while I am alive. For you are my only
son. For the other, deaf-mute one, I do not count as being mine.'

Employing a form of answering which is already found in Homer and
which consists in first repeating in negative form one's interlocutor's
suggestions before revealing all the more emphatically what is really
the case (not A, not B, but C),[35] Croesus finally tells the others about
his dream. When we compare Croesus' rendering of his dream
(a repeating internal analepsis) with the version of the narrator at
34.2, we may note verbal repetition (ὑπὸ γὰρ αἰχμῆς σιδηρέης
ἀπολέεσθαι ≈ ὡς ἀπολέει μιν αἰχμῇ σιδηρέῃ βληθέντα) but also a
difference: the dream did not explicitly say that the son will be 'short-
lived', but Croesus adds this in order to increase the rhetorical force of
his words.[36]

Croesus also repeats what the narrator had said at 34.2: Atys is his
most important son. The repetition prepares for the impact of Atys'
death soon to follow: he is not just any son, but Croesus' 'only' son.

39.1–2
(1) ἀμείβεται ὁ νεηνίης τοισίδε· 'συγγνώμη μέν, ὦ πάτερ, τοι, ἰδόντι γε
ὄψιν τοιαύτην, περὶ ἐμὲ φυλακὴν ἔχειν· τὸ δὲ οὐ μανθάνεις, ἀλλὰ λέληθέ σε
τὸ ὄνειρον, ἐμέ τοι δίκαιόν ἐστι φράζειν. (2) φής τοι τὸ ὄνειρον ὑπὸ
αἰχμῆς σιδηρέης φάναι ἐμὲ τελευτήσειν· ὑὸς δὲ κοῖαι μέν εἰσι χεῖρες,
κοίη δὲ αἰχμὴ σιδηρέη τὴν σὺ φοβέαι; εἰ μὲν γὰρ ὑπὸ ὀδόντος τοι εἶπε
τελευτήσειν με ἢ ἄλλου τευ ὅ τι τούτῳ ἔοικε, χρῆν δή σε ποιέειν τὰ

---

[35] De Jong 2001: ad 2.42–9.
[36] Differently Szabó 1978: 11: 'wie es später aus den Worten von Kroisos hervor-
geht, wurde auch mitgeteilt, dass der Junge ὀλιγοχρόνιος sein wird'; Long 1987: 83: 'All
understand the dream and still don't understand it, and the variations in their
language from the precise words of the dream reflect their misunderstanding.'

ποιέεις· νῦν δὲ ὑπὸ αἰχμῆς. ἐπείτε ὦν οὐ πρὸς ἄνδρας ἡμῖν γίνεται ἡ
μάχη, μέθες με.'

(1) **The youth** answers as follows: 'There is ample excuse for you, having
had such a dream, to protect me. But what you do not understand and
where the dream's true meaning has escaped you I am entitled to
explain to you. (2) You say that the dream says that I will die through
an iron spear. But what hands does a boar have? And what iron
spearhead, which you fear? If you had said that I was to die through a
tusk or something else like that, you would have had to do what you do.
But now it is through a spear. Since the battle therefore is not with men,
let me go.'

The son now gives *his* interpretation of the dream: the danger it
predicts cannot be related to the hunt, since a boar cannot throw a
spear. The narratees at this stage still do not know the true meaning
of the dream, but Atys' emphatic claim that his father misunderstood the dream ('what you do not understand and where the
dream's true meaning has escaped you') strongly suggests that he
himself may be wrong. His speech also contains a revealing detail: ἡ
μάχη. It would have been more logical, if he had said 'since *the hunt*
is not against men'. By using the word 'battle' he unwittingly
anticipates the true nature of the hunt: it will be some sort of battle,
in that Adrastus kills Atys with his spear. Indeed, when the fatal
accident is later reported to Croesus, this happens in the following
words: a messenger came to Sardes and reported τήν μάχην and the
death of his son (43.3).[37]

40
ἀμείβεται Κροῖσος· 'ὦ παῖ, ἔστι τῇ με νικᾷς γνώμην ἀποφαίνων περὶ τοῦ
ἐνυπνίου· ὡς ὦν νενικημένος ὑπὸ σέο μεταγινώσκω μετίημί τέ σε ἰέναι
ἐπὶ τὴν ἄγρην.'
Croesus answers: 'Son, displaying your opinion concerning the dream
you somehow persuade me. And since I am persuaded by you, I change
my mind and I let you go to the hunt.'

The verb νικάω, 'defeat', is used regularly in Herodotus in the meta-
phorical sense of 'persuade', instead of the neutral πείθω (cf. λόγῳ
ἀνάπεισον: 37.3), but here its repeated use (νικᾷς, ὡς ὦν νενικημένος)

---

[37] Long 1987: 81–2 notes that the word is 'striking as a designation of a hunt', but
merely suggests that 'its connotations lead us to think of a confrontation with human
beings'.

has an ironic ring: Atys' victory actually will lead to his own and his father's defeat.[38]

41–42

(1) εἴπας δὲ ταῦτα ὁ Κροῖσος **μεταπέμπεται** τὸν Φρύγα Ἄδρηστον, ἀπικομένῳ δέ οἱ λέγει τάδε· 'Ἄδρηστε, ἐγώ σε **συμφορῇ** πεπληγμένον ἀχάριτι, τήν τοι οὐκ ὀνειδίζω, ἐκάθηρα καὶ οἰκίοισι ὑποδεξάμενος ἔχω παρέχων πᾶσαν δαπάνην· (2) νῦν ὦν, ὀφείλεις γὰρ ἐμεῦ προποιήσαντος χρηστὰ ἐς σὲ χρηστοῖσί με ἀμείβεσθαι, φύλακα παιδός σε τοῦ ἐμοῦ χρηίζω γενέσθαι ἐς ἄγρην ὁρμωμένου, μή τινες κατ' ὁδὸν κλῶπες κακοῦργοι ἐπὶ δηλήσι φανέωσι ὑμῖν. (3) πρὸς δὲ τούτῳ καὶ σέ τοι χρεόν ἐστι ἰέναι ἔνθα ἀπολαμπρυνέαι τοῖσι ἔργοισι· πατρώιόν τε γάρ τοί ἐστι καὶ προσέτι ῥώμη ὑπάρχει.' (42.1) ἀμείβεται ὁ Ἄδρηστος· 'ὦ βασιλεῦ, ἄλλως μὲν ἔγωγε ἂν οὐκ ἤια ἐς ἄεθλον τοιόνδε· οὔτε γὰρ **συμφορῇ** τοιῇδε κεχρημένον οἰκός ἐστι ἐς ὁμήλικας εὖ πρήσσοντας ἰέναι, οὔτε τὸ βούλεσθαι πάρα, πολλαχῇ τε ἂν ἴσχον ἐμεωυτόν. (2) νῦν δέ, ἐπείτε σὺ σπεύδεις καὶ δεῖ τοι χαρίζεσθαι (ὀφείλω γάρ σε ἀμείβεσθαι χρηστοῖσι), ποιέειν εἰμὶ ἕτοιμος ταῦτα, παῖδά τε σόν, τὸν διακελεύεαι φυλάσσειν, ἀπήμονα τοῦ φυλάσσοντος εἵνεκεν προσδόκα τοι ἀπονοστήσειν.'

(1) Having said that Croesus **sends for** the Phrygian Adrastus and upon arrival says to him: 'Adrastus, I have purified you, when you had been struck with grim **misfortune**, which I do not hold against you, and having taken you into my house I cover all your expenses. (2) Since you are obliged to repay me with favours after I have first done you favours, I now ask you to become the bodyguard of my son, who is setting out for a hunt, to prevent bandits from appearing to you and doing you harm. (3) And besides, it is fitting for you too to go where you can shine through your deeds. This belongs to your standing and you also have the strength.' (42.1) Adrastus answers: 'King, in other circumstances I would not have gone to such a contest. For it is not appropriate for someone who is in the grip of **misfortune** to converse with peers who are fortunate, nor do I want to, and there are many reasons that withhold me. (2) But as it is, since you urge me to and since I need to do you a pleasure (for I am obliged to repay you with favours), I am prepared to do that and you may expect your son, whom you urge me to protect, to return unharmed as far as his bodyguard is concerned.'

[38] Hellmann 1934: 62–3: 'der Sieg des Sohnes bedeutet seinen Tod; durch den Mund des Sohnes ist Kroisos von dem Gotte besiegt und seine Gegenmassnahme zunichte gemacht.'

Once more we see how Croesus, trying to avoid the announced fate of
his son, misunderstands the dream (he now fears that bandits might
kill his son) and takes another measure that will misfire, indeed this
time fatally: he chooses Adrastus as guardian of his son. The dialogue
in which he asks him is fraught with dramatic irony. Even if the
narratees perhaps did not yet know the story of Atys' death, they will
by now sense what is going to happen, Adrastus inadvertently killing
Croesus' son. Thus Adrastus' reference to himself with the leitmotif
συμφορή (συμφορῇ πεπληγμένον ἀχάριτι) and the repeated reference
to Adrastus owing Croesus a return of favour do not bode much
good.[39] Adrastus' reluctance to accompany Atys on his hunt underscores once more his fate of unintentionally doing harm. His solemn
promise that Croesus may expect that his son will return to him
unharmed 'as far as his bodyguard is concerned' is ominous and
almost spells out the opposite.

43.1–3

(1) τοιούτοισι ἐπείτε οὗτος ἀμείψατο Κροῖσον, ᾔσαν μετὰ ταῦτα
ἐξηρτυμένοι λογάσι τε νεηνίῃσι καὶ κυσί. ἀπικόμενοι δὲ ἐς τὸν Ὄλυμπον
τὸ ὄρος ἐζήτεον τὸ θηρίον, εὑρόντες δὲ καὶ περιστάντες αὐτὸ κύκλῳ
ἐσηκόντιζον. (2) ἔνθα δὴ ὁ ξεῖνος, οὗτος δὴ ὁ καθαρθεὶς τὸν φόνον,
καλεόμενος δὲ Ἄδρηστος, ἀκοντίζων τὸν ὗν τοῦ μὲν **ἁμαρτάνει, τυγχάνει**
δὲ **τοῦ Κροίσου παιδός**. (3) ὁ μὲν δὴ βληθεὶς τῇ αἰχμῇ ἐξέπλησε τοῦ
ὀνείρου τὴν φήμην, ἔθεε δέ τις ἀγγελέων τῷ Κροίσῳ τὸ γεγονός,
ἀπικόμενος δὲ ἐς τὰς Σάρδις τήν τε μάχην καὶ τὸν **τοῦ παιδὸς** μόρον
ἐσήμηνέ οἱ.

(1) After that man had answered Croesus in such a way, they set out
presently with the elite youngsters and dogs. Having reached Mount
Olympus they started to search for the wild animal, and having found
it they stood in a circle around it and threw their spears. (2) Then the
guest-friend, that man who had been purified of manslaughter, who
was called Adrastus, throwing his spear **misses** the boar but **hits the
son** of Croesus. (3) Hit by the spear, he fulfilled the prophecy of the
dream, but a messenger ran to report what had happened to Croesus,
and having arrived in Sardis he told him about the battle and the death
of **his son**.

[39] Stein 1901: *ad loc.*: 'aus der Rede des Krösos wiederholt erscheinen diese
Worte im Munde des Adrastos wie eine ahnungsvolle Ironie'; Hellmann 1934: 64;
Long 1987: 93.

The denouement, Adrastus inadvertently killing Atys with his hunting spear, follows quickly. As usual, the narrator explicitly signals to his narratees that this is the fulfilment of the dream.[40]

At this climactic moment the Herodotean narrator displays all the tricks of his trade: historic presents; the periphrastic denominations 'the son of Croesus' and 'the guest-friend'; an internal analepsis, which recalls Adrastus' earlier murder and the fact that he had been purified of it; and Adrastus' ominous speaking name. The theme of 'the hunt turning out war' crops up again (cf. *39.1–2*), this time in the form of an intertextual echo, in that Atys' accidental death is described in an unmistakably Homeric manner. In the *Iliad* we often hear how a warrior aims at X, misses him and hits Y instead; for example τοῦ μὲν ἅμαρτ', ὁ δὲ Λεῦκον, . . . , | βεβλήκει (4.491–2). Here Adrastus aims at the boar, misses, and hits Atys instead. The theme will recur three times more: in this section, when the messenger reports τήν . . . μάχην; at 44.2, where Croesus calls Adrastus πολεμιώτατον, 'his greatest enemy' (whereas ἐχθρός means a personal enemy, πολεμιός usually is a military enemy); and at 45.3, where Croesus buries his own son, a typical feature of wartime (cf. 87.3: 'for in peace sons bury their fathers, but in war fathers bury their sons').

44.1–2

(1) ὁ δὲ Κροῖσος τῷ θανάτῳ τοῦ παιδὸς συντεταραγμένος μᾶλλόν τι ἐδεινολογέετο ὅτι μιν ἀπέκτεινε τὸν αὐτὸς φόνου ἐκάθηρε. (2) περιημεκτέων δὲ **τῇ συμφορῇ** δεινῶς ἐκάλεε μὲν Δία καθάρσιον, μαρτυρόμενος τὰ ὑπὸ τοῦ ξείνου πεπονθὼς εἴη, ἐκάλεε δὲ ἐπίστιόν τε καὶ ἑταιρήιον, τὸν αὐτὸν τοῦτον ὀνομάζων θεόν, τὸν μὲν ἐπίστιον καλέων, διότι δὴ οἰκίοισι ὑποδεξάμενος τὸν ξεῖνον φονέα τοῦ παιδὸς ἐλάνθανε βόσκων, τὸν δὲ ἑταιρήιον, ὡς φύλακα συμπέμψας αὐτὸν εὑρήκοι πολεμιώτατον.

(1) Croesus was devastated by his son's death and was all the more indignant because the man whom he himself had purified had killed him. (2) Being terribly upset by his **misfortune**, he called on Zeus 'The Purifier' to witness what he had suffered through his guest-friend, and on Zeus 'Of the Hearth' and 'Of Friendship', 'Of the Hearth' because, having taken the guest-friend in his house, he had been unwittingly feeding the killer of his son, and 'Of Friendship' because the man he had sent as bodyguard he had found out to be his worst enemy.

---

[40] Cf. e.g. 3.64: 'When Cambyses heard the name "Smerdis" he was struck by the truth of what Prexaspes had said and saw the true meaning of the dream.'

188   *Narratology and Classics*

Croesus' reaction shows that he blames the gods, specifically Zeus, for his misfortune. The point will be made explicitly in the ensuing conversation. The leitmotif συμφορή is now used of Croesus himself.

45.1–2

(1) παρῆσαν δὲ μετὰ τοῦτο οἱ Λυδοὶ φέροντες τὸν νεκρόν, ὄπισθε δὲ εἵπετό οἱ ὁ φονεύς. στὰς δὲ οὗτος πρὸ τοῦ νεκροῦ παρεδίδου ἑωυτὸν Κροίσῳ προτείνων τὰς χεῖρας, ἐπικατασφάξαι μιν κελεύων τῷ νεκρῷ, λέγων τήν τε προτέρην ἑωυτοῦ **συμφορήν**, καὶ ὡς ἐπ᾽ ἐκείνῃ τὸν καθήραντα ἀπολωλεκὼς εἴη, οὐδέ οἱ εἴη βιώσιμον. (2) Κροῖσος δὲ τούτων ἀκούων τόν τε Ἄδρηστον **κατοικτίρει**, καίπερ ἐὼν ἐν κακῷ οἰκηίῳ τοσούτῳ, καὶ λέγει πρὸς αὐτόν· 'ἔχω, ὦ ξεῖνε, παρὰ σέο πᾶσαν τὴν δίκην, ἐπειδὴ σεωυτοῦ καταδικάζεις θάνατον. εἶς δὲ οὐ σύ μοι τοῦδε τοῦ κακοῦ αἴτιος, εἰ μὴ ὅσον ἀέκων ἐξεργάσαο, ἀλλὰ θεῶν κού τις, ὅς μοι καὶ πάλαι προεσήμαινε τὰ μέλλοντα ἔσεσθαι.'

(1) Soon afterwards the Lydians carrying the body were present, and the killer followed along behind it. He placed himself in front of the corpse, stretched out his arms, and gave himself up to Croesus, urging him to take his life near the corpse, referring to his earlier **misfortune** and how, on top of that, he had now devastated the man who purified him and there was no point in his going on living. (2) Hearing that, Croesus **pities** Adrastus and, even though he was in such a great misery himself, says to him: 'I have, guest-friend, all the compensation from you (that I want), since you pass a death sentence on yourself. But in my view you are not to blame for this disaster, insofar as you acted against your will, but one of the gods, who already some time ago showed me in advance what was fated to be.'

Adrastus and Croesus together evaluate what has happened. Adrastus is significantly referred to in the form of a periphrastic denomination, ὁ φονεύς, which recalls his earlier mishap (cf. ἐφόνευσας, φονεύσας: 35.1, 3) and thereby prepares for the speech in which he himself will refer to that event.[41] In his self-incrimination Adrastus perhaps exaggerates when he says that he has 'devastated' Croesus, but in a sense he hits the nail on the head, in that the death of Atys not only means great grief for Croesus, but also is the first step in the dismantling of his good fortune: he no longer is εὔπαις (one of Solon's criteria for being fortunate: 1.32.6). Croesus, however, exonerates him and blames the gods for his misfortune. The echo προεσήμαινε τὰ μέλλοντα ἔσεσθαι ≈ ἔφαινε τῶν μελλόντων γενέσθαι κακῶν (34.2)

---

[41] Long 1987: 98.

makes clear that he is thinking back to his dream.[42] His substitution of a future infinitive for an aorist one after the verb μέλλω marks that by now it is clear that announcement and fulfilment followed quickly upon each other. Croesus is right, of course, to connect his misfortune with the gods, but wrong to blame them. He does not yet understand that he himself is to blame, that, as the narrator set out at the beginning, it was his own claim to be the most fortunate of all men that brought about divine wrath. At this stage he does what all mortals do, according to Zeus in the *Odyssey* (1.32–4): he blames the gods for what in fact is his own mistake. Indeed, Croesus' words echo those of the Homeric Agamemnon: Εἷς ... οὐ σύ μοι τοῦδε τοῦ κακοῦ αἴτιος ... ἀλλὰ θεῶν κού τις ≈ ἐγώ ... οὐκ αἴτιός εἰμι, | ἀλλὰ Ζεὺς καὶ Μοῖρα καὶ ἠεροφοῖτις Ἐρινύς, 'I am not to blame, but Zeus, Moira, and Erinys, who walks in darkness' (*Il.* 19.86–7).[43] Croesus' moment of understanding of his own role will only come much later (see §7.4).

45.3

(3) Κροῖσος μέν νυν ἔθαψε, ὡς οἰκὸς ἦν, τὸν ἑωυτοῦ **παῖδα**· Ἄδρηστος δὲ ὁ Γορδίεω τοῦ Μίδεω, οὗτος δὴ ὁ φονεὺς μὲν τοῦ ἑωυτοῦ ἀδελφεοῦ γενόμενος, φονεὺς δὲ τοῦ καθήραντος, ἐπείτε ἡσυχίη τῶν ἀνθρώπων ἐγένετο περὶ τὸ σῆμα, συγγινωσκόμενος ἀνθρώπων εἶναι τῶν αὐτὸς ᾔδεε **βαρυσυμφορώτατος**, **ἐπικατασφάζει** τῷ τύμβῳ ἑωυτόν.

(3) And Croesus buried his own **son** in a fitting manner. But Adrastus, the son of Gordias who was the son of Midas, that man who had become the killer of his own brother, and the killer of the one who had purified him, after it had become quiet around the tomb, realizing that he was the one who had to bear **the heaviest burden of misfortune** of all people he knew, **takes his own life** on the tomb.

The story ends with a highly dramatic analepsis, which recalls the two misfortunes in Adrastus' life that just before (45.1) he had referred to himself: his killing of his brother and ruining of his host (by killing his son).[44] Scholars have been bothered by the formulation 'killer of the one who had purified him', since Adrastus has not killed Croesus.

---

[42] The echo was missed by Asheri, Lloyd, and Corcella 2007: ad 45.1: 'these words seem like an allusion to Solon's speech on the instability of fortune. But Croesus here refers to "some god", not to Solon'.

[43] And cf. *Il.* 3.164; *Od.* 1.347–9.

[44] Gould 1989: 55 finds the passage 'reminiscent of the "obituary" of dead warriors in the *Iliad*', which might be a last hint of the 'hunt turning out war' theme.

Some have wanted to insert '*the son of* the one who had purified him'. But the phrase can be well explained as an intensification of Adrastus' earlier ὡς . . τὸν καθήραντα ἀπολωλεκώς εἴη, 'how he had devastated the man who purified him' (45.1).[45]

The final sentence also contains the last instance of the συμφορή leitmotif: βαρυσυμφορώτατος recalls Croesus' earlier advice to Adrastus to 'bear his misfortune as lightly as possible' (συμφορὴν ... ὡς κουφότατα φέρων: 35.4) and underscores how unsuccessful Adrastus has been in following it up. It also forms a contrastive echo of the superlative that started off the story, when Croesus considered himself 'the most fortunate of men' (ὀλβιώτατον). As often in Greek narrative, ring-composition effects closure.

7.4. CONCLUSION: HERODOTUS A TRAGIC HISTORIAN

This story illustrates, for the narratees, three important Herodotean facts of life: a mortal cannot escape fate (Adrastus, Atys, Croesus); a mortal's good fortune is never stable (Adrastus, Croesus); and too much good fortune may attract the gods' envy and hence lead to disaster (Croesus).

At the same time—and this is as important to Herodotus—it shows how mortals often fail to realize these very facts. Thus, both Croesus and Atys try to escape fate, Croesus by taking precautions that misfire and Atys by interpreting the dream in such a way that it allows him to go out on the hunt. Only Adrastus, after twice being the involuntary executioner of fate and realizing that he has to bear the heaviest burden of misfortune, takes no more chances and puts an end to his life.

When Croesus considered the unhappy life of Adrastus (who, like himself, is of royal lineage), he should have seen the truth of Solon's dictum that (even) a (rich) man's fortune is never stable. But although he loses his son and is thus confronted with misfortune for the first time in his life, he does not conclude that his good fortune has come to an end or that it was his own claim of being most fortunate which induced the gods to come into action against him. Rather, he blames

---

[45] Thus Stein 1901: *ad loc.*

the gods: *Εἷς . . . οὐ σύ μοι τοῦδε τοῦ κακοῦ αἴτιος . . . ἀλλὰ θεῶν κού τις,* 'in my view you are not to blame for this disaster . . . but one of the gods' (45.2). Only much later, when he has lost not only his son but also his empire, wealth, and freedom, will he come to see the truth. First, he will admit that Solon had been right to consider wealth no guarantee for enduring prosperity (86.5), but he will still blame the gods for the loss of his empire, since their oracles had seemingly encouraged him to wage war against the Persians: *αἴτιος . . . τούτων ἐγένετο ὁ Ἑλλήνων θεός,* 'the god of the Greeks was to blame for this' (87.3). Then, when the Pythia has explained the true nature of the oracles and criticized him for not thinking harder about them, he will finally realize *ἑωυτοῦ εἶναι τὴν ἁμαρτάδα καὶ οὐ τοῦ θεοῦ,* 'that the mistake was his and not that of the god' (91.6).[46]

What is the intended effect of Herodotus' way of telling his story? Is the pattern fatalistic, moralistic, or tragic? The narratees know from the beginning that Croesus is doomed: he has to pay for the deeds of his forefather Gyges (13.2; 91.1). But Herodotus' story is not a fatalistic one, since we see Croesus himself act and make decisions. Although some of his acts are dangerous (calling himself most fortunate) or mistaken (attacking the Persians), they are not morally wrong per se, and quite a few are even good (his treatment of Adrastus, his respect for and enriching of Delphi). His downfall therefore is not simply the result of culpable behaviour, and this makes it difficult to call Herodotus a moralist. Now, one could argue that mortals who receive warnings from dreams, oracles, and wise advisers about their (fatal) plans but pursue them all the same are morally to blame. But this thesis is qualified by the circumstance that most of these warnings are vague, ambiguous, and sometimes even misleading. As a result, characters often react to such warnings with actions that themselves bring about the very fate they had been warned about! This mortal blindness suggests that Herodotus' world-view is primarily a tragic one.[47] This is confirmed by Croesus calling

[46] For Croesus' (partial) learning through suffering, see Stahl 1975.

[47] Thus e.g. in connection with this story Immerwahr 1966: 70–1; Frisch 1968: 20; Stahl 1975: esp. 6–7; Rieks 1975 (who literally thinks that Herodotus' model was a lost tragic trilogy on Gyges and Croesus); Szabó 1978: 10; and Lévy 1995: 26. Arieti 1995: 56 has missed the function of the dream: 'If it is fated that Atys will die, what value for Croesus is there in the dream? The dream stirs the natural response to try to save his son, but if death is certain, all actions in his behalf will be in vain. Thus the dream is superfluous.'

his own act of attacking the Persians a ἁμαρτάδα (91.6), the quintessential word for tragic errors committed by mortals as a result of their limited understanding.[48] In the case of Atys, his death was fated ever since the dream, but it is Croesus' own measures that bring about the particular form his death takes: during a hunt and as a result of a banal error rather than gloriously on the battlefield like Tellus (according to Solon, the most fortunate man on earth).[49] Likewise, it was fated that Croesus would lose his power, but he himself actively brings this about by over-optimistically deciding to attack the Persians and letting himself be elated by ambiguous oracles. It is this complex interweaving of the divine and the mortal that makes the Herodotean world go round.

FURTHER READING

Narratology and historiography

Barthes, R., 'Introduction à l'analyse structurale des récits', *Communications* 8, 1966, 1–27 (republished as 'Introduction to the Structural Analysis of Narratives' in *Image–Music–Text*, trans. S. Heath (New York 1977), 79–124).

Barthes, R., 'Le discours de l'histoire', *Social Science Information* 63, 1967, 65–75 (republished as 'The Discourse of History', trans. S. Bann, *Comparative Criticism* 3, 1981, 7–20).

Cohn, D., *The Distinction of Fiction* (Baltimore 1999).

Genette, G., *Fiction et diction* (Paris 1991).

Jaeger, S., 'Erzähltheorie und Geschichtswissenschaft', in A. Nünning and V. Nünning (eds), *Erzähltheorie transgenerisch, intermedial, interdisziplinär* (Trier 2002), 237–63.

Kellner, H., *Language and Historical Representation: Getting the Story Crooked* (Madison, WI 1989).

Rigney, A., *The Rhetoric of Historical Representation: Three Narrative Histories of the French Revolution* (Cambridge 1990).

White, H., 'The Historical Text as Literary Artifact', in R.H. Canary and H. Kozicki (eds), *The Writing of History: Literary Form and Historical Understanding* (Madison, WI 1978), 41–62.

White, H., *The Content of the Form: Narrative Discourse and Historical Representation* (Baltimore 1987).

---

[48] See Saïd 1978.   [49] Cf. Stahl 1975: 8; Szabó 1978: 12.

Narratology and classical historiography

Baragwanath, E., *Motivation and Narrative in Herodotus* (Oxford 2008).

Dewald, C., 'The Figured Stage: Focalizing the Initial Narratives of Herodotus and Thucydides', in T.M. Falkner, N. Felson, and D. Konstan (eds), *Contextualizing Classics: Ideology, Performance, Dialogue: Essays in Honor of J. Peradotto* (Lanham 1999), 221–52.

Fornara, C.W., *The Nature of History in Ancient Greece and Rome* (Berkeley, Los Angeles, and London 1983).

Görler, W., 'Die Veränderung des Erzählerstandpunktes in Caesars *Bellum Gallicum*', *Poetica* 8, 1976, 95–119.

Grethlein, J., 'The Unthucydidean Voice of Sallust', *Transactions of the American Philological Association* 136, 2006, 299–327.

Grethlein, J., 'Philosophical and Structuralist Narratologies—Worlds Apart?', in J. Grethlein and A. Rengakos (eds), *Narratology and Interpretation: The Content of Narrative Form in Ancient Literature* (Berlin 2009), 153–74.

Grethlein, J., *The Greeks and Their Past: Poetry, Oratory and History in the Fifth Century BCE* (Cambridge and New York 2010).

Grillo, L., '*Scribam ipse de me*: The Personality of the Narrator in Caesar's *Bellum Civile*', *American Journal of Philology* 132, 2011, 243–71.

Hornblower, S., 'Narratology and Narrative Techniques in Thucydides', in S. Hornblower (ed.), *Greek Historiography* (Oxford 1994), 131–66.

Jong, I.J.F. de, 'The Anachronical Structure of Herodotus' *Histories*', in S.J. Harrison (ed.), *Texts, Ideas, and the Classics* (Oxford 2001), 93–116.

Jong, I.J.F. de, 'Narrative Unity and Units', in E.J. Bakker, I.J.F. de Jong, and H. van Wees (eds), *Brill's Companion to Herodotus* (Leiden 2002), 245–66.

Jong, I.J.F. de, 'The Helen *Logos* and Herodotus' Fingerprint', in M.P. de Bakker and E. Baragwanath (eds), *Myth, Truth, and Narrative in Herodotus* (Oxford 2012), 127–42.

Kraus, C.S., 'Caesar's Account of the Battle of Massilia (*BC* 1.34–2.22): Some Historiographical and Narratological Approaches', in J. Marincola (ed.), *A Companion to Greek and Roman Historiography* (Malden 2007), 371–8.

Marincola, J., *Authority and Tradition in Ancient Historiography* (Cambridge 1997).

Munson, R.V., *Telling Wonders: Ethnographic and Political Discourse in the Work of Herodotus* (Ann Arbor 2001).

Pausch, D., *Livius und der Leser: Narrative Strukturen in ab urbe condita* (Munich 2011).

Pelling, C.B.R., 'Seeing through Caesar's Eyes: Focalisation and Interpretation', in J. Grethlein and A. Rengakos (eds), *Narratology and Interpretation: The Content of Narrative Form in Ancient Literature* (Berlin 2009), 507–26.

Rengakos, A., 'Homer and the Historians: The Influence of Epic Narrative Technique on Herodotus and Thucydides', in F. Montanari and A. Rengakos (eds), *La poésie épique grecque: métamorphoses d'un genre littéraire* (Geneva 2006), 183–209.

Rood, T., *Thucydides: Narrative and Explanation* (Oxford 1998).

Strasburger, H., *Homer und die Geschichtsschreibung* (Heidelberg 1972).

Herodotus, *Histories* I. 34–45

Allan, R., 'The Historical Present in Thucydides: Capturing the Case of αἱρεῖ and λαμβάνει', in J. Lallot et al. (eds), *The Historical Present in Thucydides: Semantics and Narrative Functions* (Leiden 2011), 37–63.

Arieti, J.A., *Discourses on the First Book of Herodotus* (Lanham and London 1995).

Asheri, D., A. Lloyd, and A. Corcella, *A Commentary on Herodotus: Books I–IV* (Oxford 2007).

Frisch, P., *Die Träume bei Herodot* (Meisenheim am Glan 1968).

Gould, J., *Herodotus* (London 1989).

Harris, W.V., *Dreams and Experience in Classical Antiquity* (Cambridge, MA and London 2009).

Harrison, T., *Divinity and History: The Religion of Herodotus* (Oxford 2000).

Hellmann, F., *Herodots Kroisos–Logos* (Berlin 1934).

Immerwahr, H.R., *Form and Thought in Herodotus* (Chapel Hill 1966).

Jong, I.J.F. de, 'Studies in Homeric Denomination', *Mnemosyne* 46, 1993, 289–306.

Jong, I.J.F. de, 'Paratexts "avant la lettre" in Ancient Greek Literature (Homer and Herodotus)', in D. den Hengst, J. Koopmans, and L. Kuitert (eds), *Paratext: The Fuzzy Edges of Literature* (Amsterdam 2004), 47–59.

Jong, I.J.F. de, 'Narratologia e storiografia: il racconto di Atys e Adrasto in Erodoto 1.34–45', *Quaderni Urbinati di Cultura Classica* 80, 2005, 87–96.

Jong, I.J.F. de, 'Herodotus on the Dream of Cambyses (*Histories* 3.30, 61–5)', in A. Lardinois, M.G.M. van der Poel, and V.J.C. Hunink (eds), *Land of Dreams: Greek and Latin Studies in Honour of A.H.M. Kessels* (Leiden 2006), 3–17.

Jong, I.J.F. de and R. Nünlist (eds), *Time in Ancient Greek Literature*, Studies in Ancient Greek Narrative 2 (Leiden 2007).

Laurot, P., 'Remarques sur le tragédie de Crésus', *Ktema* 20, 1995, 95–103.

Lévy, E., 'Le rêve chez Hérodote', *Ktema* 20, 1995, 17–27.

Long, T., *Repetition and Variation in the Short Stories of Herodotus* (Frankfurt 1987).

Munson, R.V., *Telling Wonders: Ethnographic and Political Discourse in the Work of Herodotus* (Ann Arbor 2001).

Rieks, R., 'Eine tragische Erzählung bei Herodot (*Hist.* 1, 34–45)', *Poetica* 7, 1975, 23–44.

Rijksbaron, A., 'The Discourse Function of the Imperfect', in A. Rijksbaron, H.A. Mulder, and G.C. Wakker (eds), *In the Footsteps of Raphael Kühner* (Amsterdam 1988), 237–54.

Saïd, S., *La faute tragique* (Paris 1978).

Sebeok, T.A., and E. Brady, 'The Two Sons of Croesus: A Myth about Communication in Herodotus', *Quaderni Urbinati di Cultura Classica* 30, 1979, 7–22.

Shapiro, S.O., 'Herodotus and Solon', *Classical Antiquity* 15, 1996, 348–64.

Sicking, C.M.J., and P. Stork, 'The Grammar of the So-Called Historical Present in Ancient Greek', in E.J. Bakker (ed.), *Grammar as Interpretation: Greek Literature in Its Linguistic Context* (Leiden 1997), 131–68.

Stahl, H.P., 'Learning through Suffering? Croesus' Conversations in the History of Herodotus', *Yale Classical Studies* 24, 1975, 1–36.

Stein, H., *Herodotos I.1, Buch 1* (Berlin 1901).

Szabó, M., 'Die Rolle der Atys–Adrastos-Geschichte in Herodots Kroisos-Logos', *Acta Classica Universitatis Scientiarum Debreceniensis* 14, 1978, 9–17.

8

Narratology and Drama

Euripides, Bacchae *1043–1152*
(The Death of Pentheus)

8.1. INTRODUCTION

If the chapter on historiography started with the question '*Can* narratology be applied to historiographical texts?', here the question is '*Should* narratology be applied to drama?'. Some narratologists adopt a broad definition of narrative that also includes drama. Paul Ricoeur, for example, says, 'I am not characterising narrative by its "mode", that is, by the author's attitude, but by its "object", since I am calling narrative exactly what Aristotle calls *muthos*, the organisation of the events.'[1] This broader definition is sometimes followed by classical scholars.[2] Drama makes use of the same devices that are found in narrative, such as analepses and prolepses, space, and characterization. In particular, drama also revolves around a plot, a series of events caused or experienced by characters that has a beginning, middle, and end. The presence of these devices, they claim, can be explained only by assuming a central controlling and selecting mind, a 'narrator', and their working can be analysed only with the help of narratology.

In this book narrative is defined by the presence of a narrator. Manfred Pfister considers the absence or presence of a narrator as the crucial difference between drama and narrative text, respectively:

---

[1] Ricoeur [1983] 1984: 36. See also Jahn 2001.
[2] e.g. Goward 1999; Markantonatos 2002; and the general discussion by Gould 1991.

198 *Narratology and Classics*

'whilst the receiver of a dramatic text feels directly confronted with the characters represented, in narrative texts they are mediated by a more or less concrete narrator figure'.[3] In order to analyse the formal devices of drama such as prolepses, plot, and so on, we do not need a 'narrator' in inverted commas because we can connect them with the playwright. Neither do we need narratology, as we can turn to drama theory, for example that of Pfister,[4] which offers a panoply of critical terms.

But of course drama does contain embedded narratives, told by characters acting as narrators, and here narratology is fully at home. As argued in Section 2.5, these narrators are best considered *secondary* narrators, even though there is no primary narrator. The reason for this is that they tell their story to other characters, who are secondary narratees, since they are to be distinguished from the spectators in the theatre (acting the part of primary narratees), if we want to explain, for example, the working of dramatic irony. To these secondary narratees only secondary narrators can correspond.

Ancient drama features many different secondary narrators: prologue speakers, messengers, the chorus, and characters sharing a past or future with other characters. If narrative lacks the directness of drama, it has certain advantages of its own: it can evoke offstage space and expand the time span of the play by including the distant past and future. In this chapter we will explore in detail the qualities of one celebrated specimen of narrative in drama: the messenger-speech.

8.2. MESSENGER-SPEECHES

Most Greek tragedies contain one messenger-speech, some more than one.[5] A messenger enters the stage, often in a hurry or in great agitation, blurts out his news, and is then asked by the chorus and/ or one of the protagonists to recount what has happened in greater detail. What follows is a continuous speech or *rhesis* of some 80 to 120 lines in which the messenger complies with this request. His story

---

[3] Pfister [1977] 1988: 3.   [4] Pfister [1977] 1988.
[5] General discussions of the messenger-speech are di Gregorio 1967; de Jong 1991; Barrett 2002; Dickin 2009. For their linguistic and narrative structure, see Allan 2009. For an inventory of Euripidean messenger-speeches, see de Jong 1991: 179–82.

usually deals with the dramatic and bloody climax of the play: a battle, murder, or suicide. The origin of the messenger-speech seems to be the result of a number of practical factors. The chorus' permanent presence on stage precluded changes of scene (the only exceptions are found in Aeschylus' *Eumenides* and Sophocles' *Ajax*), so one way in which playwrights could include offstage events, both extra-scenic and distanced, was by making a messenger recount them. The limited cast (2–3 actors, 12–15 members of the chorus) made the depiction of mass scenes impossible and the very basic design of a Greek theatre made special effects impossible to create, but narrative could be used to report both mass scenes and miraculous events. Finally, murder could not be depicted on stage because it was considered a *miasma* in Greek society and Attic drama was performed in a religious context (at the Great Dionysia), but messengers could recount it.[6] Narrative thus offered solutions to all of these restrictions. But it also had many attractive possibilities of its own, as Aristotle argued in chapter 24 of his *Poetics*. This led playwrights throughout the ages to introduce messengers in their plays.

The messengers of Greek drama usually are anonymous figures of low social status (servants, herdsmen, sailors) who do not play a role in the action of the play itself but whose sole function is to act as messenger. In order to be able to report what has happened they have to have witnessed it, and their crucial status as focalizer is therefore often stressed explicitly:

Sophocles *Antigone* 1192–3

ἐγώ, φίλη δέσποινα, καὶ παρὼν ἐρῶ,
κοὐδὲν παρήσω τῆς ἀληθείας ἔπος.

I was there, dear mistress, and I will tell you,
and I will leave out no word of the truth.[7]

Messengers are (secondary) internal narrators in that they play a role in the events they report, and this role may vary from that of a mere spectator (e.g. the prisoner of war who watches the battle between Thebans and Athenians in Euripides' *Supplices*), a bystander (e.g. Hippolytus' servant who accompanies his master in exile and has to watch how he is attacked by a bull from the sea in Euripides'

---

[6] See Bremer 1976.   [7] Cf. S. *Ajax* 748; E. *Supp.* 650–2; E. *Ba.* 780.

Hippolytus), or an active participant in the action (e.g. the Egyptian sailor who has to accompany Helen and the 'shipwrecked stranger'/ Menelaus to sea and is defeated by them in open sea in Euripides' *Helen*). The messenger, however, is never the central person of his story. His inconspicuous nature makes him well suited to observe what happens without being noticed or becoming too involved in the action, and hence able to escape and report what he has seen.

Like all internal narrators, messengers can choose whether to narrate according to their narrating or their experiencing focalization. Experiencing focalization means that the narrator-focalizer recounts events exactly as he saw and (mis)understood them at the time they took place, while in the case of narrating focalization he uses his hindsight knowledge (see §3.5). Most messengers opt for the former: having briefly informed their narratees about the main point of their report ('X is dead'), they next, in their detailed narrative, mentally return in time and recount how this event came about exactly as they and the other characters experienced it, not knowing what would come. Only occasionally they insert a brief detail that can only derive from their hindsight knowledge (e.g. calling a victim 'unhappy' before anything has happened). But when a messenger has to defend himself vis-à-vis his master because he has failed a mission, he will turn to narrating focalization. Thus the second messenger in Euripides' *Helen*, who has to report to the Egyptian king that Helen and Menelaus have escaped, makes clear from the beginning that the two had deceived him and the other members of the crew, although, of course, he was unaware of this while it was happening.

There is ample evidence that both playwrights and actors liked messenger-speeches, the former to prove that they could handle not only the dramatic but also the narrative media, the latter to show their histrionic qualities.[8] Indeed, it has been suggested that in Euripides one and the same actor might play a heroic character early in the drama and then come back on stage in the role of the messenger who reports the death of that character.[9] Since the messenger-speech is such a treasured set piece of Attic drama, it is a fitting object of narratological close reading. Can narratology confirm

---

[8] The importance of the messenger-speech is also confirmed by its popularity on vases; see Green 1996.

[9] See Dickin 2009: 105–48.

its quality as narrative? What devices do the playwrights use to turn it into a gripping story that effectively fits its dramatic context?

A particularly thrilling messenger-speech is that recounting the death of Pentheus in Euripides' *Bacchae* (1043–1152). Dionysus has come to Thebes to introduce his cult, vindicate his mother Semele, whose affair with Zeus was denied by her family, and teach a lesson to its king Pentheus, who forbids his worship. Before the start of the play he led the Theban women, including Pentheus' mother Agave and her sisters, to Mount Cithaeron and put them under his bacchic spell. In a series of episodes in which he is disguised as a Lydian worshipper of Dionysus, he tries to convince Pentheus that Dionysus is a god: he holds a conversation with him in which he tells about the bacchic rituals; he miraculously frees himself and the Asian maenads whom Pentheus had locked up and then shakes his palace in a giant earthquake and fire; and he listens with him to the first messenger-speech, which recounts the incredible feats of the Theban maenads on Mount Cithaeron, who put snakes in their hair, suckle wild wolves and gazelles, and make wine, milk, honey, and water spring up from the ground. The messenger, a cowherd, also tells that, when they tried to capture the maenads, the women descended on their cows, ripping them to shreds with their bare hands in a spontaneous *sparagmos*. Despite all these warnings Pentheus perseveres in his rejection of the god and his rituals, but by now he has become greatly intrigued by what he has heard. 'The Lydian stranger'/Dionysus thus easily manages to persuade him to come to the mountain with him and, dressed in female attire, spy on the women. After Pentheus has left the stage, 'the Lydian stranger'/Dionysus leaves no doubt that something terrible is going to befall him (971–6):

δεινὸς σὺ δεινὸς κἀπὶ δείν' ἔρχῃ πάθη,
ὥστ' οὐρανῷ στηρίζον εὑρήσεις κλέος.
ἔκτειν', Ἀγαυή, χεῖρας αἵ θ' ὁμόσποροι
Κάδμου θυγατέρες· τὸν νεανίαν ἄγω
τόνδ' εἰς ἀγῶνα μέγαν, ὁ νικήσων δ' ἐγὼ
καὶ Βρόμιος ἔσται. τἄλλα δ' αὐτὸ σημανεῖ.

Fearsome you are, fearsome, and fearsome are the sufferings to which
   you are going,
with the result that you will find a fame that is towering to heaven.
Stretch out, Agave, your hands, and you daughters

born from the same father Cadmus. I bring this
young man to a great contest, and the winner will be me
and Bromius. The rest the event itself will make clear.[10]

His final words whet the spectators' appetite, as it were, for the
messenger-speech to follow: they know the outcome (Pentheus'
death at his mother's hands) but not the details. In the ensuing choral
song, which, as usual, is supposed to cover the time needed for the
offstage events to take place, the chorus, consisting of Asian maenads,
give more clues (982–91):

μάτηρ πρῶτά νιν λευρᾶς ἀπὸ πέτρας
†ἢ σκόλοπος† ὄψεται
δοκεύοντα, μαινάσιν δ' ἀπύσει·
'τίς ὅδ' ὀρειδρόμων μαστὴρ Καδμειᾶν
ἐς ὄρος ἐς ὄρος ἔμολ' ἔμολεν, ὦ βάκχαι;
τίς ἄρα νιν ἔτεκεν;
οὐ γὰρ ἐξ αἵματος
γυναικῶν ἔφυ, λεαίνας δέ τινος
ὅδ' ἢ Γοργόνων Λιβυσσᾶν γένος.'

His mother will be the first to spot him while
from a smooth rock †or cliff†
he is spying, and shall call to the maenads:
'Who is this searcher of the mountain-running Cadmean women,
who has come, has come to the mountain, to the mountain, o maenads?
Who gave birth to him?
For this creature was not born from the blood
of women, but from some lioness,
or from Libyan Gorgons.'

This instance of prior narration ('his mother *will* be the first') has
proleptic force: Pentheus will spy on the maenads, he will be seen by
them, and his mother will take the lead in attacking him. Her tragic
maenadic frenzy is also anticipated: she will take her son to be a wild
animal.

Immediately after their song, a messenger enters the scene and
reveals 'the headlines' of his news in the customary way (1030):[11]

---

[10] The text is that of Diggle, OCT; the translations are my own, based on those of
Seaford 1996 and Kovacs (Loeb).
[11] Cf. Allan 2009: 189–90 (abstract).

Πενθεὺς ὄλωλε, παῖς Ἐχίονος πατρός.
Pentheus, son of Echion, has died.

Next, the chorus, who are external secondary narratees since they did not participate in the events themselves, ask the typical question which triggers a messenger-speech (1041-2):

ἔννεπέ μοι, φράσον· τίνι μόρῳ θνῄσκει
ἄδικος ἄδικά τ᾽ ἐκπορίζων ἀνήρ;
Tell me, explain, how did he die,
the unjust man and perpetrator of unjust deeds?

Upon this cue the messenger will launch his detailed report. The introductory dialogue has made clear that there is a contrast between the messenger, who laments and deplores the fate of his master and the royal family to which he belongs (cf. his opening apostrophe at 1024-8: 'O house that once were fortunate [...] how I groan for you'), and his (secondary) narratees, the chorus, who as followers of Dionysus greet the news of Pentheus' death as a victory of their god over a disobedient mortal (cf. 1031, 1034-5). It remains to be seen how the spectators in the theatre, acting by proxy as the primary narratees of the messenger, are to evaluate what has happened.

8.3. NARRATOLOGICAL CLOSE READING OF EURIPIDES, *BACCHAE* 1043-1152[12]

1043-7
ἐπεὶ θεράπνας τῆσδε Θηβαίας χθονὸς
λιπόντες ἐξέβημεν Ἀσωποῦ ῥοάς,
λέπας Κιθαιρώνειον εἰσεβάλλομεν   (1045)
Πενθεύς τε κἀγώ (δεσπότῃ γὰρ εἱπόμην)
ξένος θ᾽ ὃς ἡμῖν πομπὸς ἦν θεωρίας.

---

[12] See the discussions of this messenger-speech in Dodds [1944] 1960; Buxton 1991; Seaford 1996; and Barrett 2002: 102-31. This section is a thoroughly revised version of de Jong 1992.

> After we had left the settlements of this Theban land
> and had crossed the streams of the Asopus,
> we were marching into the rocky uplands of Cithaeron,   (1045)
> Pentheus and I (for I was following my master)
> and **the stranger** who was the escort of our viewing/embassy.

Most messenger-speeches open with ἐπεί. This signals that the messenger starts his story from an earlier moment in the play, usually the moment when the main character leaves the stage to go to his offstage destination. This messenger thus picks up from 971, when Pentheus left for the Cithaeron.[13]

Like many narrators, the messenger begins his story with an indication of the place where the events will take place:[14] the slopes of the Cithaeron. This setting has thematic and symbolic functions. Mountains play a prominent role in the play, since they are the place where maenads generally perform their bacchic rituals (see the parodos at 64–169, esp. 76, 86, 116, 135), and the Cithaeron in particular featured prominently in the first messenger-speech (677–774). Indeed, the specific details that the messenger mentions, Pentheus passing *the settlements*, crossing the *Asopus*, and marching into *the uplands*, may recall to the primary narratees frightening memories of what had taken place there earlier: the herdsmen, to which the first messenger belongs, and their cattle had climbed to *the uplands* (677–8), and the provoked maenadic women had been moving over the plains near *Asopus'* waters and hurling themselves upon *the settlements* of Hysiae and Erythrae at the foot of Cithaeron (749–51).[15] The Cithaeron also has symbolic value, in that it was the place where Pentheus' cousin Actaeon was torn apart by his own dogs. This event was held up to Pentheus as a warning paradigm by his grandfather Cadmus at 337–41, who later has to conclude that Pentheus died 'in the very place where in the past his dogs tore apart Actaeon' (1291).

---

[13] See Rijksbaron 1976. Messenger-speeches that do not begin with ἐπεί usually are those found in the first half of a play: there a messenger does not continue from a given point within the dramatic plot but is an accidental witness; cf. e.g. E. *Or.* 866 ('I happened to be making my way from the country . . .') or *Ba.* 677 ('It was the hour when the sun sheds its beams . . .').

[14] Cf. Allan 2009: 190–1 (orientation).

[15] Winnington-Ingram 1948: 128. For parallels and differences between the two messenger-speeches, see Buxton 1991: 44–6.

As usual, the messenger also explains his identity at the beginning of his story (he is a servant of Pentheus) and stresses his status as eyewitness/focalizer (he followed his master on his expedition). Their guide is 'the stranger'; referring to Dionysus in this way reveals that the messenger is recounting the events from his experiencing focalization (cf. again at 1059, 1063, 1068, 1077; the instances are highlighted in bold). He now knows that the stranger was actually Dionysus (see 1079), but, suppressing this hindsight knowledge, he recounts the events from his (and Pentheus') unwitting and unsuspecting perspective. This expedient is one of the ways in which messengers make their story gripping and moving.

The messenger calls their expedition a θεωρία. He means by this no more than a viewing, such as 'the stranger'/Dionysus and Pentheus had planned at 810–16. However, the chorus as secondary narratees (and followers of Dionysus) may interpret it as a sacred embassy sent to watch religious celebrations, and the primary narratees may understand it as a sacred embassy sent to see games, that is, the final confrontation between mortal and god (cf. Dionysus announcing that he would bring Pentheus to a great 'contest', ἀγῶνα: 975).[16]

Likewise, the word πομπός has a double resonance: the messenger intends no more than escort or guide; after all, 'the stranger' knows where the maeanads are (cf. 819, where he says to Pentheus: 'Shall I take you there?'). But the spectators may recall Dionysus' ominous words at 964–6: 'contests (ἀγῶνες) lie ahead of you that have been fated. So follow me. I will go as your safe escort (πομπὸς ... σωτήριος). But from there another person will bring you back'.[17]

1048–57

πρῶτον μὲν οὖν ποιηρὸν ἵζομεν νάπος,
τά τ' ἐκ ποδῶν σιγηλὰ καὶ γλώσσης ἄπο

---

[16] See Winnington-Ingram 1948: 128, n. 2 and Seaford 1996: ad 1047. Differently, Barrett 2002: 114, who contends that the messenger 'as he embarks on his narrative quietly clothes himself with the mantle of one granted a privileged, authoritative voice. He (along with Pentheus) goes not merely to watch; he goes with the task of watching with special care. His invocation of the *theōria* implies that this is no idle mission; it is as though organised by the polis itself.'

[17] Foley 1985: 208–18 interprets *pompē* and *agōn* in conjunction with *kōmos* at 1167 as referring to the procession, contest, and festive revelry belonging to a religious festival, perhaps a primitive version of Dionysus' own festival, the Great Dionysia. She interprets the events of the messenger-speech as a 'play-within-a-play': from a spectator of Dionysus' play (cf. *theatēs*: 829) Pentheus becomes its tragic hero. Barrett 2002, too, gives a metatheatrical interpretation.

σώιζοντες, ὡς ὁρῶμεν οὐχ ὁρώμενοι.   (1050)
ἦν δ' ἄγκος ἀμφίκρημνον, ὕδασι διάβροχον,
πεύκαισι συσκιάζον, ἔνθα μαινάδες
καθῆντ' ἔχουσαι χεῖρας ἐν τερπνοῖς πόνοις.
αἱ μὲν γὰρ αὐτῶν θύρσον ἐκλελοιπότα
κισσῷ κομήτην αὖθις ἐξανέστεφον,   (1055)
αἱ δ' ἐκλιποῦσαι ποικίλ' ὡς πῶλοι ζυγὰ
βακχεῖον ἀντέκλαζον ἀλλήλαις μέλος.

First we took up positions in a grassy valley,
being careful to keep our footsteps and tongues
silent, so that we might see without being seen.   (1050)
There lay a glen with steep sides, with a stream flowing through it,
overshaded by pines, where the maenads
sat employing their hands in pleasant tasks.
Some of them were restoring the
crown of ivy to their tattered *thyrsos*,[18]   (1055)
others, joyous as fillies released from their decorated yokes,
were singing bacchic songs in response to each other.

The messenger, Pentheus, and 'the stranger'/Dionysus spotted the maenads while sitting in a glen. They are thus able to watch them from above. The messenger uses first-person plural forms (ἐξέβημεν, εἰσεβάλλομεν, ἵζομεν, ὁρῶμεν) that suggest that the focalization of both scenery and maenads is that of the three of them. The particles μὲν οὖν already hint, however, at some form of contrast. It will follow at 1058–62, when it appears that Pentheus does *not* see what the messenger sees. As always when scenery is focalized by characters we find the imperfect (ἦν).[19] What the messenger sees and describes (from his experiencing focalization) is a peaceful scene taking place in a *locus amoenus*, with trees, shade, and water. He even explicitly calls the activities of the maenads 'pleasant tasks'. Thus, he looks at the maenads without Pentheus' prejudice and sees them in a positive light, as did, at first, the first messenger (683–8):

ηὗδον δὲ πᾶσαι σώμασιν παρειμέναι,
αἱ μὲν πρὸς ἐλάτης νῶτ' ἐρείσασαι φόβην,
αἱ δ' ἐν δρυὸς φύλλοισι πρὸς πέδῳ κάρα

[18] The *thyrsos* was the typical staff carried by maenads; it consisted of a fennel, covered with ivy vines and topped with a pinecone.
[19] See de Jong 2001: ad 5.63–75.

εἰκῆ βαλοῦσαι σωφρόνως, οὐχ ὡς σὺ φῇς
ᾠνωμένας κρατῆρι καὶ λωτοῦ ψόφῳ
θηρᾶν καθ᾽ ὕλην Κύπριν ἠρημωμένας.

They all lay sleeping, relaxed in body,
some lying on their backs upon fir-tree branches,
others putting their head on the ground among oak leaves,
at random, chastely, and they were not, as you claim,
drunk from the mixing bowl and the sound of the pipe
each going her own secret way searching for love in the wood.

The primary narratees, however, recalling the dramatic change from peacefulness to aggression of that same first messenger-speech, may listen to the second messenger's words with some apprehension: are the maenads restoring the *thyrsoi* which had become dishevelled from being used as weapons against local villagers (762–4)? And the comparison with fillies released from the yoke recalls that the women have left their regular place in society: they have left behind their houses (32, 36), their usual occupations (cf. 118), and their babies (cf. 702).

1058–62
Πενθεὺς δ᾽ ὁ τλήμων θῆλυν οὐχ ὁρῶν ὄχλον
ἔλεξε τοιάδ᾽· ʽΩ ξέν᾽, οὗ μὲν ἔσταμεν
οὐκ ἐξικνοῦμαι μανιάδων ὄσσοις νόσων·   (1060)
ὄχθων δ᾽ ἔπ᾽ ἀμβὰς ἐς ἐλάτην ὑψαύχενα
ἴδοιμ᾽ ἂν ὀρθῶς μαινάδων αἰσχρουργίαν.᾽

But Pentheus, poor man, did not see the female throng/a female mob
and spoke thus: '**Stranger**, from where we stand
I cannot see with my own eyes the sick raving women.   (1060)
But if I mounted a high-necked fir on the banks
I could properly see the disgraceful behaviour of the maenads.'

What does Pentheus see? It might be that Dionysus, wishing to implicate him even further into his nets, makes him see nothing (just as earlier he made him see double: 918–22), so that he will take up a vulnerable position in order to see them. In that case we have to translate θῆλυν οὐχ ὁρῶν ὄχλον with 'he did not see *the* female throng [which the messenger saw]'.[20] Most commentators, however,

---

[20] The word ὄχλος need not carry a negative undertone, since the chorus had used it in their evocation of the Theban maenads on the mountain (117).

opt for another interpretation: as he has come to see the debauchery of the maenads (about which he so far had only heard: cf. 216–25), the sight of women occupied in domestic chores and peacefully singing does not meet Pentheus' expectations. He sees women, but he does not see *a* female mob or, as he himself phrases it, 'the sick raving women'.[21] An argument in favour of this interpretation is the paradoxical nature of Pentheus' wish to see 'properly' (ὀρθῶς) the 'disgraceful behaviour' (αἰσχρουργίαν) of the maenads. Whatever interpretation we choose, the messenger briefly uses his *ex eventu* knowledge when he calls Pentheus 'poor man' even though nothing has happened yet. He knows that his master's desire to see the maenads will become fatal to him.

Pentheus proposing to 'mount' a 'high-necked' fir introduces a metaphor that will recur throughout the messenger's report, namely that of the tree as a horse and Pentheus as its rider: compare 1072, where 'the stranger'/Dionysus takes care that the tree 'does not throw off' Pentheus, who is sitting on its 'back' (1074); and 1107, where Pentheus is called 'the wild animal mounted' (τὸν ἀμβάτην θῆρ'). Is this a first indication that the battle that Pentheus had originally envisaged with the maenads (and which arguably belonged to the original tradition of the Pentheus story)[22] in a sense will take place after all, even though it has been replaced with a spying mission? Soon the maenads will (again) use their *thyrsoi* as weapons (1098–100) and raise warlike shouts of triumph (1133).

1063–74

τοὐντεῦθεν ἤδη **τοῦ ξένου** θαυμάσθ' **ὁρῶ**·
λαβὼν γὰρ ἐλάτης οὐράνιον ἄκρον κλάδον
κατῆγεν ἦγεν ἦγεν ἐς μέλαν πέδον·   (1065)
κυκλοῦτο δ' ὥστε τόξον ἢ κυρτὸς τροχὸς
τόρνῳ γραφόμενος περιφορὰν ἑλικοδρόμον·

---

[21] Cf. Winnington-Ingram 1948: 129: 'This is not what Pentheus came to see—and he does not see it.' His interpretation is followed by Dodds [1944] 1960 and Seaford 1996: *ad loc.* We should note that Pentheus' double vision at 918–24, when he finally 'sees what he ought to see', is the closest he gets to the Dionysiac perspective; he never 'sees with the eyes of faith' (Gregory 1985: 29).

[22] Cf. Pentheus' announcement to make war on the maenads at 778–86 (and esp. his call for ἵππων . . . ἐπεμβάτας, 'riders of horses': 782 ≈ τὸν ἀμβάτην θῆρ': 1107) and earlier Dionysus' announcement that should Pentheus take up arms against the maenads he would join battle with him (50–4). Vase paintings also showed an armed Pentheus fighting with maenads. For discussion, see Seaford 1996: ad 50–2.

ὡς κλῶν᾽ ὄρειον ὁ **ξένος** χεροῖν ἄγων
ἔκαμπτεν ἐς γῆν, ἔργματ᾽ οὐχὶ θνητὰ δρῶν.
Πενθέα δ᾽ ἱδρύσας ἐλατίνων ὄζων ἔπι   (1070)
ὀρθὸν μεθίει διὰ χερῶν βλάστημ᾽ ἄνω
ἀτρέμα, φυλάσσων μὴ ἀναχαιτίσειέ νιν,
ὀρθὴ δ᾽ ἐς ὀρθὸν αἰθέρ᾽ ἐστηρίζετο
ἔχουσα νώτοις δεσπότην ἐφήμενον.

From this point onwards I see miraculous deeds from the stranger:
for taking the sky-high tip of a branch of a fir tree
he brought, brought, brought it down to the black earth.   (1065)
And it began to curve like a bow or rounded wheel
when its curved shape is being traced with a peg-and-line.[23]
In like way the stranger, bringing down the mountain stem with
    his two hands,
bowed it to the earth, performing deeds not mortal.
Having sat Pentheus atop the fir branches,   (1070)
he began to let the shoot go upright
gently, taking care that it should not toss him off,
and it towered sheer to the sheer heaven,
having my master sitting on its back.

The messenger arrives at an important point in his narrative and
marks this by explicitly demarcating it (τοὐντεῦθεν ἤδη),[24] by referring to his status as focalizer again and using a historic present (ὁρῶ).
The miraculous event of the stranger bowing a tree is marked off by a
ring-composition (θαυμάσθ᾽ ≈ ἔργματ᾽ οὐχὶ θνητά), which moreover
makes clear that this is the point when the messenger started to
suspect that the stranger might be no ordinary mortal but a god.
But above all the messenger indicates the importance of what takes
place by his slowing down of the rhythm of narration (retardation):
the fatal mounting of Pentheus on the tree and its bending and slow
release by the god take up no fewer than eleven lines.[25] The thrice
repeated ὀρθόν, ὀρθή, ὀρθόν at 1071–3 is perhaps an echo of Pentheus'

[23] Both the text and the interpretation of lines 1066–7 are heavily debated;
I follow Diggle's text, but for a full discussion refer to Rijksbaron 1991: *ad loc.*
[24] Cf. e.g. 760: οὖπερ τὸ δεινὸν ἦν θέαμ᾽ ἰδεῖν, 'then happened that dreadful sight';
E. *Med.* 1167: τοὐνθένδε μέντοι δεινὸν ἦν θέαμ᾽ ἰδεῖν, 'what happened next was dreadful
to see', and Roux 1970–2: ad 1063–5: 'le messager est conscient d'aborder un point
capital de son récit'.
[25] Buxton 1991: 45.

wish to see the maenads ὀρθῶς (1062), underscoring that his 'properly' is given a fatal twist by the god, who makes him sit 'high-up' (so as to become visible himself).[26] And can the narratees hear in Pentheus' position on a fir tree that towers towards heaven an ironic echo of Dionysus' earlier promise to give him 'a fame that is towering to heaven' (972)?[27]

1075–94

ὤφθη δὲ μᾶλλον ἢ κατεῖδε μαινάδας·   (1075)
ὅσον γὰρ οὔπω δῆλος ἦν θάσσων ἄνω,
καὶ **τὸν ξένον** μὲν οὐκέτ᾽ εἰσορᾶν παρῆν,
ἐκ δ᾽ αἰθέρος φωνή τις, ὡς μὲν εἰκάσαι
Διόνυσος, ἀνεβόησεν· 'ὦ νεάνιδες,
ἄγω τὸν ὑμᾶς κἀμὲ τἀμά τ᾽ ὄργια   (1080)
γέλων τιθέμενον· ἀλλὰ τιμωρεῖσθέ νιν.'
καὶ ταῦθ᾽ ἅμ᾽ ἠγόρευε καὶ πρὸς οὐρανὸν
καὶ γαῖαν ἐστήριζε φῶς σεμνοῦ πυρός.
σίγησε δ᾽ αἰθήρ, σῖγα δ᾽ ὕλιμος νάπη
φύλλ᾽ εἶχε, θηρῶν δ᾽ οὐκ ἂν ἤκουσας βοήν.   (1085)
αἱ δ᾽ ὠσὶν ἠχὴν οὐ σαφῶς δεδεγμέναι
ἔστησαν ὀρθαὶ καὶ διήνεγκαν κόρας.
ὁ δ᾽ αὖθις ἐπεκέλευσεν· ὡς δ᾽ ἐγνώρισαν
σαφῆ κελευσμὸν Βακχίου Κάδμου κόραι
ᾖξαν πελείας ὠκύτητ᾽ οὐχ ἥσσονες   (1090)
[ποδῶν ἔχουσαι συντόνοις δρομήμασι
μήτηρ Ἀγαυὴ σύγγονοί θ᾽ ὁμόσποροι]
πᾶσαί τε βάκχαι, διὰ δὲ χειμάρρου νάπης
ἀγμῶν τ᾽ ἐπήδων θεοῦ πνοαῖσιν ἐμμανεῖς.

And he was seen by the maenads more than he saw them.   (1075)
For he was just becoming visible sitting up there,
when **the stranger** was no longer to be seen,
but some voice from the air, I guess it was
Dionysus, shouted: 'Young women,
I bring the one who is mocking you and me   (1080)
and my rites; come, take revenge on him!'
And he said that and at the same time
a light of holy fire towered between heaven and earth.
The upper air fell silent, in silence the wooded valley

---

[26] Compare the grim use of ὀρθῶς by Dionysus at 1279.
[27] Thus, Winnington-Ingram 1948: 129, n. 2.

kept its leaves, and you would not have heard the cry of
  wild beasts.   (1085)
And they, not having heard the sound clearly with their ears,
stood upright and turned their eyes this way and that.
And he commanded them again. And when the daughters
  of Cadmus
recognized the clear command of Dionysus,
they darted off, no less in speed than a dove,   (1090)
[running with an intense effort of their feet,
his mother Agave and her sisters]
and all the maenads, and through the valley with its torrent
and over boulders they leapt, maddened by the breath of the god.

Line 1075 marks the reversal of the messenger's story: while Pentheus
had come 'to see without being seen' (1050) and mounted a tree in
order to see the maenads properly (1062), he is now more visible to
them than they are to him. This line is a kind of summary announcement of what is to follow, since the messenger proceeds to recount
what happened when Pentheus was *becoming* visible: the maenads
will first hear about his presence, then run towards him, and finally
(at 1095) see him.

The messenger, as a simple man of the people perhaps more
sensitive to supernatural events,[28] now has his moment of *anagnōrisis*: he (rightly) guesses that the stranger was Dionysus and that
Pentheus' final moment has come; Pentheus' understanding will
follow only later. The messenger's assessment is based on the dis-
appearance of the stranger, the sound of a voice coming 'from the
air',[29] the voice's reference to 'my rites' ($\tau\grave{a}\mu\acute{a} \ldots \ \check{o}\rho\gamma\iota a$),[30] and the
presence of 'a light of holy fire'.[31]

The stillness of nature may also have been taken by the messenger
as a sign of a divine presence; thus, when Odysseus approaches the

---

[28] Cf. Roux 1970–2: ad 1069: 'Les gens simples, le messager comme le berger, sont
immédiatement sensibles à l'aspect surnaturel des actes de l'étranger et reconnaissent
l'intervention d'un dieu.'

[29] At 576–84 Dionysus had likewise shouted at his followers, who hear his voice
but do not see him (cf. esp. 568–9: 'whence the voice of Euhios that calls my name?').

[30] The word $\check{o}\rho\gamma\iota a$ is used throughout the play in connection with Dionysus' rites:
34, 470, 471, 476, 482, 998.

[31] Divine epiphanies are regularly accompanied by miraculous light, cf. e.g.
H. Dem. 280: 'and the sturdy house was filled with a brilliant light like that of
lightning'.

island of the Sirens 'the breeze dropped, a windless calm fell there, and some divinity stilled the tossing waters' (*Od.* 12.168–9). But it conveys more. It indicates the calm before the storm: in a few moments the maenads will start their attack on Pentheus, which will end with his death.[32] It also ensures that when Dionysus again issues his command to punish Pentheus, the maenads (this time) will hear his words clearly. A very similar silence is found in the messenger-speech relating the murder of Neoptolemus in the temple (and at the command?) of Apollo: 'In the calm that somehow ensued, my master stood still, the brilliance of his gleaming weapons about him, until from the inmost shrine some voice uttered a dreadful and chilling sound and roused the army, turning them toward battle' (*Andr.* 1145–9).

The messenger at this moment of intensity involves his (primary and secondary) narratees by using a second-person verb-form and turning them into hypothetical focalizers (see §3.6): 'you would not have heard the cry of wild beasts'.[33] His use of a comparison ('no less in speed than doves'), although almost a cliché (cf. e.g. *Il.* 22.138–43, where Achilles running at full speed is compared to a hawk), has an ominous undertone for the primary narratees; in the first messenger-speech, too, the maenads were compared to birds when they were about to attack the villages (748). The comparison is perhaps even more than that; it suggests the maenads' miraculous physical powers or, as Dodds calls it, their 'Dionysiac effortlessness'.[34]

1095–1110

ὡς δ᾽ εἶδον ἐλάτῃ δεσπότην ἐφήμενον,   (1095)
πρῶτον μὲν αὐτοῦ χερμάδας κραταιβόλους
ἔρριπτον, ἀντίπυργον ἐπιβᾶσαι πέτραν,
ὄζοισί τ᾽ ἐλατίνοισιν ἠκοντίζετο,
ἄλλαι δὲ θύρσους ἵεσαν δι᾽ αἰθέρος
Πενθέως, στόχον δύστηνον, ἀλλ᾽ οὐκ ἤνυτον.   (1100)
κρεῖσσον γὰρ ὕψος τῆς προθυμίας ἔχων
καθῆσθ᾽ ὁ τλήμων, ἀπορίᾳ λελημμένος.
τέλος δὲ δρυΐνοις συντριαινοῦσαι κλάδοις
ῥίζας ἀνεσπάρασσον ἀσιδήροις μοχλοῖς.

---

[32] Winnington-Ingram 1948: 129 ('the flash of lightning and the utter quiet when even the birds stop singing, these are the prelude to a storm, and the storm soon breaks') and Roux 1970–2: ad 1084–5.

[33] Cf. *Andr.* 1135; *Ph.* 1150; *Ba.* 712–13, 740.

[34] Dodds [1944] 1960: ad 194. Cf. 945–6, 1173–4, 1205–10, and 1237.

ἐπεὶ δὲ μόχθων τέρματ' οὐκ ἐξήνυτον,   (1105)
ἔλεξ' Ἀγαυή· 'Φέρε, περιστᾶσαι κύκλῳ
πτόρθου λάβεσθε, μαινάδες, τὸν ἀμβάτην
θῆρ' ὡς ἔλωμεν μηδ' ἀπαγγείλῃ θεοῦ
χοροὺς κρυφαίους.' αἱ δὲ μυρίαν χέρα
προσέθεσαν ἐλάτῃ κἀξανέσπασαν χθονός.   (1110)

And when they saw my master seated on the fir tree,   (1095)
at first they threw stones, hurled with force, at him,
having climbed a cliff that towered opposite him,
and he was bombarded [lit. javelined] by fir branches,
and others threw their *thyrsoi* through the air
at Pentheus, a cruel targeting, but they did not reach him.   (1100)
For occupying a position higher than their fervour
he sat, the wretched man, trapped in helplessness.
In the end they set about tearing up the roots with levers not of iron,
thunderbolting them with oak branches.
And when they did not achieve results in their efforts,   (1105)
Agave said: 'Come, stand round in a circle
and take hold of the stem, so that we can catch the wild animal
mounted on it and prevent him from disclosing
the secret dances of the god.' And they put countless hands
to the fir and pulled it out of the earth.   (1110)

In recounting the attack of the maenads on Pentheus the messenger's focalization becomes very manifest: he pities his master (ὁ τλήμων) and his fate (στόχον δύστηνον). Indeed, referring to Pentheus as δεσπότην he intrudes upon the focalization of the maenads (paralepsis): they do not know whom they are facing. The focalization of the messenger also transpires in a more subtle and implicit way, namely in his consistent use of military metaphors: the maenads occupy a 'cliff that towered opposite him', that is, a cliff which functions as a tower such as used in sieges,[35] and use tree branches and their *thyrsoi* as javelins, their hands as levers. By now this messenger is looking at the maenads in the same (negative) way as his colleague, who had likewise stressed their warlike behaviour when he said that the maenads were 'armed with *thyrsoi*' (733), attacked cattle 'with an ironless hand' (736), and hurled themselves on villages 'like enemy troops' (752–3).

---

[35] Cf. Roux 1970–2: ad 1095–8.

At this dramatic peak the messenger employs the device of the 'speech in speech', which means that the narratees 'hear' the protagonists of his story speak, and that narrative in drama turns into drama again. First, he quotes Agave who exhorts her women to uproot the fir tree and thus catch the wild animal in it. Her focalization of Pentheus is a double one: she sees him both as a beast and as a human being who could disclose the rites of Dionysus. Some scholars have wanted to mitigate the force of θῆρα by taking it as an insult or a metaphor, which only later will become a real delusion.[36] But seeing double is a typical characteristic of the Dionysian giddiness or madness: at 918–22 Pentheus sees two suns, a double Thebes, and above all 'the stranger' as a bull; likewise, in the first messenger-speech, the maenadic women give milk to gazelles and wolf cubs, probably taking them for their babies. Thus there is no reason to doubt that Agave is taking Pentheus for a beast right from the start, either prey to be hunted (see *1137–47*) or a victim to be sacrificed (see *1111–24*).

1111–24

ὑψοῦ δὲ θάσσων ὑψόθεν χαμαιριφὴς
πίπτει πρὸς οὖδας μυρίοις οἰμώγμασιν
Πενθεύς· κακοῦ γὰρ ἐγγὺς ὢν ἐμάνθανεν.
πρώτη δὲ μήτηρ ἦρξεν ἱερέα φόνου
καὶ προσπίτνει νιν· ὁ δὲ μίτραν κόμης ἄπο   (1115)
ἔρριψεν, ὥς νιν γνωρίσασα μὴ κτάνοι
τλήμων Ἀγαυή, καὶ λέγει παρηίδος
ψαύων· ἐγώ τοι, μῆτερ, εἰμί, παῖς σέθεν
Πενθεύς, ὃν ἔτεκες ἐν δόμοις Ἐχίονος·
οἴκτιρε δ', ὦ μῆτέρ, με μηδὲ ταῖς ἐμαῖς   (1120)
ἁμαρτίαισι παῖδα σὸν κατακτάνῃς.'
ἡ δ' ἀφρὸν ἐξιεῖσα καὶ διαστρόφους
κόρας ἑλίσσουσ', οὐ φρονοῦσ' ἃ χρὴ φρονεῖν,
ἐκ Βακχίου κατείχετ', οὐδ' ἔπειθέ νιν.

Sitting high up, from high **he falls**,
hurled to the ground with innumerable groans,
Pentheus. For he knew that he was close to disaster.

[36] Cf. Roux 1970-2: ad 1106-13: 'ce n'est pas d'abord qu'un insulte à l'égard de l'espion juché dans l'arbre, comme l'étaient dans la bouche des Lydiennes [...] 543, 990; mais Agavé passe très vite de la métaphore à l'hallicunation et confond réellement l'homme avec le gibier'. Dodds [1944] 1960: ad 1106-10: 'What later becomes a fixed delusion (1141) begins as a fleeting fancy, perhaps no more than a metaphor.'

His mother was the first as priestess to start the slaughter
and **falls on** him. And he threw the headdress (1115)
from his hair, so that the wretched Agave
would recognize him and not kill him, and **he says**,
touching her cheek: 'Look, it is I, Mother, your son
Pentheus, whom you bore in Echion's house.
Have pity on me, mother, and do not
kill your own child as a result of my tragic mistakes.' (1120)
But she, exuding foam and rolling her twisted
eyes and not thinking as she should think,
remained possessed by Dionysus, and he could not persuade her.

Reaching the climax of his story the messenger starts using historic presents: πίπτει, προσπίτνει, and λέγει (highlighted in bold).[37] Falling to the ground, Pentheus regains his senses and realizes the situation he is in. Thus, for him, too, the moment of *anagnōrisis* has now arrived. His name is placed effectively at the end of the sentence and, exceptionally, after the verb (1113), which gives it emphasis. As Winnington-Ingram suggested, it may be that the narratees are to recall its ominous nature, twice explicitly spelled out in earlier parts of the play: 'take care that Pentheus does not bring sorrow (πένθος) on your house' (367) and 'you are fit, as regards your name, to suffer because of it' (508).[38] A suspenseful prolepsis ('For he knew that he was close to disaster', i.e. that his death was near) is inserted, focalized by Pentheus.

The messenger refers to Agave as 'his mother', underscoring the horror of what is taking place, a mother attacking her own son. He also calls her 'a priestess' (ἱερέα). Just as the women in the first messenger-speech performed a 'normal' Dionysian ritual, the *sparagmos* or tearing apart of animals,[39] they now turn to a perverted one, the victim of their *sparagmos* being a human being. Alternatively, we may, with Seidensticker, see the whole sequence of Pentheus' death as a perversion of an ordinary animal sacrifice: there is (1) the adornment of the victim (925–44); (2) the procession leading it to its sacrifice (1043–7); (3) the moment of silence (1084–5); (4) the collective pelting with barley groats (1096–1100); (5) the women's

[37] For the functions of historic presents in messenger-speeches, see Allan 2009: 192–5. Here we are dealing with its use to mark a climax (or peak) of the story.
[38] Winnington-Ingram 1948: 130, n. 1.
[39] It is highly questionable whether historical women ever performed a real *sparagmos*, let alone the eating of raw meat (*ōmophagia*) associated with it.

scream during the actual killing (1133); and (6) the feasting on the victim's meat (suggested at 1184, 1242).[40] Pentheus throws off his headdress, i.e. dismantles his female disguise, and once again the messenger embeds his focalization (ὥς + optative), to make clear his intentions and lead up to his speech. Pentheus will try to make his mother recognize him. Agave is called 'wretched' (τλήμων), either by the focalizer Pentheus or by the messenger intruding on Pentheus' focalization (paralepsis), who earlier had called Pentheus himself τλήμων, too (1058). If focalized by the messenger, it reflects his hindsight knowledge: he knows that Agave will kill her own son and can expect her to repent this heavily when she finds out (as indeed she does: 1259–1329; Agave is called τάλαινα no less than three times: 1282, 1284, 1306). If focalized by Pentheus, it prepares for what he is about to say, namely that in killing him Agave will pay the penalty for *his* mistake (note the deliberate contrast in ταῖς ἐμαῖς and παῖδα σόν).

The messenger now inserts the most dramatic quotation of all, Pentheus admitting his mistake and begging his mother (note the repeated vocative μῆτερ) not to kill him. Pentheus' mistake or *hamartia* is his failure to understand that Dionysus is a god, resulting in his resistance to his cult as a *theomachos*.[41] Pentheus suggests that his mother, unwittingly killing her own son, is punished for *his* mistake. Actually, the primary narratees know from Dionysus' prologue speech that Agave is being punished by Dionysus for *her own* deeds, her refusal to admit that her sister Semele slept with Zeus and that their son Dionysus therefore is a god (26–33).

> *1125–36*
> λαβοῦσα δ' ὠλέναισ' ἀριστερὰν χέρα,   (1125)
> πλευροῖσιν ἀντιβᾶσα τοῦ δυσδαίμονος
> ἀπεσπάραξεν ὦμον, οὐχ ὑπὸ σθένους
> ἀλλ' ὁ θεὸς εὐμάρειαν ἐπεδίδου χεροῖν.
> Ἰνὼ δὲ τἀπὶ θάτερ' ἐξηργάζετο
> ῥηγνῦσα σάρκας, Αὐτονόη τ' ὄχλος τε πᾶς   (1130)

---

[40] Seidensticker 1979.

[41] The word ἁμαρτία will become a key concept in Aristotle's *Poetics*. It refers to a 'tragic mistake', i.e. a mistake made through/in ignorance, with fatal consequences; for a full discussion and bibliography, see Lurje 2004. But note that at *Ba.* 29 the word is used in a more casual way, as the mistake of a woman sleeping with a man and becoming pregnant.

ἐπεῖχε βακχῶν· ἦν δὲ πᾶσ' ὁμοῦ βοή,
ὁ μὲν στενάζων ὅσον ἐτύγχαν' ἐμπνέων,
αἱ δ' ἠλάλαζον.⁴² ἔφερε δ' ἡ μὲν ὠλένην,
ἡ δ' ἴχνος αὐταῖς ἀρβύλαις, γυμνοῦντο δὲ
πλευραὶ σπαραγμοῖς, πᾶσα δ' ἡματωμένη   (1135)
χεῖρας διεσφαίριζε σάρκα Πενθέως.

Taking his left hand with her forearms   (1125)
and setting her foot against the flank of the unfortunate man,
she tore out his arm at the shoulder, not by her own strength
but the god gave ease to her hands.
And Ino was destroying his other side,
tearing his flesh, and Autonoe and the whole mob   (1130)
of the bacchants went at it. And there was crying by all at the
    same time,
he groaning for as long as he had breath,
and they raised the triumph-cry. One carried an arm,
another a foot with its shoe still on, his ribs
were bared through the *sparagmos*, and every woman,
    with bloodied   (1135)
hands, was playing ball with Pentheus' flesh.

Euripides has a certain penchant for gruesome and bloody scenes in
his messenger-speeches; thus the present passage of Pentheus' *sparagmos* (explicitly labelled as such at 1135: σπαραγμοῖς) may be
compared to the flesh of Jason's young bride being devoured by the
poison put on her mantle by Medea (*Med.* 1185–202) or the blood of
Heracles' children, hit by one of his arrows, drenching the pillars (*HF*
977–1000). We find the by now common elements of the messenger's
pitiful focalization of his master (τοῦ δυσδαίμονος), the maenads'
'Dionysiac effortlessness' (εὐμάρειαν), and the messenger's depiction
of the maenads in military terms (ἠλάλαζον).⁴³

1137–47
κεῖται δὲ χωρὶς σῶμα, τὸ μὲν ὑπὸ στύφλοις
πέτραις, τὸ δ' ὕλης ἐν βαθυξύλῳ φόβῃ,
οὐ ῥάιδιον ζήτημα· κρᾶτα δ' ἄθλιον,
ὅπερ λαβοῦσα τυγχάνει μήτηρ χεροῖν,   (1140)

---

⁴² This is the reading of the ms., which I prefer to Diggle's conjecture ἀλόλυζον.
⁴³ Cf. Seaford 1996: ad 1133: 'it [ἠλάλαζον] is often a cry of triumph in war, and so
is here one of the many expressions of the maenads' assumption of male roles. They
have become hunters—even warriors'.

πήξασ' ἐπ' ἄκρον θύρσον ὡς ὀρεστέρου
φέρει λέοντος διὰ Κιθαιρῶνος μέσου,
λιποῦσ' ἀδελφὰς ἐν χοροῖσι μαινάδων.
χωρεῖ δὲ θήρᾳ δυσπότμῳ γαυρουμένη
τειχέων ἔσω τῶνδ', ἀνακαλοῦσα Βάκχιον　　　　　　(1145)
τὸν ξυγκύναγον, τὸν ξυνεργάτην ἄγρας,
τὸν καλλίνικον, ᾧ δάκρυα νικηφορεῖ.

His body lies scattered, some part of it under rough
rocks, another in the thick-growing foliage of the woods,
not an easy search. His wretched head,
which as it happened his mother took in her hands,　　(1140)
she fixed on the point of her *thyrsos* and is carrying
across the midst of Cithaeron, as if it were the head of a
　　mountain lion,
leaving her sisters among the dancing groups of the maenads.
And she, exulting in her ill-fated hunt,
is passing inside these walls, calling on Dionysus,　　(1145)
her 'fellow huntsman', her 'fellow-worker in the catching',
'the glorious victor', through whom she wins tears as her victory prize.

The messenger ends his report with a kind of still or coda, a description of
the situation such as it was when he left the 'crime scene' to bring his news
(and still is on the moment of speaking). It brings about the transition
from the narrated world to the moment of narration: Pentheus' body lies
scattered and Agave is on her way to the palace.[44] His remark that
Pentheus' body was οὐ ῥάιδιον ζήτημα, 'not an easy search', hints at
what has to be done, collecting his remains and bringing them back, and
what we soon will hear about Cadmus has done (1216–20):

ἕπεσθέ μοι φέροντες ἄθλιον βάρος
Πενθέως, ἕπεσθε, πρόσπολοι, δόμων πάρος,
οὗ σῶμα μοχθῶν μυρίοις ζητήμασιν
φέρω τόδ', εὑρὼν ἐν Κιθαιρῶνος πτυχαῖς
διασπαρακτὸν κοὐδὲν ἐν ταὐτῶι πέδου.

Follow me, carrying the woeful burden
of Pentheus, follow me, servants, before the house,
whose body toiling with infinite search
I am bringing here, having found it in the glades of Cithaeron
torn to pieces and no two parts in the same spot of ground.

---

[44] See Allan 2009: 197.

Cadmus' 'toiling with infinite search' mirrors the messenger's 'not an easy search'.

In his description of Agave's state of mind the messenger's pitying focalization, which (perhaps) had already transpired at 1117 when she was called τλήμων, now comes to the fore fully: Agave, still in the grip of maenadic madness, thinks that she has caught a wild animal (cf. θῆρ': 1138), that is, a lion (cf. again 1190, 1196, 1215, 1278), and is extremely pleased with the success of her hunt and Dionysus' assistance in it. The metaphor of the hunt is the leading one of the *Bacchae*: first we have Pentheus (and his servants) hunting down and catching 'the Lydian stranger' and his maenadic followers (228, 352, 434, 451, 719, 732, 866–71); then Cadmus warns Pentheus that he might incur the same fate as the hunter Actaeon, who was torn to pieces by the raw-eating dogs he himself had reared (337–40); the chorus later announce that the roles have been reversed and that Dionysus will now 'cast upon the bacchant's hunter a deadly noose' (1020–1); and now we have Agave acting as hunter. For this character, however, this is no metaphor but reality: she really thinks of herself as a hunter who has caught a wild animal. Her delusion will continue on stage (cf. 1171, 1182, 1183, 1189, 1193, 1196, 1203, 1237, 1241) and be endorsed by the chorus (1200–1) until Cadmus, finally, makes her come to her senses (1277–84):

Κάδμος   τίνος πρόσωπον δῆτ' ἐν ἀγκάλαις ἔχεις;
Ἀγαυή   λέοντος, ὥς γ' ἔφασκον αἱ θηρώμεναι.
Κάδμος   σκέψαι νυν ὀρθῶς· βραχὺς ὁ μόχθος εἰσιδεῖν.
Ἀγαυή   ἔα, τί λεύσσω; τί φέρομαι τόδ' ἐν χεροῖν;
          [. . .]
Κάδμος   μῶν σοι λέοντι φαίνεται προσεικέναι;
Ἀγαυή   οὔκ, ἀλλὰ Πενθέως ἡ τάλαιν' ἔχω κάρα.

Cadmus   Well, whose head do you have in your hands then?
Agave   Of a lion, so the hunters told me.
Cadmus   Look at it properly. To look hardly takes an effort.
Agave   Ah, what am I seeing? What is this that I carry in my hands?
          [. . .]
Cadmus   Does it seem like a lion to you?
Agave   No, but I, wretched woman, hold the head of Pentheus.

The messenger, who is not deluded by Dionysian madness, immediately understands the horror of Agave's illusion and makes it come out through trenchant juxtapositions: θήρᾳ δυσπότμῳ γαυρουμένη (1144) and δάκρυα νικηφορεῖ (1146).

His quotation in indirect speech of Agave's triumphant speech, in which she compliments herself and hails Dionysus as her 'fellow hunter' and 'fellow-worker in the catching', prepares for her exultant words spoken on stage (1169–1215) but will also later be tragically reversed at the moment of her *anagnōrisis*: Διόνυσος ἡμᾶς ὤλεσ', ἄρτι μανθάνω, 'Dionysus has destroyed us, now I realize this' (1296). Her reference to Dionysus as καλλίνικον likewise is an instance of horrible dramatic irony, as the messenger himself immediately makes clear, adding, 'through whom she wins tears as her victory prize'. The primary narratees may recall Dionysus' own words τὸν νεανίαν ἄγω | τόνδ' εἰς ἀγῶνα μέγαν, ὁ νικήσων δ' ἐγὼ | καὶ Βρόμιος ἔσται (974–6), and realize that he indeed is the winner in the contest between god and mortals (see *1043–7*).

> *1148–52*
> ἐγὼ μὲν οὖν <τῇδ'> ἐκποδὼν τῇ ξυμφορᾷ
> ἄπειμ', Ἀγαυὴν πρὶν μολεῖν πρὸς δώματα.
> τὸ σωφρονεῖν δὲ καὶ σέβειν τὰ τῶν θεῶν   (1150)
> κάλλιστον· οἶμαι δ' αὐτὸ καὶ σοφώτατον
> θνητοῖσιν εἶναι κτῆμα τοῖσι χρωμένοις.

> Well, I will depart, out of the way of this disaster,
> before Agave comes to the palace.
> To be moderate and revere the gods   (1150)
> is the best thing. And I think that that is also the wisest
> possession for mortals to use.

The messenger, like his colleagues and many other storytellers, ends with an evaluation.[45] Such evaluations may be specific, as is that of the first messenger, who urges his addressee Pentheus to accept Dionysus (769–74), or that of the messenger of the *Andromache*, who on account of the murder of his master in the temple—and perhaps at the behest of Apollo—questions the wisdom of that god. Or they may be couched in general terms. Thus the messenger of the *Medea* concludes on account of the death of King Creon and his daughter that human happiness is never secure. Our messenger concludes that it is best to be moderate and revere the gods. How are we to interpret his words? As a positive embrace of the Dionysian religion?[46] As

---

[45] See de Jong 1991: 74–7 and Allan 2009: 197–8.
[46] Seaford 1996: ad 1150–3.

Euripides' implicit criticism of that religion?[47] Or as the ordinary man's typical plea for moderation, such as we know from choral songs and other messenger-speeches, too?[48] The third interpretation seems most likely.

But the messenger's evaluation is not the final one. Cadmus, who strategically accepted Dionysus and his rites at first (330–42), accuses the god of acting excessively in the exodus (1344–8):

Κάδμος Διόνυσε, λισσόμεσθά σ᾽, ἠδικήκαμεν.

Διόνυσος ὄψ᾽ ἐμάθεθ᾽ ἡμᾶς, ὅτε δ᾽ ἐχρῆν οὐκ ᾔδετε.

Κάδμος ἐγνώκαμεν ταῦτ᾽· ἀλλ᾽ ἐπεξέρχηι λίαν.

Διόνυσος καὶ γὰρ πρὸς ὑμῶν θεὸς γεγὼς ὑβριζόμην.

Κάδμος ὀργὰς πρέπει θεοὺς οὐχ ὁμοιοῦσθαι βροτοῖς.

Cadmus Dionysus, we beseech you, we have wronged you.

Dionysus Late did you know me, and what you had to know you did not know.

Cadmus We have realized these things; but you proceed against us excessively.

Dionysus Yes, but then I was insulted by you, though born a god.

Cadmus It is not right for gods to resemble mortals in their anger.[49]

As so often in Euripidean tragedy, opinions on the moral evaluation of what has happened are contradictory, and it is clear that the messenger's story is only one of many elements of what in the end constitutes a kaleidoscopic view. But whatever the value of the messenger's conclusion, his pitiful narrative of what happens to both son and mother turns him into an important instrument of a tragedian like Euripides, called by Aristotle 'the most tragic of the tragedians' (*Poetics* 13).

---

[47] Winnington-Ingram 1948: 132–3: 'Superficially it is a counsel of acceptance [. . .] But through his words Euripides takes us back to the reiterated statements of the Bacchic creed. Sanity and piety they had claimed as the distinguishing marks of their religion [. . .] Now, after the full horror of their revenge has been disclosed, the poet returns to these themes. Here is the sanity, the piety, the honour and the wisdom of the Bacchanals.'

[48] Cf. e.g. the messenger at *Hel.* 1617–18, and Dodds [1944] 1960: ad 1150–2: 'It is the same traditional moral which Sophocles' Chorus drew from the fate of Creon [. . .] (*Ant.* 1348)'; Buxton 1991: 46: 'The choral tone is again prominent: faced with overwhelming odds, it is prudent to keep one's head down [. . .] Dionysiac ecstasy may be beautiful, but it is also very, very dangerous.'

[49] Such criticism of the gods as acting petty, like mortals, is common in Euripidean tragedy: cf. e.g. E. *Hipp.* 117–20; *Andr.* 1161–5; *HF* 339–47, 1303–10; *Ion* 442–4; *IT* 380–91; and *Or.* 285–7.

FURTHER READING

Allan, R.J., 'Towards a Typology of the Narrative Modes in Ancient Greek: Text Types and Narrative Structure in Euripidean Messenger Speeches', in S.J. Bakker and G. Wakker (eds), *Discourse Cohesion in Ancient Greek* (Leiden 2009), 171–203.

Barrett, J., *Staged Narrative: Poetics and the Messenger in Greek Tragedy* (Berkeley, Los Angeles, and London 2002).

Bremer, J.M., 'Why Messenger-Speeches?', in J.M. Bremer, S. Radt, and C.J. Ruijgh (eds), *Miscellanea tragica in honorem J.C. Kamerbeek* (Amsterdam 1976), 29–48.

Buxton, R.G.A., 'News from Cithaeron: Narrators and Narratives in the *Bacchae*', *Pallas* 37, 1991, 39–48.

Dickin, M., *A Vehicle for Performance: Acting the Messenger in Greek Tragedy* (Lanham 2009).

Dodds, E.R., *Euripides: Bacchae* (Oxford 1960; first published 1944).

Foley, H.P., *Ritual Irony: Poetry and Sacrifice in Euripides* (Ithaca, NY and London 1985).

Green, J.R., 'Messengers from the Tragic Stage', *Bulletin of the Institute of Classical Studies* 41, 1996, 17–30.

Gregorio, L. di, *Le scene d'annuncio nella tragedia greca* (Milan 1967).

Gregory, J., 'Some Aspects of Seeing in Euripides' *Bacchae*', *Greece & Rome* 32, 1985, 23–31.

Gould, J. '. . . And Tell Sad Stories of the Death of Kings: Greek Tragic Drama as Narrative', in *Myth, Ritual, Memory, and Exchange: Essays in Greek Literature and Culture* (Oxford 2001), 319–34.

Goward, B., *Telling Tragedy: Narrative Technique in Aeschylus, Sophocles, and Euripides* (London 1999).

Jong, I.J.F. de, *Narrative in Drama: The Art of the Euripidean Messenger-Speech* (Leiden 1991).

Jong, I.J.F. de, 'Récit et drame: le deuxième récit de messager dans *Les Bacchantes*', *Revue des Études Grecques* 105, 1992, 572–83.

Jong, I.J.F. de, *A Narratological Commentary on the Odyssey* (Cambridge 2001).

Jahn, M., 'Narrative Voice and Agency in Drama: Aspects of a Narratology of Drama', *New Literary History* 32, 2001, 659–79.

Lurje, M., *Die Suche nach der Schuld: Sophokles' Oedipus Rex, Aristoteles' Poetik und das Tragödienverständnis der Neuzeit* (Munich and Leipzig 2004).

Markantonatos, A., *Tragic Narrative: A Narratological Study of Sophocles' Oedipus at Colonus* (Berlin and New York 2002).

Pfister, M., *The Theory and Analysis of Drama*, trans. J. Halliday (Cambridge 1988; first published in German 1977).

Rijksbaron, A., 'How Does a Messenger Begin His Speech? Some Observations on the Opening-Lines of Euripidean Messenger-Speeches', in J.M. Bremer, S. Radt, and C.J. Ruijgh (eds), *Miscellanea tragica in honorem J.C. Kamerbeek* (Amsterdam 1976), 293–308.

Rijksbaron, A., *Grammatical Observations on Euripides' Bacchae* (Amsterdam 1991).

Roux, J., *Euripide: Les Bacchantes* (Paris 1970–2).

Ricoeur, P., *Time and Narrative I* (Chicago and London 1984; first published in French 1983).

Seaford, R., *Euripides Bacchae* (Warminster 1996).

Seidensticker, B., 'Sacrificial Ritual in the *Bacchae*', in G.W. Bowersock, W. Burkert, and M.C. Putnam (eds), *Arktouros: Hellenic Studies Presented to Bernard M.W. Knox* (Berlin and New York 1979), 181–90.

Scodel, R., 'Ignorant Narrators in Greek Tragedy', in J. Grethlein and A. Rengakos (eds), *Narratology and Interpretation: The Content of Narrative Form in Ancient Literature* (Berlin 2009), 421–47.

Winnington-Ingram, R.P., *Euripides and Dionysus: An Interpretation of the Bacchae* (Cambridge 1948).

Index of Terms

acceleration, *see* rhythm
achronical narrative 73
'action-perception-reaction' motif 148
aftermath 91
anachrony 78
analepsis 79-80, 189
  actorial 83-4
  completing 81-2
  external 80, 150-2
  heterodiegetic 80-1
  internal 80, 159, 183
  narratorial 82-3
  repeating 82, 183
argument function, *see* embedded
  narratives

beginnings 87-9
  ab ovo 88
  in medias res 88
  thematized 88-9

close-up, *see* spatial standpoint
closure 90

description 112-16
  impossible 113
  mirror- 123-4
  (and) narration 113-14
  organization of 114-15
  (and) pause 114
  see also ekphrasis
dramatic irony 34, 152, 153, 163,
  186, 220
'dream' speech 158
dreams (in Herodotus) 175-6

ekphrasis 120-2
ellipsis, *see* rhythm
embedded narratives 34-7, 159-63
  argument function 35-6, 162-3
  distractive function 35
  explanatory function 35
  key function 35-6
  persuasive function 35
  predictive function 35
  thematic function 35
  see also mirror-story, *mise en abyme*

ends 89-91
  see also aftermath, closure
epiphany 146, 157

fabula, *see* levels of narrative
focalization 47-72, 157-8, 161, 170, 206,
  213, 217, 219
  embedded 50-6, 63-4, 140, 141, 145,
    146, 158-9, 170-1, 181, 207-8, 216
  experiencing 65-6, 67, 200
  (and) information 56-60
  narrating 66-7, 200
  restricted 57-9
  see also omniscience, paralepsis,
    paralipsis
focalizer:
  anonymous 69, 117
  external primary 48-9
  hypothetical 68-9, 212
  internal primary 49
frames, *see* space
frequency 99-101
  iterative narration 100
  omnitemporal narration 100-1
  repetition 99-100, 179
  singulative narration 99, 140

'god meets mortal' type-scene 146

header technique 174
Herodotus:
  narrator 172
  tragic historian 190-2
historic present 67, 68, 179, 181, 182,
  187, 209, 215
hypothetical narration 76

implicit foreshadowing 85-6
implied author 19
in medias res, *see* beginnings
intertextuality 187
iterative narration, *see* frequency

key function, *see* embedded narratives

levels of narrative:
  fabula 5, 38, 47, 77, 138

Index of Greek and Latin Passages

1.44.2 187
1.45.1–2 188–9, 190, 191
1.45.3 187, 189–90
1.51.3–4 59–60
1.201–4 96
2.44.1–2 78
3.30.2–3 37
3.65.2–3 36–7
7.5.2–6.1 55–6

HESIOD

Theogony
22–3 18

HOMER

Iliad
1.48–52 27
1.370–92 80
1.488–92 100
2.299–330 80
2.459–68 61
4.134–8 94–5
4.539–42 69
6.357–8 42
6.482–5 49
15.612–14 80
16.140–1 30
16.844–6 60
18.478–84 119–20
22.59–76 80
22.445–6 54
24.448–56 110–11
24.478–9 52
Odyssey
4.844–7 112
10.100–2 65–6
11.134–7 90
12.166–9 86
13.95–113 97
14.523 92
15.1–5 92
19.226–31 124

HOMERIC HYMNS

137–8
to Aphrodite
45–291 138–65
45–52 139–40
53–7 141–2
58–65 142–3
66–75 143–4
76–80 144–5

81–91 145–7
92–106 147–9
107–16 149–50
117–30 150–2
131–42 153–4
143–54 154–5
155–67 155–7
167–79 157–8
180–90 158–60
218–38 160–1
239–55 161–3
256–90 163
291 163
to Apollo
124–9 24

HORACE

Odes
2.19.1–4 108

JOSEPHUS

Jewish War
5.176–7 113

LIVY

History of Rome
21.32.7 51
22.7.3–4 38–9
36.18.8 76

LONGUS

Daphnis and Chloe
1.1–2 107

LYSIAS

Orations
1.5 33–4
1.7–10 66–7

OVID

Metamorphoses
1.168–76 111–12
1.218–21 50
1.717–21 24
2.748–51 82
3.407–10 124–5
4.695–701 31
5.429–37 68–9
9.225–9 107
10.152–6 74
10.519–24 95

Printed and bound by CPI Group (UK) Ltd, Croydon, CR0 4YY